Feminist Utopias

Feminist Utopias

Frances Bartkowski

University of Nebraska Press
Lincoln and London

Copyright © 1989 by the University
of Nebraska Press

First paperback printing: 1991
Most recent printing indicated
by the last digit below:
10 9 8 7 6 5 4 3 2 1

*Library of Congress
Cataloging-in-Publication Data*
Barkowski, Frances, 1948–
    Feminist utopias/Frances Bartkowski
        p.   cm.
    Bibliography: p.
    Includes index.
    ISBN 0-8032-1205-4 (alk. paper)
    ISBN 0-8032-6091-1 (pbk.)
    1. American fiction–Women authors–
History and criticism.   2. Utopias in
literature.   3. Feminism and
literature–History–20th century.
4. Women and literature–History–
20th century.   5. American fiction–
20th century–History and criticism.
6. French fiction–Women authors–History
and criticism.   7. French fiction–20th century–
History and criticism.   8. Literature,
Comparative–American and French.
9. Literature, Comparative–French and
American   I. Title.
PS374.U8B38   1989
813'.54'099287–dc19   88-37399   CIP

To the flying women of the dream
and
To the memory of my mother,
Susan Wertheimer Bartkowski
(1924–1952)

Contents

Acknowledgments, ix
Introduction, 3

1
Remembering and Inventing:
Charlotte Perkins Gilman's *Herland*
and Monique Wittig's *Les Guérillères*, 23

2
The Kinship Web:
Joanna Russ's *The Female Man* and
Marge Piercy's *Woman on the Edge of Time*, 49

3
Of Unmen and Women:
Suzy McKee Charnas's *Walk to the
End of the World* and *Motherlines*, 81

4
The Houses of Women:
Christiane Rochefort's *Archaos, ou le jardin
étincelant* and E. M. Broner's *A Weave of Women*, 111

5
No Shadows without Light:
Louky Bersianik's *The Eugélionne* and
Margaret Atwood's *The Handmaid's Tale*, 133

Afterword, 161
Notes, 167
Bibliography, 181
Index, 195

Acknowledgments

Here is the moment I have anticipated anxiously: thanking all those who have given hours and moments to the contemplation of possible futures for women, for this book, for feminism. How do I acknowledge with any specificity the last decade and the climate in which feminist discourse has flourished? For this is part of what must be recognized as setting the stages for the changing hopes and desires which I set out to track. To those many friends, mentors, and co-workers who weathered and created seasons of this climate with me, I give thanks.

I began this inquiry at the University of Iowa. Steve Ungar's support was unwavering, especially in the face of my own doubts about pursuing work with texts so recent I could not turn to experts. In the community of a feminist theory reading group I want to acknowledge the encouragements and challenges provided by Wendy Deutelbaum, Dee Morris, Florence Boos, Laura Mumford, Barb Klinger, and Kate Stearns. There was also a stimulating group of undergraduate students with whom I read some of these works in the context of traditional and contemporary utopian projections.

The invaluable environment I needed to return to this work came in the form of an Andrew W. Mellon Post-Doctoral Fellowship at the Center for Humanities at Wesleyan University. There, large lectures and small group discussions provided further challenges to the development of my thinking on utopias. It is impossible to thank each and every member of that community who contributed to the more subtle shape this project then took on. But I want to express my gratitude especially to Judith Butler, who began at the beginning and made me rethink the work as a whole, and to Neil Lazarus, Khachig Tololyan, Richard Stamelman, Judith Genova, and Jill Morawski, whose contributions to the reshaping of parts were sharp and generous.

At Carnegie Mellon University, where I brought this book to a close in the working community of the Literary and Cultural Theory Program, Paul Smith, Peggy Knapp, and Anne Hayes as well as Jim Knapp of the University of Pittsburgh provided attentive and timely criticisms. Gary Waller supplied the resources and environment for seeing the project through to another stage of closure.

Further thanks must go to those who kept the phone lines humming over ever-shifting distances. At crucial moments I was especially grateful for the help offered by Barbara Harlow and Gayatri Spivak. Two former colleagues and permanent friends whose enthusiasm and critical support never failed are Sharon Willis and Linda Singer.

For the work I did not do—the technological transformations from paper to disk—I must thank Patricia Camden, Laurie Walz, and Lisa Ehrlich.

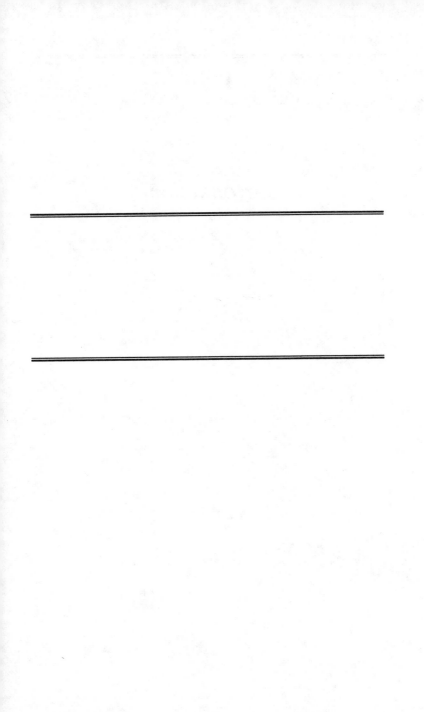

Introduction

. . . the way the story is told is the story itself.

Louis Marin
Utopiques: Jeux d'espaces

The future can only be anticipated in the form of an absolute danger. It is that which breaks absolutely with constituted normality and can only be proclaimed, *presented,* as a sort of monstrosity.

Jacques Derrida
Of Grammatology

This is a study of a group of novels, all of which aim to speculate on futures for women and men; I have chosen and juxtaposed them idiosyncratically in pairs. Two by two seems to be an organizing principle of social life, information gathering, and decision making, and many of these novels try to find ways to redistribute this kind of thinking and behavior. Clusters, groups, bands, tribes, clans, cells, even loners, all find, momentarily or eventually, a kind of effectivity in the form of a bonded pair. Yet these are not narratives based on the romantic dyad; what they are, in each and every case, are works of the political imagination which try to propose ways we might think beyond the pairs, oppositions, dualities, and polarities that we know and live and tell from along the faultlines of gender. The rift between women and men, more than any other, is germane to all the writers whose texts are read and written about here; that is what makes these fictions feminist. This perspective opens horizons not often the subject of fiction, and it does so at the cost of turning attention away from other concerns that also cloud the possible representations of desire, that hobble the capacity for hoping. By listening to feminist narratives inscribe the field of desire—the erotic, broadly conceived—we will explore the question of what women are both free and constrained to want.

To pose this question is to take steps toward that not yet inscribed into territories unsurveyed. A monstrous grandeur awaits those who walk into the unnamed, unclaimed, unknown. Each of these fictions strike some balance between the exhilaration of discovery and the diagnosis of a collectivity, defined both as castes and classes of women, too crippled to think of voyaging out. The metaphors of journey are appropriate here, for the utopian will be modeled in space as well as time. "Utopia" is anywhere but here and now. It is alternatively the good place (*eutopos*) and no place (*outopos*; think here of William Morris's *News from Nowhere*), which could also "be" anywhere. Its imagined site always implicates the here and now of its production whether implicitly or explicitly. These feminist utopian fictions tell us as much about what it is possible to wish as they do about what it is necessary to hope. They are tales of disabling and enabling conditions of desire.

Imagine then that this book means to chart representations by women writers who have asked the questions of desire cast in a mood of "as if," "what if," and "if only." Through remodeling that which is *not,* we watch the "not-yet" taking shape, what could be, might be, even what some say ought to be. The conditional and subjunctive modes ironize the tendentious voice of projection—the ought is warned by the if and produces a "grammar of desire."[1]

While eight of these novels (Louky Bersianik's *The Eugélionne,* E. M. Broner's *A Weave of Women,* Suzy McKee Charnas's *Motherlines,* Charlotte Perkins Gilman's *Herland,* Marge Piercy's *Woman on the Edge of Time,* Christiane Rochefort's *Archaos, ou le jardin étincelant,* Joanna Russ's *The Female Man,* and Monique Wittig's *Les Guérillères*) have been chosen primarily for their utopian strategies, that is to say, the what-if of hope, two of them (Charnas's *Walk to the End of the World* and Margaret Atwood's *The Handmaid's Tale*) specifically aim to ask the what-if of despair, the underside and antinomy of hope, the dystopian.[2] Several double strategies and dialectical tensions are at work both in the organization of this book and in the novels themselves. For they are all framed in the light—whether bright or dim—of the possibilities alive for feminist thought, action, fiction, and theory;

those possibilities give us not only the rhetoric of utopian speculation but also the shape that women's desires take on during the period at issue here: broadly 1969–1986, the dates of earliest and
latest publication, more narrowly the mid-1970s, the peak of literary production and political activity. It is abundantly evident in
these texts that, as Raymond Williams has put it, *community* is
the keyword of the "entire utopian mode"—the two dystopias are
as exemplary in their focus on the lack of it. A central question in
my discussion concerns the varying constructions of communities
and what constitutes them. Each novel chosen, each juxtaposed
pair of texts, naturally gives more time to some questions than
others; yet what is most apparent is the consistent redefinition of
family and kinship as the heart of the matter of bonds among and
between women, sometimes between women and men, and usually between women and children.

Each chapter deals with certain specifics of feminist desires,
those emphasized and highlighted by the juxtaposition of texts
and the concerns of each text. The "what" of the wish is set off
against the "how" of the tale. That is to say, rather than do finely
detailed schemas or anatomies of feminist utopias, I have chosen
to work across the inevitable combinations of tenses and tales:
how the future is infused with the past and present; how the romantic and the technological strains of the utopian can no longer
be separated. My questions here are not meant to produce classi-
fication; rather they are impelled by a desire to read out, tease out,
sift out the productive tensions and dialectics of feminist thought
when it takes up forms of discursive strategies that are simultaneously fictional and profoundly theoretical. The feminist utopian novel is a place where theories of power can be addressed
through the construction of narratives that test and stretch the
boundaries of power in its operational details.

Writing from the margins and coming into speech in full
knowledge of the abuses of power *over,* feminists have tended to
imagine instead about power *to*; they have needed and chosen to
take up the materiality of the language, in order to install a self as
subject, knowing that the self has also been subjected. The naiveté
of this split between notions of power over and power to (the former debased, the latter upheld) led to the need to confront other,
more dangerous (because denied) relations to power among wo-

men, finally tackled in the feminist debates of the late 1970s and
early 1980s.[3] This need had been articulated at a time when notions of empowering had suffered the reversals of feminism which
came so quickly after some of its victories. Early on in the contemporary women's movement there was a governing idea, mostly
untheorized, that the contaminating effects of power were tied to
the work, world, and politics of men. However, the struggles
among and inside women's groups belied this wish to set aside a
feminist critique of power relations. Such work began to be done
as it became clear that splits and fractures among women could
not be denied if the movement was to continue to develop: splits
defined by combinations of difference—race, age, class, religion,
ethnicity, education, urban and rural background, occupation,
employment, sexual orientation, marital status, those with children and those without, ability, disability, language, region, culture, world. These limitless structures of difference remain and
must remain resistant to overarching analysis that founds difference only along lines of sexual difference, for even there, analysis
has proven inadequate to the complexity and complications of
how we live our lives as gendered. The need for empowering strategies whether in language, literature, or life remains crucial, because it has only become more evident how readily feminist strategies of empowerment can be undermined. A single powerful
example is the headiness of the relatively quick and early victory
of the struggles for legalized abortion which have since become
mired in the equally necessary work to hold off the political force
of what was problematically named the pro-life movement. With
such work feminism struggles to stay in place when it might have
further developed other concerns of equal importance to women
of different ages, races, and classes. This book is not a study in the
political history of contemporary feminism. Yet that history must
be understood as in the process of being staged, rehearsed, and
performed even as the novels discussed here are being written.
And the process of their production needs to be understood in
terms of those concurrent as well as previous histories.

A frame around this group of novels gives this study some of
its historical constraints; this frame is constructed by the limits
and possibilities of literary forms like the utopian, which comes in
spurts and is responsive to a social history of times of reorganiza-

tion, upheaval, revolution, and, perhaps more likely, reform. Utopian literature is a genre that arises refashioned for specific epochs. The periodization of utopian writing and thought would seem to chart certain moments or ruptures in Western social history—those times when utopian desires/projective longings are driven by both hope and fear, those times particularly marked by anticipation and anxiety. This can be seen clearly in the phenomenal production of utopian literature in the last decades of the nineteenth century, when the costs and benefits of urban industrialization and concomitant forms of family and social life had drastically changed urban life, when American populist and foreign forms of socialism seemed to hold promise yet to be delivered, and when the millennium loomed.[4]

This book is a cross-cultural (France, the United States, Canada) study of feminist utopian theory and literary practice. Although its central focus is on the 1970s, some distinctions from earlier and also more recent periods of feminist writing and political activity are made; another axis of this inquiry is an examination of generic changes in the utopian form as practiced by self-consciously feminist writers. Whereas the utopian socialists of the early nineteenth century, such as Henri de Saint Simon, Robert Owen, and Charles Fourier, systematize the revolutionary ideals ("liberty, equality, fraternity") and theories of the late eighteenth century not yet carried through in social practice, the later utopian novelists, such as Edward Bellamy and William Dean Howells, imbued with these philosophical backgrounds, offer less systematic and more imaginative versions of how these ideals might be put into practice, mapping the future over a newly chosen past.

The greatest number of utopian fictions were written at the end of the nineteenth century; the first half of the twentieth century saw fewer of them, and they were different: it is a negative moment, the time of antiutopia or dystopia. The future still holds all that imagination may shape, but the visions are much more uniformly grim. The nightmare fears of technology which often led to regressive, pastoral, anti-industrial images in the late nineteenth and early twentieth centuries are confirmed by a realization that the machine will not be banished from the garden. The two global wars early in the twentieth century produced strong dystopian strains in popular and pulp science fiction as well as the popular success of novels such as *Brave New World,* 1984, and *Walden Two,* all deeply cynical visions of where social planning could take the white, Western world. During this period, from 1900 to 1950, the genres of utopian and science fiction are no longer so easily separable, leading later to the more inclusive term, speculative fiction.

Critical works on utopian thought claim a lack of utopian writing since 1950, even as new utopias were taking root.[5] In the 1960s the revolutionary and messianic tensions in utopian thought begin to clash again, producing texts such as Herbert Marcuse's *Eros and Civilization* (1966), Norman O. Brown's *Love's Body* (1966), and Paul and Percival Goodman's *Communitas* (first published in 1947 and revised in 1960), all responsive to the promissory economy and politics of the post–World War II epoch, all also warning of the darkness that would later become "Vietnam" as U.S. involvement in that war increased. Simone de Beauvoir's *The Second Sex* (1949) and Betty Friedan's *The Feminine Mystique* (1963) articulate the philosophical and sociological contexts of a postwar dystopian situation for women. By their very force they will inspire utopian sketches and, as such, become the foremotherly pre-texts for feminists writing in the decade of change discussed here. The political movement for women's liberation grows out of the situations these voices diagnose in order to anticipate the desires of women. Historically, utopia is an imaginative site of economic and affective abundance. The storytellers or history makers of utopia define their own notions of perfection and plenty in the good society which is "nowhere" but might also be "anywhere."

Just as the adjective "socialist" can be used to group a number of nineteenth-century utopian novels by both men and women, the term "feminist" is apt to describe the utopian fictions of the 1970s. Feminist utopias all posit societies which women have shaped themselves or in concert with men, though these words may no longer be in use. Because of changes in linguistic practice, certain words no longer serve as and in exchange, and these words and the ways of thought they represent are thus rendered obsolescent. The inhabitants of Morris's England in *News from Nowhere* do not know the word "politics," and "poor" is understood only in the context of health, not economics; similarly in

Bellamy's Boston of the year 2000 in *Looking Backward,* the "labor question" no longer exists. In the feminist utopias some of the words that fall into disuse because they no longer signify are "prostitution," "father," "rape," "heroism," "love," "madness," "homosexuality." The shift in perspective from late nineteenth- to late twentieth-century utopian critiques is the shift from capitalism and its discontents to patriarchy.

The utopian voice is always tendentious; it has designs on the reader. Often its didactic points are made in the form of long monologues and polemics and are just those aspects by which literary critics have often deemed it a marginal kind of fiction—a crossbreed of tract made palatable as literature through a poorly and hastily constructed romance. The nineteenth-century popular success of Edward Bellamy's *Looking Backward* is exemplary here. Another kind of writing to which utopian narrative has always had close ties is travel literature—the island lost in time and space. The traveler-narrator is traditionally a man who, through dialogue with an inhabitant of utopia or with an interlocutor from the present, poses the questions which this "nowhere" has answered by its re-vision of social practices. Beginning with Thomas More's *Utopia* the question of women in utopia is always asked and usually summarily answered. Their "condition" is usually seen as improved relative to the narrator's present, though women themselves tend not to participate in shaping this future in any dramatic way. While there were numerous all-female utopias produced in the nineteenth century, they were far from feminist, in that they tended to idealize the "true" woman of the domestic sphere, not the "new" woman.[6]

To assume the tendentious voice of utopian projection takes a certain amount of confidence and a sense of power to imagine collective change. While women writers have been fewer, more closeted, and often silenced by literary history, they have nevertheless contributed to most forms of literature. It is not at all surprising that contemporary feminist writers have also begun to speak the language of utopia, thereby rewriting the genre and its history, past and present. This desire to speculate for and on the future and how it might be shaped we can read as a feminist eros, speaking the language of female desires.

The three operative terms, then, are "feminist," "utopian,"

and "fiction"—feminist in that the everyday life of women becomes an exercise of willful imagination, demanding revolutionary transformation; utopian in that longing and desire, anger and
despair, are reshaped by hope; fiction in that a narrative sets the
pattern of these desires and transformations as if a potential future had erupted into the reader's present. This future coming to
inhabit the present is what Ernst Bloch has named the not-yet.
Bloch's major philosophical work, *The Principle of Hope*, first
published in German in 1959, situates the mode of utopian consciousness: always fictive and always speculative, it brings the
imaginative possibilities of what is not into the concrete realm of
what could be.[7] Thinking the not-yet is of particular importance
for feminists, as it is here that freedom and necessity meet; for
feminists working with narrative the not-yet can rewrite views of
the past and present even as it projects possible futures. It is
Bloch's formulation that I find the most provocative. Other theorists of utopian thought name the utopian out of various vocabu-
laries: for Darko Suvin it is the place of "cognitive estrangement";
for Joanna Russ, the realm of "subjunctivity"; for Rachel Blau
DuPlessis, the time of the "future perfect"; for Paul Tillich, "the
negation of negation"; and for Louis Marin, "the ideological critique of the ideological."[8] All of these terms indicate a dialectical
node in the very form and gesture of utopian projection.

The dialectical tension between time and text will move the
reader into discussion of contradiction and hope, where hope is
understood, Bloch reminds us, as that which is always thwarted.
Fredric Jameson, reading Bloch, explains, "the future is always
something other than what we sought to find there"—it never
comes.[9] Utopia is the work of anticipation motivated by anxiety,
its correlative; plenitude imagined out of scarcity; the messianic
out of the apocalyptic, to paraphrase Jameson. It is precisely the
absence of plenitude and satisfaction (dystopia) which will constantly and radically transform desire into utopia.

The utopian impulse in thought and narrative may be conceived as an aesthetically organized and politically motivated day-
dream. Sometimes it verges on fable or actively produced myth.
Freud, in "Creative Writers and Day-Dreaming," clarifies the ties
between narrative and time:

The relation of a phantasy to time is in general very important. We may say that it hovers, as it were, between three times—the three moments of time which our ideation involves. Mental work is linked to some current impression, some provoking occasion in the present which has been able to arouse one of the subject's major wishes. From there it harks back to a memory of an earlier experience (usually an infantile one) in which this wish was fulfilled; and it now creates a situation relating to the future which represents a fulfillment of the wish. What it thus creates is a day-dream or phantasy, which carries about it traces of its origin from the occasion which provoked it and from the memory. Thus past, present and future are strung together, as it were, on the thread of the wish that runs through them.[10]

The metaphor of weaving suggests these fictions as tapestries of an invented and remembered future. Where the unconscious is the organizing agency of the dream of sleep and night, the ego, Freud specifies, is the hero of "every day-dream and every story" (p. 150). Freud speaks of the daydream and the aesthetic component of art as offering us a kind of "fore-pleasure." "It may even be that not a little of this effect," he writes, "is due to the writer's enabling us thence-forward to enjoy our own day-dreams without self-reproach or shame" (p. 153). And the daydream, engaging the future, knows "how not to forgo," according to Bloch. What *The Interpretation of Dreams* does for nightdreams and the workings of the unconscious, Bloch's *Principle of Hope* does for consciousness and daydreaming. Where Freud explores the territory of the no-longer-conscious (what we need to remember), Bloch's major work focuses on the not-yet-conscious (what we need to invent).

The political and philosophical advocacy inherent in the term "feminist fiction" has by now appropriated and transformed a variety of literary genres.[11] The utopian literary tradition with its emphasis on social planning and collectivity is the locus of a fictional practice which posits a future and simultaneously interrogates the present moment of its production as a text, and thus in positing a future also illuminates the past. Suvin has done a critical reworking of utopia; one of his axiomatic statements which we will want to keep in mind is that "utopia explicates what satire implicates and vice versa."[12] Some feminist utopian fictions mix satire and utopia as a way of bringing the here and now into the future of possibility. Utopian thinking is crucial to feminism, a movement that could only be produced and challenged by and in a patriarchal world. Joanna Russ notes the predominance of pessimism in contemporary science fiction, which is not, however, shared by women writing in this genre. Russ names some of the writers gathered here as a group that has produced "classless feminist utopias."[13] In *New French Feminisms,* the first collection of French theoretical writings made widely available to readers of English, the texts included are grouped for presentation as demystifications, warnings, creations, manifestos, and finally utopias; all these forms of action are the work of feminism.[14] Feminist fiction and feminist theory are fundamentally utopian in that they declare that which is not-yet as the basis for a feminist practice, textual, political, or otherwise.

Utopian practice decenters questions of time and history, the angle of long-standing criticism from the Left. Traditionally, literary utopias have been set in specified past or present times and places—the golden age, the lost island—effacing their present condition of production. Feminist utopias also reject the specific naming of where and when of utopia and stake their interests in the interplay of the varying "here" of the writer and reader and the "there" of the fiction. Few feminist utopias of the 1970s take on a total revision of the world women might make; the social planning of earlier utopias is instead transformed into an extensive social critique which exposes and makes use of the dystopian as well. Affective and economic scarcity is refigured as abundance. Feminists have chosen to specify the contradictions of the "now" and the intensity with which they are felt rather than to totalize in order to make the utopian impulse one of potential, not project. This is not to say that contemporary feminist utopian fiction is never didactic, for it is. Yet the refusal of hierarchy at the core of contemporary feminist theory arises from the knowledge that women have been spoken both for and about, and in this speaking for, their experience and subjectivity have been falsified. The caution about speaking *for* others makes for a didacticism that is at best ironic and at least self-critical. Didacticism, after all, could not be completely absent from a literary genre and mode of thought which is basically moral, philosophical, and political.

Where some critics have denigrated the utopian for its tendency to privilege the political over the formal demands of narrative, others have criticized the politics of the genre for the ways that the utopian often crudely collapses the political and the religious. This tension in utopian thought between the religious and the political has a long history; a counterpart to utopia may be apocalypse and its messianic, even chiliastic, kernel.[15]

In the mid-nineteenth century modern feminism and socialism began to take shape, separately for the most part. Yet early on, Karl Marx acknowledged in a crude but apt analogy that bourgeois is to man as proletarian is to woman.[16] Soon Marxism would create a terrain for those who wished to pursue this insight, for Marx himself did not. Friedrich Engels and then August Bebel laid the theoretical groundwork for discussing "the woman question" as appropriated by Marxism for decades.[17] Inherent yet ghettoized within the theoretical confines of socialism, feminism grew its own roots and branches. Engels set utopian socialism aside, but not scientific socialism.[18] Only in the later Marxist work of the Frankfurt school, especially that of Herbert Marcuse and Ernst Bloch, is the utopian impulse again considered and recognized. Bloch, Marcuse, and feminist utopian writers do not evade or deny the question of class struggle as the utopian socialists had done in the early nineteenth century. What they share is an emphasis on the work of consciousness as a path to the "good place" (*eutopia*) which is still "no place" (*outopia*). Feminism has done much to bring together the theoretical differences and similarities of the struggles among classes and between the sexes. A history of the polemics of the contemporary women's liberation movement demonstrates that the priority given to sex, class, or race as a basis for theorizing is a regular source of factions and rifts and often works to bring theory and experience into productive conflict.

Within feminist literature, a small but significant group of writers has revived the fictional genre of utopia. Whereas earlier utopian writers devoted some time and space to the place of women in their social planning for a fictional future, like thought on the "woman question," these creators of utopias make a "place" *for* women that seems only to mask oppression while imagining patriarchal utopias. Like these earlier writings, feminist utopian fictions have responded to social and political movements of transformation. Given the gap between feminist theory and everyday struggle, the utopian mode is both useful and logical for writers who self-consciously place themselves within a feminist (i.e., partisan) literary practice. The utopian genre, with its implicit reference to the world of the reader is perfectly suited to its didactic function. In an essay of 1973 a prefeminist Joanna Russ draws the Brechtian implications of utopian and science fiction: "the reader carries his frame with him . . . the reader himself performs the paradoxical movement into and out of the work . . . . science fiction practices the alienation effect, sometimes straightforwardly, sometimes inside-out, as it were."[19] In utopian fiction a structural three-way splitting always exists between the "here" of the reader and the narrator and the "there" of represented possibilities. In a definitive essay Suvin explains the genre as "a gesture of pointing, a wide-eyed glance from here to there, a 'travelling shot' moving from the author's everyday lookout to the wondrous panorama of a far-off land."[20]

The earlier utopias, however, most often lack any indication of the process of change necessary to move from here to there; this constituted much of Engel's critique of utopian socialism as distinct from scientific socialism. Most contemporary feminist utopian fiction refuses to avoid this very process of transformation— whether economic, sexual, or political. As distinct from the genre as practiced by Sir Thomas More or Edward Bellamy, an extraordinary attention to language and linguistic change marks feminist utopian fiction, whether the language of kinship, ritual, history, the dictionary, or that which delimits gender.

Feminism makes a practice of questioning hierarchical structures and divisions of labor, power, and discourse. The feminist texts gathered here will also pose these questions and in so doing interrogate some of the generic distinctions that operate in literary criticism. What I am calling utopian fiction also verges on science fiction, myth, history, and theory. During the decade at issue here utopian fiction has constituted the potential site of a radical feminist practice both textual and political. That site demands a long, close look, for it is the "place where ideology is coiled: in narrative structure," in Rachel Du Plessis's fine formulation.[21]

The novels discussed here all are based on: 1) a model of static and/or dynamic utopian rhetoric and its embodiment in the structures of narrative; 2) to a limited extent, the status of the national and historical differences in the development of feminist thought in France, the United States, and Canada; and 3) the long-standing and productive tension within feminism between the discourses on sexuality and on reproduction as it shapes representations of kinship systems and desires for community while it also arranges more general modes and relations of exchange. These investigations raise questions, crucial to current Western feminist theory, about the establishment and recognition of gender categories, the distinction made between "women" and "mothers", and the conflict and violence in these fictive feminist worlds.

I have assumed throughout that tacit rather than reified models of the state can be read within the discourse on the family. Classic utopias of the state, masculinist utopias, as it were, keep the question of the family on the level of an analogy that must finally be sublated. Lacking in those texts is a theory of the family as the place where the inhabitants of the projected utopian state would be formed. It is presumed that the governing of one's own conduct and that of others cannot be tracked from the domestic sphere but instead must be displaced and reproduced in the civil.

The opening chapter rewrites Charlotte Perkins Gilman into the literary and feminist history of the 1970s, the decade in which we can chart a proliferation of utopian writings by women, the decade of intense and multifarious forms of political activity on behalf of women. The ending, for here and now, will come with Margaret Atwood's *The Handmaid's Tale,* published in 1986, a coda to this striking phenomenon of literary production. Rather than offer another version of the not-yet, *The Handmaid's Tale* says, "not-so-fast" and interrogates implicitly some of the imaginative renderings of the re-solutions presented in the previous novels. Dystopian novels are crucial to a full engagement with the problematics of utopian thought, often too easily dismissed as synonymous with naive wish-fulfillment. My aim in including two dystopias is to attempt to give voice to that which the utopian leaves unspoken in order to do its work. Most of the utopian novels give space to what is wrong that they "mean" to right. But the systematic forms of oppression and repression on the basis of gender are not fully drawn out. That is what Suzy McKee Charnas and Atwood both delineate in narratives as nightmarish as the utopias are daydreamy. By the mid-1980s Atwood writes from the vantage point of already being able to see the force of feminist history recuperated by global, economic, and reproductive constraints on freedom for even a relatively small number of women in the world. Control over their own bodies and their own labor is wrested from them first—precisely what the utopian fictions, written in a mood of greater promise, had worked hard to construct and reconstruct, privileging the modes of reproduction, as do most of these works, for reasons discussed specifically in Chapter 2.

Chapter 1 links the twentieth-century histories of late first-wave American and early second-wave French feminism through a reading of two novels: Charlotte Perkins Gilman's *Herland* and Monique Wittig's *Les Guérillères*. *Herland* (produced serially in 1915) is the prototype for later feminist utopias, while *Les Guérillères* is the first example of the production of utopias which appeared in response to the women's liberation movement. They each represent forms of the genre which I define in this chapter in order to be able to read from the literary to the social text: the static utopia (Gilman) and the dynamic utopia (Wittig). The former adheres to and enacts the generic conventions crystallized in late-nineteenth-century utopian novels, and the latter manipulates convention only to break out of limitations set by traditional utopian structures. A central theoretical and practical issue already established here is the representation of reproduction. Gilman attends to this explicitly, while Wittig addresses it by negation. To amplify their differences it is necessary to situate the feminist politics of mothering in the early and late twentieth century and the dominant ideologies on the family and sexuality by which these politics were shaped. Wittig's work also opens discussion on the debates about the relation of women to violence, both as subjects of the enactment of violence and as its victims.

Chapter 2 enlarges on the question of narrative and political strategies through a discussion of two novels produced at the same historical time and place, the United States in 1975: Marge Piercy's *Woman on the Edge of Time* and Joanna Russ's *The Female Man*. Here the static and dynamic models will be linked to critical discussions of realist versus postmodernist texts and readerly versus writerly texts. Piercy's *Woman* is a contemporary rewriting of the nineteenth-century genre in late-twentieth-century dress, whereas Russ's *Man* stretches conventions and draws on the tradition of science fiction, thereby offering a more subtle feminist model of temporality and historical possibility. Both these texts work out thorough critiques of kinship structures, dominant forms of sexuality, and ideologies of romance. In terms of the questions of reproduction both authors draw on technological debates and fantasies of the 1970s which by now have been surpassed. We can see that they reproduce in fiction the theoretical analyses of Shulamith Firestone and Gayle Rubin and open onto the issues of intergenerational and interracial conflicts and their resolutions.

Chapter 3 works with two novels by the same author, *Walk to the End of the World,* a masculinist dystopia, and its feminist utopian sequel, *Motherlines,* by Suzy McKee Charnas. In this chapter it becomes possible to address the issues of narrative and kinship in a more thoroughgoing manner because of the development of a single character central to both novels: a slave in the first novel, she becomes an embodiment of hope in and for the utopian future. Charnas also demands a reading of utopian longings by way of the dystopia that makes change necessary and desirable. Within the story she represents a temporal scope that shows a more problematic relation to ideology than the earlier works studied. In the dystopia ruled by older white men, women are breeders and inarticulate slaves. The setting is postnuclear conflagration, where rumors and legends circulate that some women have escaped and found refuge outside the territories of the men. The sequel then explores the flight of Alldera, the courier in possession of language, and her subsequent encounter with these women of legend. More than other utopian fictions, this one fully addresses the conflicts of shared and diverse histories. Differences of age, race, and history are reformulated through a kinship structure that grows out of a nomadic economy.

Chapter 4 pairs one French and one American novel again. These two fictions represent aspects of the relationship utopian rhetoric has often had to the discourse of religion. They also recast utopian temporality: Christiane Rochefort's *Archaos,* set in a nostalgic arcadian past, and E. M. Broner's *Weave of Women,* set in a geographically specified and dynamically evoked present. Here the patriarchal underpinnings of religious "states" are disclosed and overturned through the rewriting of already established structures rather than their abandonment. In a balance with what would appear to be the most conservative narrative choice is the play with textual irony that is made to work within entrenched religious traditions. The very nature of the sacred and the spiritual, found to be lacking in the joyousness they were once meant to provide, must be scrutinized. Both Rochefort and Broner want to infuse the secular network with a sense of community. As a result, readers are presented with everyday ritualized moments. This allows a closer look at the family-state relationship, since both narratives dramatize potential takeovers of regimes that remain in place though their rulers have been removed.

Chapter 5 comprises another bilingual pairing: two Canadian novels. Louky Bersianik's *The Eugélionne,* where a woman traveler searches for the perfect planet, was first published in French in Canada in 1976; it is set beside Margaret Atwood's 1986 dystopian novel *The Handmaid's Tale.* Like the leap demanded in the move from Gilman to Wittig, the juxtaposition of the two works allows for a provisional closure that Atwood's novel suggests, both by the muted utopian rhetoric it criticizes and demystifies and the dystopian discourse it brings out of the darkness. The fact that both writers are Canadian, one anglophone, one francophone, gives a geopolitical texture to the questions of marginality, identity, and difference which each novel takes up. Where Gilman's work reminds us how the utopian story could be told, Atwood's warns us that we cannot simply tell the utopian tale any longer, and that if we dare to, we forget her cautionary fable at our own risk. It is in this sense that these two novels serve as frames for the movable feminist selves and communities in the arena where the eight other novels are staged.

To date, the topic of feminist utopian fiction has been mapped out in special sessions at national and regional conferences, special issues of journals, collections of essays, and numerous articles.[22] This book formulates and groups such writings as a particular kind of narrative and political projection in order to situate the most recent manifestation in fiction of what is a transhistorical and cross-cultural need of feminist work: the ability to specify and articulate social change. Such projects and projections are produced within the discourse of activism, as well as that of theory and fiction, and come to function as ideological artifacts of what stories are and can be told at particular historical junctures. These works, deeply concerned with theory, simultaneously generate representations of wish, fear, and hope for change.

Chapter One

Remembering and Inventing

Charlotte Perkins Gilman's *Herland*
and Monique Wittig's *Les Guérillères*

History makes the exemplar . . . . the original text is, in effect, recreated by its progeny. It follows that generic exemplars are usually read according to an anachronistic set of conventions. . . . it is really the *second* work of a genre that creates the genre.

Gary Saul Morson
Boundaries of Genre

The master-warrior-speaker . . . needs a frontier to conquer and savages to civilize. . . . One should not attack him head-on but wage a guerrilla war of skirmishes and raids in a space and time other than those imposed for millennia by the masculine logos.

Jean-François Lyotard
"One of the Things at Stake in Women's Struggles"

Charlotte Perkins Gilman's *Herland* is among those last texts of the early-twentieth-century wave of feminism, and Monique Wittig's *Les Guérillères* is the first in a series of utopian fictions of a 1970s feminist cast.[1] Both are exemplary generic texts, written some fifty years apart, which shed light on each other and on the historical moments in which they were produced permitting us to chart the connections between early- and late-twentieth-century feminist theories and fictional practices.

Gilman's *Herland* has had a sleeping-beauty history that is linked to the selective memory of the marketplace. First written as a serial novel in 1915 for Gilman's newspaper, *The Forerunner,* it was rediscovered and published as a book for the first time in 1979. It returns to us valued and marketed as a "lost feminist utopian novel." Our reading of *Herland* is doubled by its history, we might say. Despite its "lost" history, in 1979 Gilman's novel joined the group of texts it unwittingly spawned. We can think of Gilman's *Herland* as the "mother-text" and Wittig's novel as the first of the contemporary "amazon-texts," to take up one of the operative distinctions for this chapter.[2]

Gilman's novel will be read as a feminism of the past, speaking to the present about a still and always deferred future, and Wittig's *Les Guérillères,* as a contemporary feminism that replies to this invented and remembered past. Such a reading interweaves time and history and parallels the tasks of feminism and utopia: to seek out a past, to examine the present critically, to posit a future, and to tell a tale of and for that imagined future. Gilman's and Wittig's voices are strikingly different; these differences will be our guide as we disclose and examine two literary and political situations tied by history yet separated by time. Such a gap in time will not necessarily reveal notions of progress; what we are looking for are shifts of emphasis, argument, and interest. The limits reached and tested by these fictions will tell us a great deal about the situation of feminism at its high-water marks of this century.

What makes these utopian fictions feminist is that women are not dismissed as one question among many, as in classical utopias; their place is everywhere. Although Gilman's novel serves here as the exemplar, as Ann J. Lane's introduction to the reprinted edition of *Herland* indicates, Gilman was certainly not the first woman to write a utopian novel. Utopian fiction was a genre at the height of its popularity in the last two decades of the nineteenth century, and Charlotte Perkins Gilman, a young woman who in other texts used other voices, chose this utopian voice to embody her view of feminism as a philosophy of growth. Such a philosophy was conceivable only if it posited the full humanity of women as subjects, not objects, in the world.

Gilman's productivity as a writer and lecturer was prodigious. Her "rediscovery" points to one of the major tasks of feminism, one Wittig also upholds: the need to remember. In a study of theory and history written in 1917 and titled simply *Feminism,* Correa Moylan Walsh calls Gilman "the foremost American female feminist."[3] Walsh groups Gilman with Olive Schreiner and Ellen Key as the "foremost living leaders in English-speaking lands."[4] Gilman's autobiography, *The Living of Charlotte Perkins Gilman,* describes her years of national and international travel in the cause of socialism and feminism.[5] It is difficult to imagine, from the activity chronicled in *The Living,* that this is the same woman who in 1899 published "The Yellow Wallpaper," a short fictional piece whose autobiographical heroine undergoes the infamous rest-cure of S. Weir Mitchell, a nerve specialist in the era of neurasthenia and hysteria.[6] With its fictional documentation of Gilman's actual nervous breakdown after the birth of her daughter, "The Yellow Wallpaper" might be placed in Gilman's body of work as the inverse of the world of fulfilled and exalted motherhood portrayed in *Herland*. Gilman herself only began Mitchell's cure. That Gilman has been rediscovered as theorist and utopian novelist is in part a result of her refusal to follow the "experts' advice."[7] Mitchell advised Gilman never to leave her child and never to touch pen to paper; he was not alone in linking women's increased intellectual activity and the spread of nervous disorders, documented in the United States in his work and in that of George Miller Beard, for example, and in Europe by Sigmund Freud, Josef Breuer, and Jean Charcot.[8]

During her lifetime Gilman's best-known work was *Women and Economics*, first published in 1898, translated into seven languages, and used as a college textbook in the 1920s.[9] It is here, and in her articles in *The Forerunner,* that her socialist and feminist visions merge. The interdependence of socialism and feminism was widely acknowledged by some of the early-twentieth-century feminists. Both movements were internationally active, and they sometimes worked together. Women like Gilman, Emma Goldman, and Crystal Eastman, and their European counterparts Clara Zetkin and Alexandra Kollontai, were as well known for their socialism, anarchism, or communism as for their feminism. Gilman fervently pamphleteered against a world war that threatened to affect the intellectual scope and expansion of the new century. Ironically, that very antiwar activity would subsume the suffrage issue she supported with equal fervor. Though writers like Crystal Eastman were active in the interests of feminism and socialism, emphasis in the postwar years turned primarily to reformist and personal ends until the granting of suffrage in 1920 brought to a stall the long-active feminist debates.

If 1970s Western feminism grew out of "new left" politics of the advanced capitalist societies of Western Europe, one of its first moves was to reject the masculinist or phallocentric orientation of those movements. One need only read Marge Piercy's essay, "The Grand Coolie Damn," to see catalogued the sexist dynamics of radical student politics of the late 1960s in the United States.[10] Not until the socialist feminist conference at Yellow Springs, Ohio, in

1975 did American feminists begin systematically to rejoin the struggles of class, sex, and race.[11] Despite such attempts, feminism continues to maintain a separate set of intellectual questions precisely because the earlier "marriages" of socialism and feminism failed to confront the patriarchal heart of socialism. This was apparent even in Walsh's 1917 history of feminism: "The woman movement has been almost synchronous with socialism (like Jill, tumbling after)."[12] The following quotation is from Gilman's autobiography, on which she worked until her suicide ("I prefer chloroform to cancer") in 1935. In the chapter entitled "Home" Gilman comments on feminism and socialism as they have been transformed in the postwar decade:

> There is now nothing to prevent women from becoming as fully human in their social development as men; and although just now they seem more anxious to exhibit sex than ever, the real progress in humanness is there and will gradually overcome this backwash of primitive femininity. . . .
>
> Socialism, long misrepresented and misunderstood under the violent propaganda of Marxism, has been fairly obliterated in the public mind by the Jewish-Russian nightmare, Bolshevism. . . . It may be years before that legitimate and gradual social advance can be presented with any hope of understanding.[13]

What Gilman calls "primitive femininity" underlies her discussion of women's condition and the ways overdeveloped sex-distinctions inform women's tasks and functions. We are also able to read within Gilman's radical politics the progressivism, racism, and nationalism common to reformist, even radical, thought during the early twentieth century. Not only does the quotation expose her anti-Semitism and xenophobia, it also demonstrates her belief that feminism had accomplished its goals, that women were already free to be all they might wish.

The masculinist biases of radical thought were not always apparent to radical feminists of the nineteenth and early twentieth centuries. Variants of "woman's sphere," "feminine nature," and the "eternal feminine" form the essentialist underpinnings of feminist theory of the time. All of these notions depend on the biologism of late-nineteenth-century thought represented by the Social

Darwinism of free thinkers such as Lester Ward, Gilman's mentor and her probable model for a male feminist. The philosophical implications of such views of woman as "other" and immanent were systematically reexamined only in 1949 in Simone de Beauvoir's *The Second Sex*.[14] The excessive faith in science and progress that permeates literary and critical work at the turn of the century also informs the teleological arguments of Marxism and Darwinism.

Feminists like Gilman believed that feminine qualities would tame masculine ones and create the balance necessary for cultural and natural *growth,* the key word of Gilman's vocabulary. In *Women and Economics* Gilman uses analogies to the animal world to describe male and female characteristics. The religious and medical institutions of Gilman's time put forth views of women as passionless and sexually disinterested. While Gilman does a great deal to prove that such concepts of sex distinctions are socially transmitted, she also accepts certain distinctions as biologically and psychically immutable. For our purposes one of Gilman's most significant assumptions is that women's essential tendency is to *protect,* as opposed to men, whose tendency is to *fight.* Contemporary feminism must repeatedly undertake the self-critical task of checking theory and practice so that they do not succumb to the same trap of positing essentialist notions of femininity. This is the impasse reached and risked by feminist theories of the 1970s. At the (apparent) impasse presented by demands for equality *and* acceptance of différences, it is necessary to continue to strive to rescue the idea of difference from its connection with other hierarchical and dualistic systems of thought.

In *Women and Economics,* at a certain moment we can see the wish-fulfillment impulse behind utopian thought. At one point in this book Gilman imagines "an extraterrestrial sociologist, studying human life and hearing for the first time of our so-called 'maternal sacrifice' as a means of benefiting the species."[15] Some seventeen years later another sociologist, Vandyck Jennings, appears as the narrator of *Herland*. In a reversal of the earlier character, Van is of the Earth, and Herland is somewhere else, exotic and mysterious in the minds of Van and his two fellow explorers, Jeff, the genteel survivor of the chivalric hero, and Terry, the wealthy womanizer. *Herland* gives a feminist twist to the woman's sphere elaborated by late-nineteenth-century ideologues who dealt with the "woman question." It is not surprising that Van, the modern sociologist, is our guide and narrator in *Herland*. It is also Van who gives this women's world its name. When we realize that we are to view this feminist utopia through the gaze and voice of a man—albeit the most receptive of the three male characters— some of the ideological trappings of early-twentieth-century feminism are set in relief for us.

Herland is presented to its readers from the outset as a text "written from memory." Therefore it is meant to be seen as inherently flawed, misrecorded, and even misremembered by the narrator. Van and his friends in the course of their travels have heard stories of a land of women. Excited by the challenge of such an idea, they become obsessed with finding "Womanland," giving this place a variety of names before establishing its "true" existence. In this sense Herland is very much a country of the mind, a mythic and perhaps terrible place: "Fraid the ladies will eat you?" (p. 6). They baptise it Feminisia, Ladyland, and finally Herland, the possessive marking it as named by an outsider. We never know what the women themselves call their country. The narrative and ethnocentrically American point of view is further reinforced by the title of Gilman's sequel, written the following year, *With Her in Ourland*; Ourland is Van's world, the United States, though that novel includes world travel.[16]

Gilman's choice of a male narrator is revealing in many ways. The choice is one which might make male readers of *The Forerunner* more comfortable by giving them the privileged place of observer or storyteller; for female readers, however, Van and his friends are the objects of humor, and even humiliation. The choice also gives Gilman a great deal of space in which to play, for this is one of her few truly lighthearted pieces of writing. *Herland* maintains its humor through the constant and repeated exposure of the men's preconceptions about what a world of women would or could be. Female readers are situated with Van as outsiders but also distanced from him in their responses to a women's world. Yet giving Van narrative control reasserts his dominance—he reconstructs by memory the events which took place somewhere, sometime, outside the text.

Van, Jeff, and Terry approach Herland "manfully." They arrive by plane and powered boat, armed with the instruments of voyeuristic power: camera, binoculars, and guns. They are easily captured by unarmed, cautious women whom they perceive as more like "intent boy[s]," but who are "all moved by precisely the same feelings" (p. 22). When Terry, the headstrong one of the three, fires his revolver, he turns their welcome into a capture. Mutual observation begins when the three men are surrounded by a large group of women. Sex distinctions immediately create confusion and panic. We will encounter throughout this study such moments of seemingly desperate need to determine sex and recognize and maintain gender differences. The large group of women is perceived as hostile, like an army. But since they are "only" women the men cannot fight them. Their consternation is managed in this series of judgments: "Never, anywhere before, had I seen women of precisely this quality. Fishwives and market women might show similar strength, but it was coarse and heavy. These were merely athletic—light and powerful. College professors, teachers, writers—many women showed similar intelligence but often wore a strained nervous look, while these were as calm as cows, for all their evident intellect" (p. 22). Appearances to the contrary, these cannot be women as Van has learned to see and recognize them.

The tension of this crucial moment of the men trapped by the women is broken by the sound of Terry's gun. At this sound the women subdue the men with anesthesia as the chapter closes. Rendered thus passive and now observed by the women, the men are transformed: "We felt like small boys, very small boys, caught doing mischief in some gracious lady's house" (p. 19). The women appear neither young nor beautiful. They cannot be lured by the jewels and brightly colored cloth Terry has brought to support his bid to become king of Ladyland. De-sexed in the eyes of the men, the women are variously referred to as "aunts," "colonels," and "sturdy burghers." Van, the enlightened man, explains for the reader what the very word "woman" suggests: "'Woman' in the abstract is young, and, we assume, charming. As they get older they pass off the stage, somehow, into private ownership mostly, or out of it altogether. But these good ladies were very much on the stage, and yet any one of them might have been a grandmother" (p. 20).

Just as the appearance of these women renders them asexual as far as the men are concerned, the indigenous clothing they find in place of their possessions when they awaken after their capture leaves them "feeling like a lot of neuters." After a second escape attempt, the men's and the reader's in(tro)duction to Herland begins in earnest. This time each man is brought back under the surveillance of five women. On the return trip, expecting punishment, they are treated only as "truants." This also provides "a good opportunity to see the country . . . perfect roads . . . endless lines of trees" (p. 43). Everywhere they stop, women gather to see the men, for news of their arrival has already spread. And again looks are exchanged, each group seeking out the other. Herlanders, we soon learn, have not seen men for 2000 years, and Van, Jeff, and Terry "caught many glimpses . . . no boys. We all looked, carefully" (p. 43). The reader may wonder just what they are looking for, given the non-gender-specific clothing of Herland.

While the men and the women have yet to master each other's language, Van reports by the next morning a conversation which opens up the question of reproduction in Herland. The misapprehensions begin to multiply and the customs clash. Finally Terry asks, " 'Ladies . . . are there no men in this country?' " Terry, indicating his beard and throwing back his broad shoulders, says, " 'Men, real men' " (p. 45). It is Terry who uses the term "parthenogenesis," creating immediate confusion when he explains the idea of virginity and attaches the term to females but not to males. The conversation moves rapidly from reproduction to history to domesticated animals and the carnivorous diet of the world the men inhabit. But the reproductive practices of Herland take up more than one conversation; in fact the rest of the novel continually returns to motherhood as the primary institution and even the religion of this society.

Through Gilman's exposition of motherhood in *Herland,* the reader can begin to distinguish some characteristics of turn-of-the-century feminist political theory. *Herland* is written in between what Linda Gordon has located as two distinct periods of feminism: a mid-nineteenth-century "sexual ideal which I shall call domesticity," and a period surrounding World War I emphasizing "sexual liberation" and "romanticizing the importance of sexual pleasure."[17] Gilman's possibilities of representation are caught precisely between these two ideological moments. She has broken with the reactionary cult of "woman's sphere" but has not come to grips with speaking of sexual pleasure. Gilman's late-Victorian sexual ethics are apparent in all her writings. These contradictions are obvious in *Herland* and finally express not only the author's blindness but a historically determined blind spot as well. We can read her emphasis on motherhood through parthenogenesis as a compromise with her ideological double bind.

The *Herland* discourse on motherhood goes beyond what we might imagine this word to mean: "Every woman of them placed motherhood not only higher than other duties, but so far higher that there were no other duties, one might almost say" (p. 140). It becomes especially significant after the marriages of Van and Ellador, Jeff and Celis, and Terry and Alima. The triple marriage ceremony is cause for celebration in Herland. It is heralded as the "great change," though it is the men who insist on the need for a ceremony. They feel they have little to offer these women, and they assume that giving them their names will be very much appreciated. Since the Herlanders have no notion of marriage, the only ideas available to them come from the men of "Ourland." The men's ideas about marriage are expressed in words that have no currency here: home, privacy, possession, wife. The men assume they will live with their "wives"—the women cannot imagine why this would be desirable or expected. In much of the last two chapters Van constantly revises his expectations about marriage with Ellador. Ellador understands sexuality as it is connected with reproduction but not as anything more or other than that; Van says, "these people had . . . not the faintest idea of that *solitude à deux* we are so fond of" (p. 125). Van regrets that he "could not sweep her off her feet by [his] own emotion as [he] had unconsciously assumed would be the case" (p. 126). In trying to explain his difficulties the following comments and questions from Ellador are reported:

> "Do you mean . . . that with you, when people marry, they go right on doing this in season and out of season, with no thought of children at all? . . ."
>
> "There is something very beautiful in the idea. . . . It has—I judge from what you tell me—the most ennobling ef-

fect on character . . . and, as a result, you have a world full of
continuous lovers, ardent, happy, mutually devoted, always
living on that high tide of supreme emotion which we had
supposed to belong only to one season and one use. And you
say it has other results, stimulating all high creative
work. . . ."

She was silent, thinking.

So was I. (P. 127)

Terry, the would-be ruler, rejects the Herland notions of asexual
marriage and tries to rape Alima. This act precipitates the ending
of the novel, because the women decide that he must leave, and
Ellador takes this occasion to voyage out with Van.

Van learns to love "up" in loving Ellador, thus transforming
his ideas about sexuality and returning again to motherhood: "I
found that loving 'up' was a very good sensation after all. It gave
me a queer feeling, way down deep, . . . that they were right
somehow—that this was the way to feel. It was like—coming
home to mother. . . . It was a sense of getting home; of being clean
and rested; of safety and yet freedom . . . a love that didn't irritate
and didn't smother" (pp. 141–42). We ought not to be surprised
that Van translates Herland's ideas of motherhood into terms he
had known earlier in his life, nor by his repeated perceptions of
feeling like a child vis-à-vis the women of Herland. In *Women and
Economics* Gilman critiques the accepted notions of motherhood
in the following way: "More sacred than religion, more binding
than the law. . . . This matriolatry is a sentiment so deep-seated,
wide-spread, and long-established as to be dominant in every
class of minds. It is so associated with our religious instincts, on
the one hand, and our sex-instincts, on the other, both of which
we have long been forbidden to discuss—the one being too holy
and the other too unholy."[18]

Herland accomplishes a dialectical turn in the context of
motherhood, making it no less a social value but rather the primary social function, since it includes the highest good of all, education. Gilman replaces religion with sacred motherhood and
eliminates sexuality. She changes the object of worship and does
away with the unholy and unhealthy animal instinct that made

the drives toward sex and food (a repeated analogy in *Herland*) allied instincts.

A distinctive characteristic of 1970s feminism, according to Gordon, is an attention to "women's own sexual pleasure" in relation to the "norms of sexual behavior which are distorted by male supremacy."[19] Though theories and speculations about matriarchy reemerge, often in the hands of feminists more radical than Gilman, Gordon notes the essential conservatism that accompanied the popularity of matriarchy theory among nineteenth-century men and women. She helps us to situate Gilman's work in light of an ideological double bind. Gilman is a twentieth-century feminist who, as an apologist for the cult of motherhood, reminds us that the issue of motherhood was argued passionately by feminists and antifeminists alike. This remains a source of tension in contemporary feminist theory, which continues to rewrite its own attitudes toward reproductive freedom and parenthood. Like Gilman, contemporary feminists attempt to disentangle the biological mother from the function of mothering.

Just as the nineteenth-century women's movement privileged motherhood and denied sexuality to the detriment of a fuller conception of women's lives, the privileging of sexuality in the 1920s was, in its own way, as partial an account of women as the earlier version. While rejecting a limited view of women's capacities and desires, the ideological critique of the family initiated by feminists of the 1920s still masked a pro-male attitude. De Beauvoir's insight into woman as other in *The Second Sex* was only worked out decades later, for the male was still viewed as "the human type." Demands for sexual liberation were articulated within an accepted heterosexual ideology—a single rather than double standard, a desire for freedom clearly defined within male norms. In this sense, Gilman's feminism was in many ways more woman-centered than the radical birth-control movement of the World War I era. Not until the 1970s did political and theoretical questions converge to examine the need for "woman-defined kinds of sexual activity" and to separate sex from reproduction. Finally lesbian feminism emerged as a strategy to break away from previous definitions of sex as allied to reproduction.

My focus on Gordon's analysis of the birth-control debate as a path to trace the development of feminist theory points to one of the sadly ironic, long-term effects of what was, in the early years of this century, a radical program of education and a grass-roots political movement. Gordon clarifies how most revolutionary demands for reproductive freedom are easily assimilated by capitalist patriarchy. As early as the 1920s, Gordon shows, opponents of birth control claimed it would lead to "race suicide," deliberately confusing birth-control demands with questions of reproductive freedom and women's rights. The parallels with today's prochoice versus pro-life abortion debate are clear. Then as now, feminism inevitably interpreted the family as a social, not merely a biological or economic, institution. Gilman's novel, set in a world of women, keeps its critique of capitalism and patriarchy implicit until the men's view of marriage leads to open conflict. The changes Gordon enumerates find their counterparts in contemporary utopian novels and the social planning they envision. Predictably, the emphasis on alternative family and kinship structures is a primary aspect of these fictions.

Another key to understanding the changes which have occurred between early- and late-twentieth-century feminism is found in the narrative strategies available to Gilman and Wittig. In Gordon's distinctions in examining the issues connected with reproduction and sexuality, the mother-amazon split I mentioned earlier characterizes the lesbian-feminist political position elaborated only by late-twentieth-century feminists. While *Herland* represents a world of mothers, *Les Guérillères* and *Lesbian Peoples* represent a distinctively new world of daughters and "companion lovers."[20] To make a political issue of lesbian love marks the exile of the Amazons throughout the ancient world charted by Diner. In *Lesbian Peoples*, written after *Les Guérillères*, Wittig and Zeig rework and reinvent that exile imposed by the mothers who have been compromised by heterosexual, patriarchal marriage. The mothers of Herland are outspokenly unsexual women; their passion is for a motherhood they themselves have institutionalized. *Lesbian Peoples* and *Les Guérillères* speak of female sexuality and desire through an explosive language that has come to be a part of the "novum" of contemporary feminism. Where violence is unnecessary and unthinkable in Gilman's world because Herlanders are seen as untainted by conflict, hostility, and aggression, the feminism of the 1970s first responds to this conceptual failure with a historical and epistemological position that requires a discussion of women's relation to violence. Where current feminist discussions of violence focus primarily on its use against women by men, Wittig's novels ask the questions about violence among women and against men. *Les Guérillères* represents women warriors both at play *and* at war.

In *Lesbian Peoples,* Wittig charts a history of the wanderings of the companion lovers under the dictionary entry "deserts": "Once, an arid land, an expanse of sand, every place which was not inhabited by lesbians. From which comes the expression, 'to go into the desert' " (p. 42). Gilman and Wittig know exile in both personal and political terms. Gilman was publicly maligned as an "unnatural mother" when she chose to have her daughter live with her husband and his second wife, Gilman's close friend, Grace Channing. This fact may help explain Herland's vindication of motherhood, especially in forms that transcend biological ties. Another exile, Wittig emigrated from France (Gaul) to the United States (Large Country, as it is renamed in *Lesbian Peoples*). Her choice to leave Paris responded to a radical split within the French women's movement in which she felt her position was no longer heard by her opponents, the "politics and psychoanalysis" group. This group chose to privilege a feminist rereading of Marxist politics and Lacanian psychoanalysis, while its leader, Antoinette Fouque, espoused a position emphasizing voice or speech over writing.[21] Wittig's own politics are best described as anarchistic, not a popular political position after the student revolts of May 1968, when psychoanalysis came to predominate in the cultural and intellectual context.

The foreclosed sexuality of *Herland* erupts in *Les Guérillères* as a shared erotic play and display which negates the mother and ignores the question of reproduction. The lesbian peoples, a later name for these guerilla warriors, are not defined in "relationship," except insofar as they are "companion lovers." Among the words designated as obsolete in the (present) Glorious Age are "to have," "wife," and "woman." Wittig's definition of the word "mother" is instructive for a rereading of Herland's "maternal pantheism":

During the Golden Age, everyone in the terrestrial garden was

called amazon. Mothers were not distinct from daughters. . . .

   After the first settlements in the cities everything continued as before. . . .

   Then came a time when some daughters, and some
mothers did not like wandering anymore in the terrestrial garden. They began to stay in the cities and most often they
watched their abdomens grow. This activity brought them, it
is said, great satisfaction. Things went so far in this direction
that they refused to have any other interests. In vain, their
friends asked them to join them in their travels. They always
had a new abdomen to watch. Thus they called themselves
mothers. . . . The first generation of static mothers who refused to leave their cities, began. From then on, they called the
others "eternal, immature daughters, amazons. . . ." At that
time the mothers stopped calling themselves amazons and the
mothers and the amazons began to live separately. (*LP*, pp.
108–9)

The rejection of the amazons by the mothers defines the history
separating the Golden Age from the Glorious one. The "lesbian
people's" dictionary represents an attempt to reinstate an amazon
continuity for the companion lovers, the new amazons. The utopian slogan of May 1968, "*l'imagination au pouvoir*" (power to
the imagination), lives on in the lover's dictionary where the lesbian peoples reproduce "by the ear" and little companion lovers
sprout among the cabbages.[22]

   The textual and political practices represented in *Les Guérillères* are as anarchic as the companion lovers' reproductive techniques. Some feminist critics cite Wittig's work as exemplary of
écriture feminine, a writing which disrupts, disturbs, and de-
ranges the language of a culturally embedded patriarchy. Against
logocentrism and phallocentrism, which privilege unity and the
word while they deny the presence of the body in language,
French feminist theorists have advocated plurality, voice, breath,
and the presence of the female body in the text itself.[23] Wittig herself rejects the essentialism of this position. Her essay "One Is Not
Born a Woman" borrows this primary insight from de Beauvoir
and constructs the case for a materialist feminism.[24] This position

placed her outside the French feminist debate preoccupied as it had been with the status of words like "feminist," "psychoanalysis," "politics," "the unconscious," and "the Symbolic." Since 1968 these words of the "fathers" have become the disputed terrain of the daughters. Living as she now does in the United States, Wittig has become a displaced voice in both the French and American contexts. Her contributions have been written out of contemporary feminism as recorded in the *Histoire du feminisme français*.[25] Wittig's work aims to cultivate those deserts not yet visited by the lesbian peoples. She finds herself in the uneasy position of having rejected both American cultural feminism *and* French psychoanalytic politics: "Warning to the companion lovers, if you have an unconscious, you know all about it. But if you have one, all the more reason to be careful of the traffickers of the unconscious" (*LP*, p. 157). French feminist theory, though not the French women's liberation movement, shared and explored territory similar to that explored by what has been named poststructuralism. This placed the development of French feminism in the difficult and ambivalent situation of self-definition in relation to the *maître-penseurs*. Some of these magisterial presences had to be integrated to a greater or lesser extent. Aspects of this context could not be avoided by women thinkers. To wit: while rereading Freud, Jacques Lacan reinvented a new patriarchal discourse on femininity and female sexuality. Jacques Derrida developed a metaphor of the hymen to displace phallocentrism and spoke of a text endlessly unfolding itself. Michel Foucault discussed the institutionalization of madness, the clinic, and the discourse of sexuality. And Roland Barthes explored sexual difference as it affects both libidinal and narrative economies. French feminists found themselves both within these masterful discourses of their culture and wanting to deconstruct them. They learned to speak these languages *and* to name the inability of these discourses to give voice to "the feminine."[26] In response to this dilemma, some women refused to write because writing was seen as a phallocentric mode; they only spoke. Some became preoccupied with the status of voice and breath, rather than the work; with the process of language rather than its products.

Wittig's preoccupation with process and overthrow (*renversement*) is signaled in the opening poem of *Les Guérillères*. In the narrative, both history and story occur in a dynamic present tense; only the final fragment shocks by its move into the past. This is not so much a circular text as one which alternately spirals back to a revolution already made by Alexandra (K)Ollontai, "the aged grizzled woman soldier," and forward to revolution, defined as a refusal of closure. The past is only seemingly hidden by the present; *Les Guérillères* finally reminds and challenges us to renew our efforts to recount our histories. It reminds us that the crucial choice of what will be remembered is ours to make. *Les Guérillères* and *Lesbian Peoples* can also be read as compendiums of the amazon myths which recall and invent a potential past to suggest a utopian future. When we read Wittig, we are already within the Glorious Age.

One of the shocking moments of *Les Guérillères* occurs when the women (*elles*) burn the feminaries, texts of received knowledge in need of being reconceived and rewritten. The celebration attending the auto-da-fé of the feminaries demonstrates a narrative and political break from the inherited, false continuity of history. Orthodoxy names heresy. Though at first seen as texts of overthrow and discontinuity, the feminaries supply the women with words, images, archetypes, and icons for their bodies drawn from the symbolic preserves of patriarchy. The body catalogued by the feminaries is a body-in-parts. When they reject the feminaries, the women reject a fragmented body and the metonymy which denies the whole in order to privilege its parts. Replacing the feminaries is the "great register":

> Every now and again one of them approaches and writes something therein. . . . it is useless to open it at the first page and search for any sequence. One may take it at random and find something one is interested in. This may be very little. Diverse as the writings are they all have a common feature. Not a moment passes without one of the women approaching to write something therein. Or else a reading aloud of some passage takes place. It may also happen that the reading occurs without any audience, save for a fly that bothers the reader by settling on her temple. (Pp. 53–54)

Here the women are portrayed as speakers, knowers, and bearers of fables. They change from readers of orthodoxy to writers of texts cast against the canon. When Gilman's Herlanders rewrite history without undue reverence for the past, they attempt a progressive revision the guérillères reverse, revolutionize, and subvert. Once the feminaries have fulfilled their function they are burned and reborn, phoenix-like in the great register: the amazons are dead, long live the companion lovers! Where Gilman writes the book of mothers, Wittig writes the book of daughters, amazons, and lesbians.

Les Guérillères, in contrast to *Herland,* may be said to be without a discernible narrator, though narration as the writing of history is one of Wittig's structural and polemical concerns. The narration of *Les Guérillères,* always in the present tense, the now in which history must be written, comes to us first from the feminaries and then from the great register. Where the feminaries contain history as and from the past, the great register contains the new histories written as we read them. The war fought in the second and third parts of *Les Guérillères* is also being written into history, simultaneously inscribed as text.

The contrast between *Herland* and *Les Guérillères* can be delineated with equal sharpness by considering the ways the two fictions conclude. In *Herland* closure and resolution come about when the wonderwoman of them all, Ellador, now married to Van, voyages out to his world of Brotherhood. Again as reversal, in *Les Guérillères,* a few young men come to join the women after the "longest war," that imaginary war in which the women of Herland fought some 2,000 years before. In *Les Guérillères* militancy is overt and violent. In *Herland,* despite the fact that physical culture is an important facet of the education of its citizens, the use of force occurs only when the text deals with Terry, the man's man, who resists the women until he is finally exiled.

While the novels are taken as autonomous productions when we speak of Gilman and Wittig as authors, neither novel can be removed from the political and ideological structures dominant at the time of its appearance in the literary marketplace. Utopian fiction invites us to consider at another level the problems encountered in dealing with representation. In its textual practice as in its portraits of social behavior, utopian fiction may present a challenge to the dominant modes of representation, testing and stretching their limits of possibility. Time and history intervene both in Gilman's writing and in the reading, which permits us to be appalled by her race of Aryan Overmothers, (un)surprised by her thoroughly integrated Victorian view of the "sex instinct," and amused by Herlanders calling that other, outside world "bisexual." If we examine exactly which limits are explored we may then attempt to read (from our own determined and determining moment) a connection between the fictional practice of feminist utopian writing and contemporary feminist theory. It is easy to see the gaps between Gilman's then and our now. And though we may be closer to feminists of Wittig's late 1960s re-generation, we already cast a retrospective glance at this first new feminist utopian fiction.

In *Herland,* generations after the parthenogenetic miracle first occurs, motherhood is still the object of worship. Laws are always updated as these women learn from their history, not viewing the past as sacred. Motherhood and early education of the daughters are the supreme tasks in this society. Van pays rapt tribute to this "Maternal Pantheism" and is exalted by the comparison of "Mother Earth, bearing fruit," all this just after he has realized that "feminine charms" are "mere reflected masculinity." He also informs us that "children were the—*raison d'être* in this country" (pp. 59, 51). Joanna Russ cuts through this preoccupation with motherhood when she notes that Gilman "creates a Utopia with a gap in its passions."[27] For us, that gap is what Russ aptly terms "the trade-off of sensuality for freedom," at least a sensuality that would also include sexual passion. For the women of Herland do not lack passion; they channel it into work, mothering, physical exercise, and various forms of play and pageantry. While the guérillères laugh wildly, the Herlanders giggle gently. Russ remains puzzled and curious about the underscoring within the text of the many pockets in the women's layered articles of clothing. Once again it is Van who reminds us of how well-placed they are, "the middle one in particular," adding later that they also allow for "decorative lines of stitching." We are then told with condescension how this shows "a practical intelligence, coupled with fine artistic feeling" (pp. 38, 74). What is suggested by the middle pocket, and the fact that both Gilman and Wittig describe their women's movements as being like those of kangaroos? In *Lesbian Peoples,* kangaroos carry the little companion lovers in their pouches, evolutionary middle pockets presenting a "natural" instant of duality in unity and vice versa. Clothing in Gilman's day occupied both hands, one to lift the skirts, the other to carry a reticule. But in Herland, clothing allows freedom of movement, and items to be carried can be distributed throughout the various pockets. The hands are then free—for access to the body, which, though it is not mentioned, is something we may assume in our disbelief in a society of asexual women whose desires are limited, we are told, to those months of "utter exaltation" when an "inner demand for a child began to be felt" (p. 70). This "child-longing" must eventually be subject to population control in the manner of negative eugenics, a preeminent feature of the patriarchal response to feminist demands for birth control and contraceptive methods. To expect a utopia from 1915 without this "gap in its passions" is, perhaps, to ask Gilman to deliver the impossible, given the ideological circumscriptions of the time and her own resistance to speaking about female sexuality.

Les Guérillères and *Herland* both depict a society of women and female children, but with palpable differences in their modes of representation and textual practice. When we read *Les Guérillères* its graphic diversity assaults us. In the original French edition, a large O fills the first page, followed by a poem; then begins a litany of women's names as poems, and at intervals, two repetitions of the large O, and another poem just before the last fragment. (The English translation curiously reverses the first O and poem.) The first section, the circle, or O, of *Les Guérillères*, sets forth a radical attitude toward language and sexuality. This section ends with the burning of the feminaries mentioned earlier. Before the feminaries fulfill their function we read that the women are "prisoners of the mirror" (p. 31). They tell stories, a privileged and pleasurable activity, and they also begin to ask "how to decide that an event is worthy of remembrance" (p. 28). The song of the siren, a continuous O, "evokes for them, like everything that recalls the O, the zero or the circle, the vulval ring" (p. 14). And the "feminaries privilege the symbols of the circle"; it is there that the women learn the repertoire of names and designations for their genitalia. Erika Ostrovsky has traced Wittig's cyclical narrative of creation and destruction in which, we are reminded, "all action is overthrow."[28] For Wittig, the burning of the feminaries is "an excuse for celebrations": "The women say that it may be that the feminaries have fulfilled their function. They say they have no means of knowing. They say that thoroughly indoctrinated as they are with ancient texts no longer to hand, these seem to them outdated. All they can do to avoid being encumbered with useless knowledge is to heap them up in the squares and set fire to them" (p. 49).

From now on the stories chosen to be remembered will become history as entered into the great register. And we readers are cautioned by the words "it is useless to open it at the first page and search for any sequence." Now the women "must stress above all their strength and their courage." And this requires abandoning the images of a body-in-parts: "The women say that they perceive their bodies in their entirety. They say that they do not favour any of its parts on the grounds that it was formerly a forbidden object. They say that they do not want to become prisoners of their own ideology" (pp. 57–58).

The women warriors learn the "ancient texts" of history the better to overthrow them. Wittig writes less "against meaning" than against certain texts—"WHICH IS TO WRITE VIOLENCE / OUTSIDE THE TEXT / IN ANOTHER WRITING." But *Les Guérillères* is not just another writing. It is another utopia; one in formation which includes a war and not just the aftermath of some natural or social holocaust, as in other utopias such as *Herland* and Gilman's earlier novel, *Moving the Mountain* (1911). Wittig writes violence in her "other text"; she presents a utopia in which women do violence. Not simply a text of rage, *Les Guérillères* portrays women at war with men more openly than in earlier feminist writings. Although Gilman wrote in the midst of a world war, *Herland*'s war of the women against the already decimated male population is not represented in the text. Two thousand years later, the need for violence is long extirpated. Wittig's women gather their strength for war as they had done in pre-feminary history. They are warriors who get drunk, dance, sing, and, with the "integrity of the body their first principle, advance marching together into another world" (p. 72).

Unlike Gilman's advanced feminist state in which the process of change has led to a renewed curiosity about that outside world where things "must be better," *Les Guérillères* is a dynamic utopia represented in the process of actively rejecting the dominant ideology. The guérillères gather their knowledge carefully as they rewrite the dictionary that later "becomes" *Lesbian Peoples.* They reject dualistic and hierarchical modes of thought which had previously named them only negatively in terms derived from the norms of masculinity. At the same time they receive reports of casualties from the front and tell stories, such as the one of Julie, another woman killed in the struggle for knowledge. The laughter of the guérillères incites and is ferocious—a victorious laughter of the body made whole, a sound of strength and courage which brings down the bricks in the ceiling but "does not lessen" (p. 92). The women remember the strictures of the past, as they remember freedoms of the past—to make war, to walk alone, to bathe bare-bellied. This is the motive of Wittig's utopia: to invent and remember. At the same time, she overthrows and exhorts with rage, channeling support for the war and a "concern for strategy and tactics" (p. 94).

As we come to the third O we are asked to "look at" the first of the male victims "ambushed in his towns"—while "he begins to cry" the "women laugh, baring their teeth" (p. 97). This is a long way from the world of rosy-cheeked babies portrayed in *Herland.* Recitations of what the "domineering oppressors" have said about "negroes *and* women" encourage those returning to the battlefield, "singing without pause." Other groups of women join the war. Each is named with the proliferating O's, as is the ospah, a "most formidable weapon," which rotates in a green circle but is invisible when not in use. (It is worth remarking that the Land Mother in *Herland* is given the honorary prefix to her name, O-dumera, meaning "the great.") The women of Herland and the victorious guérillères are both in power. Yet each group uses its power quite differently and treats its male captives correspondingly. Terry, Van, and Jeff make one foolhardy attempt to escape the captors whom they can hardly bring themselves to call "women." Once recaptured, they are not punished, only more carefully guarded. The prisoners taken in *Les Guérillères* are often tortured while the "women stop their ears with wax so as not to hear their discordant cries." Wittig's women are not primarily defined as mothers, a fundamental difference from traditional utopian fictions and one which indicates some directions Wittig's later feminist texts will take. This speaking and writing of feminism in 1969 is one where "paradise exists in the shadow of the sword" (p. 111).

Toward the end of the novel the zero, O, the perfect circle, imprisons and overthrows the oppressors. Their rage spent from another battle, the women now mourn the men who have died. Formerly prisoners of the mirrors held up by men, the women now kill with mirrors they station along the roads. The war over, they learn again to laugh and move, as they had been represented earlier. This ever-historical present reminds the reader of the great register which may be opened at any page. In this war, a new language is sought out—"every word must be screened" (p. 133). Now a few men learn the women's songs and their language as the war goes on. In the final passage of the novel, the past tense and the first-person plural intrude abruptly; echoing the Russian Revolution, Alexandra (K)Ollontai sings the "Internationale" and a final funeral march for the "women who died for liberty . . . a melancholy and yet triumphant air." Wittig's utopian fiction is both dynamic and dialectic—the war is over and still goes on.

Like Gilman's utopia, and as is prototypical and problematic for the genre, Wittig's fiction serves a didactic purpose. We, the readers, learn the lessons and legends simultaneously with the guérillères. Where Gilman's narrator lumbers through his own naturalist, essentialist rhetoric about his spiritually uplifting life with Ellador in Herland, Wittig's narrative is laconic and poetic, disruptive and orchestrated. Where Gilman offers a utopian image of what she believes to be innately feminine functions and tasks in a world women *might* create, Wittig represents women performing functions which have not historically been theirs. The guérillères remake war, language, body, and history in the formation of new collectivities.

Fredric Jameson has suggested that utopian fiction may be represented as either technological and organizational, *or* libidinal and aesthetic.[29] We witness feminist utopian writing in the process of rejecting such dualities. However, I *am* suggesting a textual and ideological opposition: Gilman's static utopia of projection and planning where all is in place, as opposed to Wittig's dynamic utopia of potential and process where we read change in progress. This opposition is as much a matter of literary history as it is one of political history. The novels reread here extend the boundaries of generic conventions, particularly those of the codified utopia of the late nineteenth century, though some of those conventions are still apparent in *Herland*. While some of these novels are more akin to science fiction, all are speculative attempts to bring together the technological *and* libidinal utopian possibilities. We see women as warriors *and* mothers confronting and overturning the contradictions in which such terms had been set. The politics of gender require just such a continuing challenge to remember and invent again.

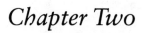

Chapter Two

The Kinship Web

Joanna Russ's *The Female Man* and
Marge Piercy's *Woman on the Edge of Time*

Of course, the biological family is ubiquitous in human society. But what confers upon kinship its socio-cultural character is not what it retains from nature, but, rather, the essential way in which it diverges from nature.

Claude Lévi-Strauss
Structural Anthropology

The discussion of the novels by Gilman and Wittig in Chapter 1 has given a historical view of the utopian genre and of twentieth-century feminism, both projects in thinking the "not-yet." Whereas historical and national differences were crucial to comparisons between Gilman and Wittig, another issue could be discerned in examining how the novels were produced as generic models, static and dynamic. Keeping each of these novels in mind we continue to ask the questions of narrative and ideology in light of two more recent works which carry on and elaborate the tradition of feminist utopian fictions. If *Herland* stands as foremother to the genre, then Marge Piercy's *Woman on the Edge of Time* picks up this line of matrilineal descent, and Joanna Russ's *The Female Man* might be considered "sister" to *Les Guérillères*.[1]

Reading *The Female Man* and *Woman on the Edge of Time* for their utopian and dystopian similarities helps to clarify their differences both as fictions and feminist representations of desire. Here, simultaneity of production highlights the heterogeneity of a specific historical moment—feminism in the United States in the mid-1970s. Generic strategies place Piercy's work in the tradition of utopian writing, while Russ's text borrows from the conventions of science fiction. They offer their readers journeys through time and space by different modes of transport. A list of the specific utopian practices of Piercy's and Russ's future visions would reveal variations in the reconception of housing, work, family, pleasure, and ritual; a primary difference is that Russ's utopia is all women whereas Piercy's is a genderless world of biological males and females. Both, however, are contemporaneous feminist texts. It is the manner in which such practices are discovered and explained that places the reader in the position of passively receiving Piercy's fiction while having actively to reproduce Russ's narrative trajectory. The reader can consume Piercy's novel, which arises out of a tradition of moral realism. The active reader of Russ faces a disjunctive, dialectically motivated novel.[2] Similarly, Piercy continues in the static line of Gilman while Russ picks up the dynamic practice of Wittig.

Russ and Wittig also cast their narratives in an epic mode through a plurality of narrators (Wittig's "*elles*," "the women say"). In the first chapter of *Mimesis,* Erich Auerbach discusses the language of representation in the epic form, choosing *The Odyssey* and the Bible as representative texts. Schematically, it could be said that the classical narrative is spatially and temporally set in a fixed present, while the biblical epic presents a process, a simultaneity of layers of consciousness and history.[3] Russ fuses these two epic modes of representation in the four female characters who populate the novel, each appearing with attentive descriptions of external historically indicative details; they are brought together to create the effect of a multiplicity of female histories and narratives. In Russ's novel each character inhabits a different present, all of which collide to form multilayered pasts, presents, and futures. The authorial presence interrupts suddenly, as does the primal voice of God in the Old Testament epic. What Auerbach says about the possibilities inherent in the biblical form, Rachel Blau DuPlessis also notices in Russ's text: that is, it permits the presentation of conflict within the didactic mode.[4]

This godlike and prophetic voice is apparent in two passages I will cite in part. The first occurs very early in the novel, where Russ presents her narrative strategy and lays bare a particular view of history. The citation is from chapter 6, the keystone to the

structure of time and place in this novel, and is presented as a theoretical interlude on probability and eventuality:

> Every choice begets at least two worlds of possibility . . . or
> very likely many more. . . . It's possible, too, that there is no
> such thing as one clear line or strand of probability, and that
> we live on a sort of twisted braid. . . . Thus the paradox of
> time travel ceases to exist, for the Past one visits is never one's
> own Past but always . . . creates another Present (one in which
> the visit has already happened) and what you visit is the Past
> belonging to that Present—an entirely different matter from
> your own Past. . . .
>
> Thus it is probable that Whileaway—a name for the
> Earth ten centuries from now, but not *our* Earth, if you follow
> me. . . .
>
> Whileaway, you may gather, is in the future.
> But not *our* future. (Pp. 6–7)

We can see here that Russ produces a fiction where the time of
narration and historical time are envisioned in the complex ways
the novel will then reproduce. The naive reader will not be allowed an easy, leisurely stay on Whileaway. Russ moves characters and readers through time and shifts between and among characters in an attempt to reproduce the twisted braid, as we will see
in the structure of the opening chapters. The textual structure of
the twisted braid can be read to suggest a feminist reworking of
the Freudian myth of origins, in which the sole contribution of
women to civilization was that of weaving, an invention arising
from the imagined necessity of covering the so-called "wound" of
castration.[5] From text to braid, web to network, the metaphor re-
curs in many feminist works of theory and fiction. Russ's use of
the metaphor is fully drawn out in her casting of character, plot,
and narrative structure. The textually ironic use of history is again
apparent in the closing paragraphs of the novel, where Russ addresses the book itself in a parody and play with the Renaissance
envoi convention:

> Go, little book . . . behave yourself in people's living rooms
> . . . take your place bravely on the book racks of bus terminals
> and drugstores. . . . recite yourself to all who will listen. . . .

Do not complain when at last you become quaint and old-
fashioned. . . . Do not get glum when you are no longer understood, little book. Do not curse your fate. Do not reach up
from readers' laps and punch the readers' noses.
    Rejoice, little book!
    For on that day, we will be free. (Pp. 213–14)

This mixture of sublime and quotidian diction is something
Auerbach notes as available to history but not to the language of
legend in the classical epic. The final phrase, "we will be free" signals what DuPlessis sees in feminist narratives as an attempt to
write beyond the ending, as the author of any novel which specu-
lates about the future must attempt to do.

The narrative structure of *Woman on the Edge of Time* in its
mode of time travel shuttles the reader between New York City,
circa 1975, and Mattapoisett in the year 2137. Unlike Russ's web
woven by a narrator in control of threads spun out by four characters, Piercy presents us with one visitor to utopia (in the manner of
More, Bellamy, and Morris), Connie Ramos, who will be transported first from her home to Bellevue Hospital and from there to
the future of possibility, which is Mattapoisett. Her confinement
to Bellevue is foretold in the opening paragraph of the novel:
"Connie got up from her kitchen table and walked slowly to the
door. Either I saw him or I didn't and I'm crazy for real this time,
she thought" (p. 9). The "him" of this sentence is not explained
until the closing lines of the chapter: "Perhaps she deserved punishment for the craziness none had guessed, the questions no one
had asked, the story no one had pried from her: that all of the
month before she had been hallucinating with increasing sharpness a strange man. That she had dreamed and then waking-
dreamed and finally seen on the streets that same smooth Indio
face" (p. 31).

The status of utopia as waking dream is clear in Piercy's
novel. Connie's need and desire for fantasy are briefly mentioned
in the middle of this first chapter. A woman displaced and dispossessed, Connie's closest association is with her niece Dolly, who is
pregnant: "Like figures of paper, like a manger scene of paste-
board figures, a fantasy had shone in Connie since her conversation with Dolly that morning: she and Dolly and Dolly's children

would live together. She would have a family again, finally" (p. 14). But Connie's reverie and her relationship with Dolly are disordered by Dolly's dependence on her pimp. When she arrives at Connie's door, battered by Geraldo, his arrival some moments later leads to Connie's first represented act of violence. Trying to defend Dolly from further assault by Geraldo, Connie smashes him in the face with a wine jug. The scene shifts suddenly to the hospital ward where Connie lays strapped to a bed, heavily drugged.

From the start Connie questions her own mental stability. But the shift from self-doubt to her institutionalization and the diagnoses of the medical professions cause the reader less to question the reliability of Connie's narrative than to identify with her. Connie's voice is always validated against the "voice" of the state institutions through which she is transported and "translated." Like the traditional utopian novel—and unlike Russ—Piercy chooses a representative traveler from the present to visit and report on the future. As a feminist utopian fiction the traveler is not a white male but a thirty-seven-year-old Chicana whose life is exemplary in its experience of forms of oppression, who is without a job or a spouse, and whose daughter has been placed in foster homes. The first sudden shift and shock which presents Connie as a violent patient under sedation is duplicated throughout the novel each time Connie travels to Mattapoisett and repeatedly awakens to find herself again in the ward. Rather than Russ's version of a multiplicity of time frames colliding and coinciding, Piercy's rougher but simpler rhythm moves the reader back and forth, increasingly disturbed by the dystopian present, and, with Connie, soon anticipating the unfamiliarity of the future.

More starkly than many other novels grouped as utopian fictions, Connie's present makes obvious the need for a concretely imagined future. Connie's present, though elaborated through the novel, is sketched out in this first chapter; it includes battered women, child abuse, street drugs, and the betrayal of women by women through a reliance on men who rule by force. Piercy chose Connie to narrate her own story because her life is one in which many of the social practices criticized by contemporary feminism are brought to light. Through her personal struggle the political is laid bare; her circumstances are dire—fantasy keeps her hoping.

And her special receptivity brings her into contact with the imagined future of Luciente, where "higher" mental functions have been learned. Travel to the future is merely a matter of psychic concentration and the pressing together of foreheads. In its emphasis on character and psychology, *Woman on the Edge of Time* rests easily in the realist tradition and replicates the tendentiousness of utopian narratives. Piercy's use of time travel through extrasensory perception updates Edward Bellamy's Julian West, the voyager of *Looking Backward,* an adept at mesmerism. Russ's twisted braid is a more treacherous and more exhilarating form of time travel, which, furthermore, works to estrange the reader.

For Russ, as for Piercy, the future presents a vision of hope (the future of Janet) but also one of fear (the future of Jael). But since the past, present, and future are not easily separated we are forced to read with a simultaneous awareness of both product and process. Who is the "female man"? The oxymoronic title already sets forth the contradictions and copresence of opposites within consciousness. Through a dramatization of female men Russ arrives at a full-scale feminist critique in which the political is subtly drawn out of the personal through an array of self-images evolved in the hall of mirrors which masculinist, heterosexist society offers to women. The four J's of the novel are, in order of appearance, Janet Evason, Jeannine Dadier, Joanna, and Jael Alice Reasoner, functioning together as a "cluster protagonist." Each of the four presents a possible reading of the novel's singular title worked out in multiple in the text that presents us with paradoxes and unions of contraries.

"I was born on a farm on Whileaway" is the first sentence of *The Female Man.* It is spoken by Janet Evason, who is also the narrator of Russ's short story "When It Changed," first published in 1972, which contained the seed for this novel.[6] The story is set on Whileaway six centuries after a plague killed off the male population, and the subject is the arrival of four Earth men who are in search of new gene pools. Chapter 5 of *The Female Man* abbreviates the story of "When It Changed" and the arrival of men, but in the novel, rather than poignantly resigned, the women of Whileaway are in control and it is the last we hear of the men, who are presented as curiosities, not as threats as in the earlier story. A first play on the name Whileaway occurs in this chapter; we read that the youth sport long hair affecting an indolence reminiscent of Lotusland "to while away the time" (p. 6). The ending of "When It Changed" presented a rather different twist to the name: "Sometimes at night I remember the original name of this planet, changed by the first generation of our ancestors, those curious women for whom, I suppose, the real name was too painful a reminder after the men died. I find it amusing, in a grim way, to see it all so completely turned around. This, too, shall pass. All good things must come to an end. For-A-While" (p. 239). Chapter 1 of part 1 of *The Female Man* is narrated in the first person by Janet Evason, a visitor to Earth from the future. The novel opens in a clear, expository fashion with Janet telling the readers about her family, her work history, her Stanford-Binet scores, how many duels she has fought, and how many times she has killed. A simple preposition announces the extraterrestrial setting—Janet is born not in but on Whileaway, where, we are told, one comes across bands of "wandering children."[7]

Janet's appearance in the streets of New York City creates front-page headlines: "WOMAN APPEARS FROM NOWHERE [utopia?] ON BROADWAY, POLICEMAN VANISHES." Jeannine's quiet world in the Tompkins Square Library, Young Adult section, is shattered, though she does not yet know it, when she reads them. She begins to reassure herself of the secure things in her life: "I have my cat, I have my room, I have my hot plate, and my window and the ailanthus tree" (p. 3), all the while repeating to her coworker, "I don't believe it." Jeannine is the female as victim; she usually perceives herself through the look of the other, who is male. (Later when Janet approaches her sexually she cannot recognize the gesture because it comes from a woman.) We read that it is "the third Monday in March of 1969," but our bearings betray us when it soon becomes apparent that in this 1969 the wartime routine of rations and government stores never ended. Chapter 3 is only a few paragraphs long and journalistically recounts Janet's quick appearance-disappearance in New York.

Chapter 4 returns us to the title; it is once again in the first person but a new "I" speaks and time shifts again. I quote the chapter in its entirety:

When Janet Evason returned to the New Forest and the exper-
imenters at the Pole Station were laughing their heads off (for
it was not a dream) I sat in a cocktail party in mid-Manhattan.
I had just changed into a man, me, Joanna. I mean a female
man, of course; my body and soul were exactly the same.

    So there's me also. (P. 5)

Joanna, the third of the J's, all of whose names, as DuPlessis has
pointed out, mean "gift of god," is the one who, bearing the author's name, inhabits a world most like the world of the novel's
time of publication itself. It is again 1969, and Joanna, unlike
Jeannine, is painfully aware of her situation and existence as a "female"; that she turns into a man at certain moments is something
she rails against. While Jeannine thinks only to "please the Man,
comfort the Man," Joanna is angered that her sex blocks perception of other aspects of herself:

    I'll tell you how I turned into a man.

    First I had to turn into a woman.

    For a long time I had been neuter, not a woman at all but
One Of The Boys, because if you walk into a gathering of
men, professionally or otherwise, you might as well be wearing a sandwich board that says: LOOK! I HAVE TITS! . . . If you
get good at being One Of The Boys it goes away. . . . so they
split me from the neck up; as I said, it demands a certain dis-
embodiment. . . . I'm not a woman; I'm a man. I'm a man
with a woman's face. I'm a woman with a man's mind. . . .
Nothing can put you above this or below this or beyond it or
outside of it, nothing, nothing, nothing at all. . . . I howled
and wrung my hands as people do only in medieval romances. . . .

    I had a five-year-old self who said: *Daddy won't love you.*

    I had a ten-year-old self who said: *the boys won't play
with you.*

    I had a fifteen-year-old self who said: *nobody will marry
you.*

    I had a twenty-year-old self who said: *you can't be ful-
filled without a child.* . . .

    O of all diseases self-hate is the worst and I don't mean
for the one who suffers it! (Pp. 133–35)

Joanna's female self is built only to be denied. Her self-hatred echoes Connie's in *Woman on the Edge of Time*, a self-hatred that Piercy also connects to Connie's experience of herself as a woman in the world, a primary structure of what Frantz Fanon named internalized colonization. It is Joanna who will serve as Janet's primary guide during her visit.

But Joanna's anger, directed at her split social self, is no match for Jael, who remains unnamed (but repeatedly invoked) until part 8, some 136 pages into the novel. Where Joanna's anger is turned inward and transformed into self-hatred, Jael, like her biblical namesake who kills a man by forcing a stake through his head, has taken the weapons, tactics, and strategies of masculine power and made herself a steel-ribboned mouth and wrinkled hands which, when she is filled with adrenaline, become claws that tear. Jael is a late-twentieth-century avatar of the most ghoulish aspects of the nineteenth-century femme fatale. Only later does it become clear that it was Jael speaking at the end of Joanna's tirade: "Listen to the female man. If you don't . . . I'll break your neck" (p. 140). Jael lives in a world divided into Manland and Womanland, where real women are so separated that the specifications for their manufacture are suspect; it is necessary to know that Manland is populated not only by men, but also by those called "the changed," and the "half-changed," feminized men, surgically transformed for the pleasure of the "real" Manlanders, who demand sexual difference, as long as it is the result of artifice. Real women are taboo and abhorred, though, in fact, unknown. For Jael, a central question about her visitors, the three other J's, is whether they have ever killed anyone. Jael is all too recognizable as a representation of agonistic heroism.

The immediate affinity Jeannine feels for Jael might at first surprise us. Yet Jael knows how to win Jeannine to her fight. She seduces, flatters, and is coy. Jeannine grows under her gaze, awed by the idea that she might be thought to have killed someone. Her long-repressed anger comes into play at the possibilities offered by Jael, her radical opposite. Jeannine is the vision many have created of enslaved women suddenly given power and using it to devastate a past and annihilate the future of possibility. Jeannine is the most eager to offer Jael "bases" in her world for the final takeover which Jael seeks. They are each other's worst fears and profoundest hopes. Recalling the phrase from Wittig, it becomes apparent that Jeannine could not have invented Jael; Jael could not have remembered Jeannine, though she tells us many times, "I'm really just an old-fashioned girl." These are the polarities glimpsed by Janet and Joanna, who reject their implications but who could not have come to be as character or as consciousness without either of the other two.

In addition to the four J's another reading of the "female man" becomes possible when the reader encounters Davy, Jael's blond, blue-eyed, "monster-pet." Her "female manhood" is given a new turn as the other three J's observe their lovemaking, rather lyrically described. What strikes the observer is Davy's passivity in response to Jael's controlling caresses, with Janet responding, "Good lord! Is *that* all?" The mechanical aspects of Jael's sexuality become clear when we realize that Davy is a machine, like those artificial females that populate literature from the Marquis de Sade to Lawrence Durrell. Davy, on his back, in the traditional position of women in the sexual act, becomes the "female man"/"male woman" in this coupling with Jael, where the more extreme attributes of sexual difference collide.

Though it seems agreed that gender identity is learned in the first few years of life, the assumption of gender roles does not become socially mandatory in most cultures until adolescence. Russ presents us with one more female character, Laura Rose Wilding, shuddering on the threshold of adulthood. She is the daughter of the American family Janet visits during her exploration of Earth. Laura can only imagine herself a "female Genghis Khan," because she does not know how to express the sexual desires that she begins to feel, but for which she has no names because the heterosexual cultural scripts available to her are so limited. Laura offers Janet an opportunity to break one of the few taboos of Whileaway, cross-age sex; Janet offers Laura the means of expression of sexual desires and pleasures which no high school biology text will reveal. This allows Laura to negotiate the twisted path to adulthood with the help of some signs that Jeannine could not have read even if they were presented to her, and which Joanna will not entertain.

The twisted braid is made of these threads, and the weaver is the "I" who makes brief appearances as the author-in-person.

Elsewhere in the text this extranarrative voice occurs as a string of blurbs from reviews of the book in the reader's hands: "Shrill . . . vituperative . . . no concern for the future of society . . . selfish femlib . . . needs a good lay . . . this shapeless book . . . another of the screaming sisterhood . . . violently waspish attack . . . the predictable fury at anatomy displaced to . . . we 'dear ladies,' whom Russ would do away with, unfortunately just don't feel . . . ephemeral trash, missiles of the sex war . . . a female lack of experience which . . ." (pp. 140–41). These characters with female names are more than themselves and *parts* of each other; women at a number of the edges of time, they form multiple, collective protagonists. The twisted braid makes no attempt to be what Barthes terms the seamless, readerly, classical text. Rather, it displays the knotting together of spatial and temporal frames by emphasizing a structure that is disruptive to the reader and reminds us that utopian fiction with its inherent otherworldly setting is deliberately estranging. In sum it allows a "dynamic transformation rather than a static mirroring of the author's environment."[8]

The Female Man frames in multiple the questions, What if all of these women coexist? What if their histories do not permit a facile leap of consciousness but require four manifestations of "femininity?" What if the twisted braid can only be negotiated with long rests in order to undo the knots which constitute it? A clue can be found in the epigraph to the novel, taken from R. D. Laing's *Politics of Experience*: "If Jack succeeds in forgetting something, this is of little use if Jill continues to remind him of it. He must induce her not to do so. The safest way would be not just to make her keep quiet about it, but to induce her to forget it also. . . . In order for such transpersonal invalidation to work, however, it is advisable to overlay it with a thick patina of mystification."

In this passage we can read the invalidation of women's memory, history, and perceptions. Like Wittig, Russ is concerned to remember and to remove some of the layers of mystification. This utopian fiction is not only contradictory and paradoxical but also dialectical; and as such, it offers its readers the work to be done, while its purpose is, like Brecht's, "to entertain the children of the scientific age and to do so with sensuousness and humour."[9]

Russ's debt to Brecht is apparent in a number of ways, not

least of which is the fact that Russ earned an advanced degree at the Yale Drama School before becoming an English professor (like Joanna of *The Female Man*). In her essay "The Subjunctivity of Science Fiction" Russ cites Brecht, and in his "Short Organum" something of Russ's practice is announced in fragment 50: "He [the actor] narrates the story of his character . . . knowing more than it does and treating its 'now' and 'here' not as a pretense made possible by the rules of the game, but as something to be distinguished from yesterday and some other place, so as to make visible the knotting-together of the events."[10]

In fragment 67, "The Use of Titles," Brecht relates this usage to the tone of a chronicle, ballad, newspaper, or morality play. In her essay on the aesthetics of science fiction Russ notes a relationship to the genre of the medieval exemplum, and says, "science is to science fiction (by analogy) what medieval Christianity was to deliberately didactic medieval fiction."[11] The humor and rage so delicately balanced by Russ is often clearest in passages accompanied by didactic titles. Chapter 5 of part 6 of *The Female Man* bears the title, "The Great Happiness Contest (this happens a lot)." Here nameless women compete in dialogue in their management of home, work, family, love, sexuality, community, and social activities. The contest ends thus:

> I know that somewhere, just to give me the lie, lives a beautiful (got to be beautiful), intellectual, gracious, cultivated, charming woman who has eight children, bakes her own bread, cakes, and pies, takes care of her own house, does her own cooking, brings up her own children, holds down a demanding nine-to-five job at the top decision-making level in a man's field, and is adored by her equally successful husband because although a hard-driving, aggressive business executive with eye of eagle, heart of lion, tongue of adder and muscles of gorilla (she looks just like Kirk Douglas), she comes home at night, slips into a filmy negligee and a wig, and turns instanter into a Playboy dimwit, thus laughingly dispelling a canard that you cannot be eight people simultaneously with two different sets of values. She has not lost her femininity.
>
> And I'm Marie of Rumania. (Pp. 118–19)

The serious breathlessness of the critique of bourgeois domesticity and its monological quality are instantly pierced by the lighthearted self-critical afterthought. We can see here how Russ has adapted the tonality of Brechtian techniques of alienation and estrangement in order to bring to consciousness the desires and fears of her audience of readers.

One of the keynotes of feminist utopias as distinct from earlier ones is the inclusion of alternate futures, "wrong," "false," atavistic futures which signal the possibility of nightmarish backlash to the "fact" of women's liberation. We have seen how Russ chose to integrate her false future in the figure of Jael and her war between Manland and Womanland in such a way as always to threaten the present of Jeannine and Joanna as well as the future of Janet. In *Woman on the Edge of Time* the "false" future comes as an aberration, a fault in Connie's telepathic messages to Luciente. This takes up a chapter in which, alongside the peaceable realm of Mattapoisett, there is a world where the outdoors is represented on projected screens, human beings made out of flesh are fast disappearing, in favor of those put together with prostheses made to specifications, and where women ("fems") are confined to the activity of prostitution, their status depending on the length of their contract to one man. These "people" are all owned by "multis," food comes from "factory-farms," and intelligence is genetically controlled. This dystopia, though an aberration, is related to the one which is part of life in Mattapoisett. Connie makes the connection when she finds herself back in the hospital ward: "so that was the other world that might come to be. That was Luciente's war, and she was enlisted in it" (p. 301). Piercy reveals information slowly about the military status of the tribes in Mattapoisett. We learn that people take turns going out "on defense."

Life in Mattapoisett is situated in a peasant economy where high-level technology functions to provide information and service. Piercy's version/vision of utopia includes an array of conflict, aggression, war, madness, rivalry, and competition. In these situations experienced by persons of the future, we readers are moved by and with Connie Ramos in transit between here and now and there and then, as the doctors in New York and the healers of Luciente's tribe struggle for control of Connie's mind.

Bringing together the subject of women and the naming of

madness, Piercy's novel is narratively structured through a process of gaining and losing consciousness. The theory and practice of contemporary American feminism were formulated in the context of consciousness-raising, arising out of "new left" readings of the Chinese revolutionary practice of "speaking bitterness" and its compatibility with the focus on consciousness and ego central to the practice of psychology in the United States. Connie, the narrator, is impoverished economically, emotionally, and educationally. The novel opens at a moment where "light" (Luciente) first appears in her life, and one which precipitates her encounter with madness and the ways it is medicalized and institutionalized by a society which doubts, and often does not hear, the words of women. That Connie is a Chicana single mother makes her words even more susceptible to remaining unheard and denied at Bellevue Hospital, a state institution administered by white, professional heterosexists. This hospital has a status in the minds of New Yorkers reminiscent of that once accorded to Bethlehem Hospital in London; it functions as a voyeuristic setting where the repressed may return, contained and confined. Along with schools, medical workers, a variety of "helping" professions, and the church, the mental hospital is one of the institutions which helps to contain violence, disorder, chaos, and fragmentation.

"Spring in the violent ward was only more winter"; so begins Connie's movement within the institution, a movement that at first seems to be leading progressively toward freedom. This chapter ends as Connie is moved to a mixed male and female ward for those who have been chosen as subjects for experimentation with new psychopharmacological and surgical techniques funded by the government. The movement between the present and her trips to the future always returns us readers with a shock to the wards of a variety of New York's mental hospitals, each specializing in its own type of control device. Connie moves from isolation to the mixed ward, with its "luxurious" accommodations where the most horrific treatments are conducted. The exercise in contrast meant to jolt both Connie and the reader occurs each time she voyages to Mattapoisett "in touch" with Luciente, and she/we enter a world of light where a sense of mobility and access to life are preeminent. The world of the ward is everywhere confining, in its very structure, to be sure, but also in what is possible in thought.

Friendship is suspect, touch prohibited; matches, for example, are unavailable, and communication is always blocked by drugs and regulations.

Most writers of feminist utopian fictions have gathered some wisdom from the political activity in which seeds were sown for their own struggles. In Ken Kesey's *One Flew Over the Cuckoo's Nest,* a popular novel of the late 1960s counterculture, we also find a critique of the "Combine," the mental institution's machinelike control of body and mind.[12] Piercy's novel adds a feminist component missing from the earlier book. Where Kesey's text is blatantly woman-hating, Piercy condemns the men and women who run such institutions and their exploitive treatment of women and men of all cultures. In Kesey's novel, the symbol of control is a grotesque character, Big Nurse, an incarnation of the terrible mother. Piercy's agents of repression, in contrast, are a collection of professional men and women who work together at classifying and experimenting with those like Connie who are displaced in and by the dominant culture. The connections between hospital, school, and church are apparent in the following interview which Connie undergoes:

> Clearing her throat with nervousness, she sat in a chair facing them lined up behind a table. Doctors and judges, caseworkers and social workers, probation officers, police, psychiatrists. . . . What were they looking for? Would it be better to fall into their net or through it? . . . She was taking a test in a subject, and she didn't even know what course it was. The young doctor who had picked her out of the ward did most of the questioning at first. . . . It was like saying the responses at Mass. . . . What were they listening for, inasmuch as they listened at all? How that Dr. Redding stared at her, not like she'd look at a person, but the way she might look at a tree, a painting, a tiger in the zoo. (Pp. 91–92)

Connie's dehumanization and objectification under these gazes is as apparent as the lack of a common language. Piercy's novel needs to be situated within a countercultural critique of institutions developed in widely read works of the 1960s such as those by Paul Goodman (*Growing Up Absurd*), Norman O. Brown (*Life against Death, Love's Body*), and Herbert Marcuse

(*Eros and Civilization* and *One Dimensional Man*). In adding to this line of radical thought, like Kate Millett, Shulamith Firestone, Phyllis Chesler, and Dorothy Dinnerstein, feminists had the further task of rereading these earlier works for their unspoken assumptions of privileged patriarchal positions. Marcuse, for example, a philosopher of utopia, whose roots like Bloch's were in the Frankfurt School, served as gray eminence for many radical leftists in the United States. Only in the years before his death in 1979 did Marcuse speak and write about feminism as "perhaps the most important and potentially the most radical political movement that we have."[13] Marcuse's version of the political effectivity of feminism is rather heavily imbued with a romanticized understanding of women's subjectivity and their relation to memory reminiscent of many nineteenth-century male feminists. Marcuse's works of the 1960s do not refer to feminism; nevertheless, American feminist activists were certainly aided in their quest for liberation by a climate of thought that questioned the split between work and play, public and private, labor and repression of sexuality, and the effect of such splitting on human gender arrangements.[14] Many of the countercultural practices of the late 1960s are replayed with a feminist spin in Piercy's novel.

In their focus on language American feminists have conceived it as a social practice and a system that is both open and resistant to change. An American-spirited need to invent has given us new words and new usages subject to a degree of antifeminist derision that matches and masks the threat this force represents. The language spoken by Luciente, her "mems" and "sweet friends," in *Woman on the Edge of Time* is both poetical and practical. The most obvious non-gender-specific usage is the word "person," which refers to individuals as subjects, and "per," as objects of verbs. As Luciente tells Connie, "we've reformed pronouns" (p. 42). If such usage at first seems awkward, it rapidly becomes accepted by and even acceptable to the reader. Other Esperanto-like inventions are easily assimilated and immediately comprehensible.[15] We never heard Gilman's Herlanders speak in their language; rather, it was learned and translated by Vandyck Jennings. We do not know if their language was informed by a sexual politics, only that it was foreign, other, and different. The male explorers seem to master it without any apparent difficulty. In *Wo-*

man on the Edge of Time, in contrast, we actually learn some of Luciente's language, a language verbally and gesturally enriched compared with ours, we are told.

Perhaps Luciente's people have reformed pronouns because, as Connie experiences them, they create factitious divisions. Connie is thinking here of her white middle-class social worker, Mrs. Polcari, whose distinction is exemplified by the fact that she "smelled of Arpege":

> Envy, sure, but the sense too of being cheated soured her, and the shame, the shame of being second-class goods. Wore out fast. Shoddy merchandise. "We wear out so early," she said to the mirror, not really sure who the "we" was. Her life was thin in meaningful we's. Once she had heard a social worker talking about Puerto Ricans, or "them" as they were popularly called in that clinic . . . saying that "they" got old fast and died young. (P. 35)

In another grammatical drama Connie misunderstands Luciente's misuse of the plural "you." She mistakenly takes it as an attack on her status as a nonnative speaker of English when Luciente explains the reasons for having made contact with Connie:

> I'm what we call a sender. . . . I'm running hard over too much, but where to begin so you'll comprend? So you'll relax and begin to intersee. A catcher is a person whose mind and nervous system are open, receptive, to an unusual extent. . . . Your vocabulary is remarkably weak in words for mental states, mental abilities, and mental acts. . . . You plural— excuse me. A weakness that remains in our language. (P. 42)

These additional words and concepts for mental states are what make Luciente's people able to travel through time, and Connie's receptivity is the reason she has been chosen as the explorer of the future.

All writers of utopias must confront the question of the family. However broadly the term is conceived and imagined, it is that social grouping of adults and children where the structures of and desires for recognition are ideologically shaped. Feminist utopian writers are in a unique position to reformulate such social needs and desires as informed by the politics of the 1970s. Piercy's utopia is one in which the world of activity, enterprise, discovery, and mastery is conceived as an adult world where tasks are as unspecific to gender, age, and class as was imaginatively possible for a mid-1970s feminist vision. Whereas Gilman anatomizes a devotional and pragmatic notion of motherhood, Piercy takes on questions of parenthood and structures of the family more broadly. Parthenogenesis, with its inevitable Christian connotations, is replaced in 1975 by "birthing chambers," where a new embryo is begun when someone dies, and three comothers decide to "kidbind." *Woman on the Edge of Time* is as much a dystopia of the structures of class, race, and sexual divisions embodied in Connie's diagnosed madness as it is a utopia of the family.

Connie's is an extended family with roots in Mexico, Chicago, and New York; she is abandoned by both her family of origin and the larger social family or community. In Mattapoisett, she gradually becomes a member of Luciente's extended "tribal" family. Connie's status in the future is anomalous—at first she mostly offers proof of a "real" past to these imagined persons of the future to whom her "facts" are "history." Her means of transport between here and there is the time travel which literalizes a basic metaphor of utopia. Connie's movement from city to village is also a movement from "social system" to "community." The circumference is drawn in, while the radius moves concentrically out. Connie's familiarity with extended village and ethnic structures eases her entry into the future family; she is often reminded of her childhood in Mexico. In the future, questions of property, privacy, propriety, and place are worked through in new ways. Luciente's family is seen in conflict and at play, mourning and celebrating.

The family is also the ideological realm in which sexuality, gender identity, and self-image are framed. These interrelated questions are kept in sharp focus during the dramatic representation of Connie's predetermination of Luciente's sex. This occurs as they prepare for Connie's first "trip" to Mattapoisett: "Time had begun to slide forward" (p. 59). Language between Connie and Luciente breaks down over the missing concept of "prostitution" in Luciente's vocabulary. Her kenner, a high-tech encyclopedic wristwatch, fills in the historical aberration of selling one's body for sex.

"I've read of this and seen a drama too about person who sold per body to feed per family!" . . .

"We don't buy or sell anything."

"But people do go to bed, I guess?" . . .

"Fasure we couple. Not for money, not for a living. For love, for pleasure, for relief, out of habit, out of curiosity and lust. Like you, no?" (P. 64)

Until this moment Connie has assumed Luciente is a man, though somewhat "girlish and queer." When she now asks Luciente, "do you like women?" the misrecognitions proliferate: "He had shown no signs of sexual interest. . . . Perhaps being crazy was always built on self-hatred and she would, of course, see a queer." But to travel through time Luciente and Connie must press their foreheads together. They try, as Luciente is unsure "if I can really pull you into my time." The scene merits lengthy quotation, for it gives us a paradigm of woman's sense of self in the dystopic present. If read as psychodrama we see here Connie's movement from fear to disavowal to loss of fear in her discovery. Such misrecognitions are inevitable in a culture where heterosexuality is the norm, and where biological sex is immediately trained into a cultural gender identity.

> Luciente gently drew her against him and held her in his arms so their foreheads touched. . . .
>
> Pressed reluctantly, nervously against Luciente, she felt the coarse fabric of his shirt and . . . breasts! She jumped back.
>
> "You're a woman! No, one of those sex-change operations. . . ."
>
> "Of course I'm female." . . . Luciente looked a little disgusted. . . .
>
> A dyke of course. That bar in Chicago where the Chicano dykes hung out. . . . Yet they had never given her that sense of menace a group of men would—after all, under the clothes they were only women, too. . . .
>
> Luciente spoke, she moved with that air of brisk unselfconscious authority Connie associated with men. Luciente sat down, taking up more space than women ever did. . . . Connie no longer felt in the least afraid of Luciente. (Pp. 66–68)

Scenes such as this one that move from misrecognition and fear to disavowal and finally to recognition and loss of fear are repeated in these novels. They constitute a body of material from which one could begin to ask the questions of sexual difference, and of gender, identity, and desire as rewritten for a feminist agenda. Luciente's world is one of two sexes and no gender. A set of three comothers is constituted by a variety of biological combinations, and birth occurs outside the body, separating genes and culture.

> we decided to hold on to separate cultural identities. . . . We want there to be no chance of racism again. But we don't want the melting pot where everybody ends up with thin gruel. We want diversity, for strangeness breeds richness. . . .
>
> It was part of women's long revolution. When we were breaking all the old hierarchies. Finally there was that one thing we had to give up too, the only power we ever had, in return for no more power for anyone. The original production: the power to give birth. . . . So we all became mothers.[16]

Coupling in the future refers only to sexual activity, and the "couple" has expanded to become a "core." The future family like the past and present family as we have come to know it through psychoanalysis is not without its oedipal drama. So that the children "will not be caught in love misunderstandings," comothers are usually not also "sweet friends" (part of the expanded vocabulary of friendship and affinity).

Mothering may become overzealous "kidbinding." At a ritual pubescent moment the children of the future, alone and capable and equipped for a week's time, leave their village and return with a new, self-chosen name. Innocente is the child of Luciente, Otter, and Luxembourg, and as she prepares to leave for her "naming," Luciente explains to Connie:

> "This is how we transit from childhood to full member of our community. . . ."
>
> "For a week. Then the aunts person selected—advisers for the next years—return for per. Not us. . . ."
>
> "But *they* won't be able to speak to me for threemonth when I come back. . . . They aren't allowed to."
>
> "Lest we forget we aren't mothers anymore and person is

an equal member. Threemonth usually gives anyone a solid footing and breaks down the old habits of depending. . . ."

"We have found no way to break dependencies without some risk. What we can't risk is our people remaining stuck in old patterns—quarreling through what you called adolescence."

"A rite of passage that doesn't involve some danger is too much a gift to create confidence. . . ."

"We set our children free." (Pp. 115–16)

Piercy gives us an imaginative projection of what human sexual arrangements might be without the profound and passionately felt malaise examined in a text such as Dorothy Dinnerstein's *Mermaid and the Minotaur,* which is profoundly utopian in its wishfulness, but more profoundly dystopian in its analysis.

The sexual rearrangements of Piercy's vision allow her to construct a comprehensive alternative family: a non-gender-specific world in terms of tasks, functions, behavior, yet still a world of people biologically male and female. The males of the future, however, have a lactating capability, literalizing Dinnerstein's exhortation that parenting needs to be done by both men and women so that we no longer create people for whom women represent the one person responsible for the limitations of human enterprise, the source of joy and fear, desire and dread.

The future family, however, also contains and constructs rivalry, jealousy, and power struggles and their attendant conflicts. We are witness to a "worming," where Luciente and Bolivar, both sweet friends of Jackrabbit, are forced to confront their difficulties with each other in this triangulated interpersonal conflict (the transactional rhetoric is deliberate: it haunts Piercy's "new language").

"Luciente and Bolivar have not been communing. Meshing badly. Sparks and bumps. . . ."

"Aren't people allowed to dislike each other?"

"Not good when they're in the same core. Jackrabbit is close to both. Such bumping strains per. They compete for Jackrabbit's attent. . . . When they crit each other, it does not hold up under scrutiny as honest—but self-serving."

"Suppose after a worming they still can't stand each other?"

"Jackrabbit may choose to see neither for some time. Both may be sent into temporary wandering. We may impose invisibility. We resort to that after bad quarreling. . . . We put a mother-in-law taboo on—drawn from old-time practice. Persons aren't allowed to speak for two months to or about each other. Such a time often releases bumping. Besides, it's such a nuisance, frequently each longs to be done with it and speak to the other again" (P. 207).

Later, at Jackrabbit's death, Luciente and Bolivar are brought together again; this time they are able to share their grief as they had struggled over their private joys with Jackrabbit. His status as artist in the community is recognized as someone who brought joy to many. As a result of this the council has decided that "genetic chance will be born again. . . . Though we will never know where or who, we know some part of Jackrabbit lives. . . . Very rarely that is done. When somebody dies young who was unusually talented, as a kind of living memorial their exact genetic mix is given to a new baby. You never know where. Nobody knows. Records are not kept" (p. 323).

Jackrabbit is an artist who produces "holies" (holographic techniques are prominent in the visual arts of Mattapoisett). The question of the status of art in utopia is not always asked. However, unlike Morris's *News from Nowhere,* where all "become" artists, Piercy gives the artist a place of privilege and even chooses those genes to be reproduced. Piercy's classless utopia does not jettison differences determined by capacities and talents. It is not a world without privileges or differences in status in the community.

In order to examine further Piercy's radical feminist imaging of the future family we can pursue some insights of Veronica Beechey's in "On Patriarchy." Beechey argues that radical, revolutionary, and Marxist feminism all tend to privilege as their object of analysis modes of reproduction rather than modes of production. The reason for this privileging is motivated by their wanting "to avoid a mechanistic version of Marxism which concentrates solely upon the production/labour process" and in order to deal specifically with women's familial activities which Marxism has consistently ignored.[17] Beechey's primary theoretical concern is with the articulation of patriarchy and capitalism. The separation of these two concepts, thus treated as "independent structures," arose out of the earlier theoretical impasse which too easily equated them, first apparent in Firestone's *The Dialectic of Sex,* a rereading of Engels in a reductive and technologically humanistic direction.

Beechey accurately points out that in the area of theoretical discourse "Marxist analysis of production is untouched and un-criticized by feminist thinking"; almost as an aside she writes, "Maybe our desire to do this [focus on reproduction to the exclusion of production] merely reflects the way in which we ourselves fetishize reproduction."[18] The intimate connection between the modes of production and reproduction is demonstrated by Piercy in an electoral slogan of the Shapers:

Do you value yourself lower than zucchini? Vote the SHAPERS!
"What's all this business about Shaping?" Connie asked. . . .
"The Shapers want to breed for selected traits," Luciente said. "It's a grandcil-level fight." . . .
"We don't think people can know objectively how people should become. We think it's a power surge." (P. 226)

If, as Beechey offers, "we ourselves fetishize reproduction," it is also because that is where women have been historically involved and oppressed. That position, always both privileged and abased, ought to provide some perspectives on the need for transforma-tions of a revolutionary kind. We may vainly wish to escape the full-scale epistemological critique of the family undertaken by contemporary feminism. This is what Beechey does not fully ap-preciate. In her desire to see the struggle well maintained on all fronts she underestimates the force and breadth of feminist think-ing on reproduction. Citing others and wanting to give "rigorous meaning to the various uses of the term reproduction," she seems indirectly to offer us such a meaning by way of reading Edholm, Harris, and Young in "Conceptualizing Women":[19] "They suggest that we should separate out three forms of reproduction: (i) social reproduction, that is, reproduction of the total conditions of production; (ii) reproduction of the labour force; and (iii) biological reproduction" (p. 78). I would suggest that Piercy's fiction succeeds best where Beechey finds theory lacking. We can see in these preceding and some following readings of the novel that Piercy not only opens wide the definition of modes of reproduction, she examines it economically, socially, and biologically as well as politically. As Beechey herself knows, perhaps undercutting her own outline of a problematic, "it is impossible to have a notion of production which does not also involve reproduction" (p. 79).

The Shapers' slogan encapsulates such ties between production and reproduction by an agricultural metaphor. Where better do production and reproduction become dialectically entwined? Both Gilman's and Piercy's utopias concentrate strongly on an economy in which agriculture is a primary form of labor, and historical and anthropological accounts routinely name agriculture as an early realm for women's activity. We have seen earlier how growth is the key concept in Gilman's feminism and socialism; Gilman seems at times to equate economic and spiritual growth, which lead to (capitalist) production, another irony in her "socialist" views. But growth in Mattapoisett as opposed to growth in Herland is subject to control of a scientific and consensual kind. The power surge sought by the Shapers is recognized by the Mixers as a desire in the direction of hierarchy, and more basically pride (to slip into a moral category). The Mixers want to use their technology carefully: "Now we only spot problems, watch for birth defects, genes linked with disease susceptibility" (p. 226). This is best seen by the value given to the new embryo begun after Jackrabbit's death—a collective tribute to an individual.

Where Gilman's future family is one of overmothers, land mothers, mothers and daughters, with a final bow to heterosexual biology, Piercy's family is an extended one in which notions of motherliness have replaced motherhood. The literature on the mother is abundant both from feminists and antifeminists alike. Piercy's word, concept, of "kidbinding" translates simply what has filled volumes on both the wonder and terror of the mother. Only preadolescent children need this degree of watchfulness; at a certain time in the future, as we read in the ceremony of the naming, the children of Mattapoisett no longer need or want this kind of binding.

The first chapter of part 1 of *The Female Man* (where we met Janet) also reveals a great deal about the social reproductive practices of Whileaway. We know Janet "bears" a child, marries, has a wife and daughter, and that her family numbers nineteen. Not until part 3 are these details and terms expanded, when Russ begins by saying, "this is the lecture. If you don't like it, you can skip to the next chapter." Part 3 consists of twelve chapters; the first three have Janet and Joanna at a cocktail party in Manhattan; the following chapters vary in length from one sentence to five and a half pages and tell the reader more about Whileaway. Not until part 5, the intersection of this chiasmatic structure, is the reader's curiosity about Whileaway fully satisfied.

From the beginning of chapter 6 of part 3, the longest and a purely expository chapter, we learn that on Whileaway the time of mothering is also the time of leisure.

> On Whileaway they have a saying: When the mother and child are separated they both howl, the child because it is separated from the mother, the mother because she has to go back to work. Whileawayans bear their children at about thirty—singletons or twins as the demographic pressures require. These children have as one genotypic parent the biological mother (the "body-mother") while the nonbearing parent contributes the other ovum ("other mother"). . . . Little Whileawayans are to their mothers . . . the only leisure they have ever had—or will have again until old age. (P. 49)

Whileawayans complain frequently about how much of their time is spent working, though this same chapter ends with the statement that "the Whileawayan work-week is sixteen hours" (p. 56). Though they work hard, with the help of "induction helmets," which do the labor of many hands, the people of Whileaway are clearly pleasure lovers. (And Russ's reader must work with her textual play in order to obtain pleasure.) The five years of intensive mothering stand out as idyllic to most. It should come as no surprise that Russ's prose is most succinct and matter of fact in the exposition of Whileaway; where the usual utopian fiction fabulates is where Russ leans most heavily on genre convention so that she may play elsewhere.

Janet's introduction also mentions four duels. Her pugnacity is not aroused on Earth until a man named Ginger Moustache calls her "baby" at the cocktail party. He had been trying to engage her in conversation about the "new feminism" while Joanna hoped to herself that Janet would be "ladylike." But "baby" is an insult in Janet's world, and so she fights him while Joanna searches in her "pink book" for instructions: *"Man's bad temper is the woman's fault. It is also the woman's responsibility to patch things up afterwards"* (p. 47). This fight leads to a discussion of conflict on Whileaway, where, as in Mattapoisett, "the cure for that is distance" and raising a hand to someone is "[f]or sport, yes, okay, for hatred no" (p. 48). But Janet, Safety and Peace officer, has no regrets about hurting the man who called her "baby." And the transition from the drama of the cocktail party is made in the one sentence of chapter 4, "Whileawayans are not nearly as peaceful as they sound."

The progression of life stages on Whileaway are marked as Middle (puberty), Three-Quarters (age seventeen), and Full Dignity (age twenty-two). Between puberty and age seventeen is when most Whileawayans go into wandering:

> There's no being out too late in Whileaway, or up too early, or in the wrong part of town, or unescorted. You cannot fall out of the kinship web and become sexual prey for strangers, for there is no prey and there are no strangers. . . .
>
> You can walk around the Whileawayan equator twenty times (if the feat takes your fancy and you live that long) with one hand on your sex and in the other an emerald the size of a grapefruit. All you'll get is a tired wrist. (Pp. 81–82)

At age seventeen they begin to work at jobs where they are needed, not necessarily where they wish. At twenty-two more permanent work and a geographical "home base" are chosen even though "Whileawayans travel all the time," hence the expression "My home is in my shoes."[20]

Returning us to Bloch's thoughts on the sources of utopian longings, Russ's insights about the psychology of Whileawayans clarify the impulses which project a future in the very act of masking an insistence on a once-fulfilled moment in the past:

Whileawayan psychology locates the basis of Whileawayan character in the early indulgence, pleasure, and flowering which is drastically curtailed by the separation from the mothers. This (it says) gives Whileawayan life its characteristic independence, its dissatisfaction, its suspicion, and a tendency toward a rather irritable solipsism. . . .

Eternal optimism hides behind this dissatisfaction, however; Whileawayans cannot forget that early paradise and every new face, every new day, every smoke, every dance, brings back life's possibilities. Also sleep and eating, sunrise, weather, the seasons, machinery, gossip, and the eternal temptations of art. (P. 52)

Bloch alone sees the utopian impulse arising out of the infantile dissatisfaction first experienced as absence.

When Janet seduces Laura we learn the Whileaway taboo on sex with anyone much older or younger. But there are other, less predictable, taboos as well: "waste, ignorance and offending others without intending to" (p. 53). The same early lesson in distrust leads to Whileawayan ideas about love and marriage. There is no legal arrangement for monogamous marriage, and there is a "reluctance to form a tie that will engage every level of emotion . . . [a]nd the necessity for artificial dissatisfactions" (p. 53). The reply to these ideas is from Dunyasha Bernadetteson, known as the Playful Philosopher, who reminds Whileawayans that without these dissatisfactions, "we would become so happy we would sit down on our fat, pretty behinds and soon we would start starving, nyet?" (pp. 53–54). When Janet tells Laura about falling in love with Vittoria (her wife) she refers to love as "A dreadful intrusion, a sickness . . . a nervous parody of friendship. . . . Poisoned with arrows and roses, radiant Eros coming at you out of the dark. . . . the pleasure of pain, the dreadful longing. . . . Love is a radiation disease. Whileawayans do not like the self-consequence that comes with romantic passion. . . . I felt it leave me two and a half months later. . . . I swallowed philosophically and that was that." (Pp. 75–79)

Russ's utopian inhabitants work and play equally hard, and avoid self-consequence whenever possible. In chapter 15 of part 5, one of the few chapters with a title and a number, we learn "What Whileawayans Celebrate":

The full moon
The Winter solstice (You haven't lived if you haven't seen us running around in our skivvies, banging on pots and pans, shouting "Come back, sun! Goddammit, come back! Come back!")
The summer solstice (rather different)
The autumnal equinox
The vernal equinox
The flowering of trees
The flowering of bushes
The planting of seeds
Happy copulation
Longing
Jokes
Leaves falling off the trees (where deciduous)
Acquiring new shoes
Wearing same
Birth
The contemplation of a work of art
Marriages
Sport
Divorces
Anything at all
Nothing at all
Great ideas
Death. (Pp. 102–3)

Here finally the playful seriousness and serious playfulness are clear. A list is given to the reader rather than a description of a utopian pageant. Whileaway, neither here nor now, exists in the time of the festival with its "arcadian anarchy."[21]

In terms of the social mode of reproduction, Piercy and Russ both rewrite the psychoanalytic family romance. Three "co-mothers" and a "core," or two mothers and a self-chosen family of twenty to thirty members offer variations on the bourgeois nuclear model. Consent and commitment bind the parents who may not be "sweet friends." Parenting, not pair-bonding, is the basis of these families. And "coupling" refers to a sexuality no longer tied to reproduction. These extended families lack what Juliet Mitchell and Gayle Rubin—glossing Claude Levi-Strauss—call the exchange of or traffic in women.[22]

Piercy and Russ frame utopias which eliminate this form of exchange. In these cultures based on ties other than those of blood, women's bodies and their sexuality are no longer primary areas of appropriation. The portrayal of these alternate systems of kinship subverts a fundamental law of the patriarchal sex-gender system with its overdetermined concern for paternity. The utopian models of Russ and Piercy recast the terms of kinship in a social, economic, and biological sense. This universal exchange of women by men through exogamy underwrites the variations on the incest taboo and heterosexual marriage. What Beechey, following the usage, calls patriarchy, Gayle Rubin names the sex/gender system, saying that "feminism must call for a revolution in kinship." Rubin's landmark essay of feminist theory, "The Traffic in Women," was also published in 1975 and has as its opening gambit a subjunctivity like these two novels. Rubin says the need to examine the situation of women's oppression is "not a trivial one," since it shapes "our evaluation of whether or not it is realistic to hope for a sexually, egalitarian society." In a kind of conditional imagining she then writes:

> Thus, if innate male aggression and dominance are at the root of female oppression, then the feminist program would logically require either the extermination of the offending sex, or else a eugenics project to modify its character. If sexism is a by-product of capitalism's relentless appetite for profit, then sexism would wither away in the advent of a successful socialist revolution. If the world historical defeat of women occurred at the hands of an armed patriarchal revolt, then it is time for Amazon guerrillas to start training in the Adirondacks.

Rubin's essay ends by stating the need to examine how marriage systems intersect with state making. I think that a reading of feminist utopias and the utopian discourse of feminism as the obverse of the traditional examples of the genre would lead to the conclusion that a nascent theory of the state is implicit in the varieties of restructured kinship systems and relations of affinity. This turns inside out the classical, Renaissance, and late-nineteenth-century utopias, where the concern is primarily to address state-making and only much less explicitly the marriage system. In the chapters that follow, critiques of dystopian patriarchal states become much clearer. Still, the liberatory possibilities of the utopian remain local, partial, specific, and strategic. These writers focus on questions of governance, of the self, and of related and dependent others, because they remain aware that to proffer more totalizing panoramas of possible futures is to participate in those gestures by which women, among "others," have been left out of the making of forms of governing.

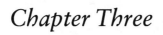

Chapter Three

Of Unmen and Women

Suzy McKee Charnas's
Walk to the End of
the World and *Motherlines*

> . . . who can tell, how many generations may be necessary to give vigour to the virtue and talents of the freed posterity of abject slaves?
>
> Mary Wollstonecraft
> *A Vindication of the Rights of Woman*

In the novels examined thus far, the social problems to which the feminist utopia proposes a response have only been implied, as is conventional for the genre. What the novels represent are changes in social practice; from these the reader may deduce the need among women for imagined collectivities to define themselves. The only writer who has chosen to precede her feminist utopia, *Motherlines*, with a fully imagined masculinist dystopia is Suzy McKee Charnas, whose *Walk to the End of the World* announces itself self-consciously with a curious pre-text. Set in a box on a page otherwise reserved for blurbs and excerpts to stimulate interest in buying the book in hand is this statement in quotation marks:

> "For too long science fiction has been dominated by masculine/sexist writing, but in recent years a group of women writers has been bringing new life and maturity into the field. These women are explicit and committed feminists. We're proud to be among them."
>
> Joanna Russ
> Suzy McKee Charnas

Russ's postmodern strategy of the twisted braid of narrative in *The Female Man* takes on new intertextual life in this context of the shared efforts of women writers of science fiction. I spoke earlier of the exhilaration of Russ's forms of space and time travel, which rely on conventional generic possibilities and even expectations. Charnas leads us on a trail very painstakingly blazed; this is not space travel, it is earth travel. The way this story is told knows ages both geological and nuclear. Both of Charnas's novels, announced as part of a collective effort on the part of women writing science fiction, have long been out of print. Their relative unavailability leads me to try to do two kinds of work at the same time: to retell their stories of rivalry, conflict, and power struggles, and to link those narratives with the theoretical issues raised by the texts discussed earlier.

Charnas's novels present themselves with pride and a rhetoric of pamphleteering appropriate to the environment of mid-1970s radical feminism.[1] Charnas's dystopia, a patrilineal quest narrative, represents a world of men and their enslaved women, known as fems. It marks a trail into a future that arises after the Wasting, an environmental and ecological holocaust. The men who have survived the Wasting have written it into history as the maleficent effect of the activity of women of the past. When that past is then recounted, the contemporary reader realizes that this is an imaginary future fashioned by men as backlash to the feminism and radical politics of the late twentieth century. In a dystopian gesture that prefigures Atwood's writing of *The Handmaid's Tale,* Charnas's narrative of forbidden and therefore desired knowledge of paternal origins, is based on a world where women have been the class of victims blamed for a global cataclysm. The older white men who now rule have silenced and confined them in many ways, though they continue to function as slaves, pets, workers, and breeders.

The mid-1970s, when Charnas worked on these two books, published four years apart, was a fractious time for feminists: lesbian separatism was a break from strategies of accommodation, which would privilege reform instead, as promised by passage of the Equal Rights Amendment. Varieties of American feminism, radical to bourgeois, would take hold most firmly in limited, local forms of women working for and with women. In her representation of daily struggles among women, those who escaped before the Wasting, and their battles with fems, those enslaved after, Charnas has offered for consideration imaginary pages from the history of these women. In her recast stories, first of the "prince in search of his father," and then of "Amazons of the future," Charnas suggests some histories that must be rewritten for a potentially new order. Like most of these narratives it is a series of radically simple suggestions. There must be an exchange of capacities acquired under freedom and slavery before we can make common cause with our own and other kind or kindred. The women and the fems speak different languages, given their split histories, and are therefore reluctant to see in each other anything but differences. They have each heard and imagined so many tales of the others' exploits and humiliations during the years since the Wasting that encounters between them are fraught with hostility, misapprehension, and even fear. These are women of different classes and histories with all this suggests of the work they must do before they can ever begin to imagine coexistence. The capacities they will need to exchange are linguistic (Bek listening to Alldera, women listening to fems' tales), economic (fems paving the granary floor, women taking fems into their families), political (women and fems taking up their futures together), and even biotechnological (fems and women finding successful means of reproduction). *Walk to the End of the World* is a tale of adventure and flight; *Motherlines* responds as a set of consolations offered by the discovery of a new community where the struggle is to enter rather than to find a way to leave.

The "what-if" premise of all speculative fiction operating in this novel is laid bare in the prologue to *Walk*:

> The predicted cataclysm, the Wasting, has come and—it seems, gone. . . . Who has survived? . . .
>
> A handful of high officials . . . thought to bring women with them. . . . As the world outside withered and blackened, the men thought they saw reproach in the whitened faces of the women they had saved and thought they heard accusation in the women's voices. . . . These women said to one another, let's do what they say for now. . . .
>
> It is their male descendants who emerge from the Refuge

to find the world scoured of animal life and beggared of resources. . . . They call their land the Holdfast,[2] after the an-
choring tendril by which seaweed clings to the rocks against
the pull of the current. . . . Nothing is abundant, but men live.

What else do they remember? They remember the evil
races whose red skins, brown skins, skins all the colors of
fresh-turned earth marked them as mere treacherous imita-
tions of men, who are white; youths who repudiated their fathers' ways; animals that raided men's crops . . . and most of
all the men's own cunning, greedy females. Those were the re-
bels who caused the downfall of men's righteous rule: men
call them "unmen." Of all the unmen, only females and their
young remain, still the enemies of men. (Pp. 3–5)

The cost of questioning this history as it has been written and spoken is nothing less than death.

In an inversion of the conventions of patriarchy, where the
name of the father must be known, the primary taboo question in
the Holdfast is to ask, "who is my father?" Fathers and sons are
believed to be natural enemies: "no blood ties were recognized. . . . Thus, men avoided the fated enmity of fathers and
sons. . . . To know your father's identity would be to feel, however
far off, the chill wind of death" (p. 26). From this taboo follows
the fictional development of government by a white, male geron-
tocracy. Separated from their "dams" (breeder fems) during early
childhood, male offspring are raised in the Boyhouse, where hierarchy is learned through a system of competitive struggles for positions of power both within and across age groups. "'In discipline
is belonging,' the Teachers said. 'In discipline is solidarity among
men against the sly evil of the void with which your dams have in-
fected you' " (p. 123).

Crossing the age line is the form of sexual taboo always broken because everything in the social system conspires to this end.
If two men manage to escape the Boyhouse and its lessons, in order to establish friendship and trust, the price they pay for such an
escape is having to perform the least envied "jobs" in this society.

The first Dreaming is a Boyhouse ritual. Order and its constant companion, repression, are maintained through these collective sanctioned dreams practiced in public.[3] What is unsanc-

tioned is private dreaming. Yet there are those who are unsatisfied with the public spectacle; they may hire a Dark Dreamer to enact their visions. Servan d Layo lives off the fears of those Seniors empowered enough to command his services and he is, of course, despised because he knows their dark desires. Boys like Servan who demonstrate a compulsion and ability to dark dream are coerced, brutalized, and shamed into accepting the order of things. Few oppose their Seniors in this regime; d Layo is one who continues his struggle.

Homophobia together with the always unmoored signifier of paternity drive men to rule in ways that debilitate and impoverish their own lives as well as the lives of others. Kinship is rewritten along military lines of blood; a share in the same history of discipline (the Boyhouse rigors and routines) and power relations binds the allegiances of men. In a stroke, being born, and of woman, is rendered unspeakable, unmentionable. Clandestine meetings occur in the Boyhouse library which houses the records of the unmen and serves as the locus of liaisons across age lines. The library walls are covered with graffiti like the spiral—"the sign of the void, of fems, of everything inimical to the straight line of manly, rational thought and will" (p. 135).

The necessity for young boys to "outgrow the fem-taint in their souls passed on by contact with fems" rewrites in fiction the point in Hélène Cixous's theoretical essay "Laugh of the Medusa" that the unrepresentability of the female sex and death in Western culture serves the phallocratic "need for femininity to be associated with death"; it also recalls a tradition of psychological and psychoanalytical writings that emphasize men's dread of women's fertility.[4] Holdfast fems are not granted a ritualized death: since "they had no souls . . . their deaths had no significance" (p. 64).

Freud's *Totem and Taboo* (1913) offers yet another insight into how specifically Charnas rewrites the underside of the patriarchal quest narrative of Western literary tradition. The narrative movement of *Walk to the End of the World* intermittently alludes to classical texts from the initial oedipal quest for the father to his finally being discovered within the walls of 'Troi. In *Totem and Taboo* Freud reworked Darwin's idea of the primal horde in the following imaginary scenario. Society is organized as a "patriarchal horde" in which the father possesses the women and so creates sexual rivalry among the sons. By killing and devouring the father (the totem meal) the sons are each invested with some of his power and form a fraternal clan. Borrowing from J. J. Atkinson, an ethnologist and contemporary of his, Freud finds that there was "an ever-recurring violent succession to the solitary paternal tyrant, by sons whose parricidal hands were so soon again clenched in fratricidal strife" which would preclude any real reorganization of society.[5] The final drama of *Walk to the End of the World* reenacts this scenario in reverse, since the fraternal horde knows no father, only internal strife among Seniors and Juniors. As Freud pointed out in a later essay, "parricide according to a well-known view [his own] is the principle and primal crime of humanity."[6] What Holdfast Juniors fear is the obverse of this threat: that sons would be killed by their fathers in order to prevent their succession to seniority.

What strikes the reader as absent from Charnas's myth of origins is the traditional notion of sexual rivalry for women as motivation of the crime. Fems are a source of wealth, objects of exchange, and necessary for the reproduction of sons. But there is no question of rivalry of a sexual nature, since it is considered deviant for Holdfast men to desire women. They only visit the "breeding rooms" when necessary. One of the cardinal virtues of the Holdfast is "manliness," and scars are prized as marks of heroism. The men always fear darkness and solitude in the open air. Rivalry itself remains omnipresent and codified by duels in the Streets of Honor in a "defiant glorification of . . . corporal punishment."

Walk to the End of the World is divided into a prologue and four sections named after each of the travelers and narrated through their respective points of view, with a final section called "Destination"—Alldera's tale. The men have taken on Alldera as a passenger; although her ability to speak, rare among fems, is threatening to the men, she is valuable to them as a speed runner. Alldera's narrative reveals for the first time more than just the simple dullness she defensively displays before the men. Now we learn of her plans. Her interactions with the laboring carry-fems, who bear the camper in which they travel, reveal hierarchies among fems that mock and imitate those among men. Alldera, who speaks more than "femmish soft speech," is a slave like them, but her intelligence sets her apart from them at the same time. It is intelligence, particularly, which the men have tried to breed out selectively. Her intelligence separates her from the labor-fems, and her lack of beauty separates her from the pet-fems, nevertheless, Alldera's identity is inevitably bound up in her slave status:

> The trouble with pet-fems was that they came to take pride in their disfigurement—a technique of survival practiced by most fems to some extent. But in its more blatant forms, when it extended to identification with the interests of masters rather than with the interests of fems, it sickened her.
>
> Besides, Alldera had a strong contempt for and distrust of the merely decorative. Her own tough body, small in breasts and hips and well muscled, predisposed her toward valuing utility. She had learned to be glad of her broad pan of a face, which served both to mask her intelligence and to repel the interests of men perverse enough to pursue fems for the gratification of sexual appetites. There were times when she wished herself beautiful, of course; her own kind took their standards of beauty from those of the masters, and Alldera had spent lonely times because of that. Generally, though, she was well pleased with the virtues of her looks, and she continued to prefer the company of hard-used labor-fems like these, battered and stupid though they were. (Pp. 164–65)

We have read of this self-hatred and hatred for those of one's "kind" in earlier textual examples of (mis)recognition among women, a feature of subjectification and rivalization. Like her three male traveling companions, Alldera has managed to break through some of the training in the Holdfast. The above passage demonstrates a continued and vehement self-identification with fems against great odds. This protofeminist consciousness marks her as that fem who will set out into the future of *Motherlines*. In a society as segregated by sex as the Holdfast, it would seem "natural" for Alldera to identify with the fems among whom she has spent her life. Yet this same segregation as a class of slaves idealizes and privileges identification with the class of those (older men) in power. This tension created in the psychic and social positioning of fems in the Holdfast divides them from each other and against themselves. The economic basis of scarcity and survival in the brutest physical sense forces dependence on men and offers security through the performance of hard labor or the enforced harem status of the ornamental pet-fems.

The political and theoretical practice of feminist conscious-ness-raising includes a primary identification with women. The reclamation of a sense of self is an empowering act. Alldera, who has intelligence and skills uncommon for both her sex and class, will be transformed when she says "I," but this will come at the cost of exile both by the masters and their female overseers, the Matris, the most co-opted of fems, those who train young females in enslavement. Alldera's exile will be literal by the novel's end.

While in a special position as a speaking fem, her nights are nevertheless spent among the carry-fems, who ask her for the words to songs that mourn the death of their lost companions. The songs, which are among the only common possessions of fems, are occasional or compressed history-cycles of the Holdfast; there are also proscribed songs, one of which Alldera dares to sing until it makes the others uneasy.

She is raped first by d Layo and also by Bek; after the second time this exchange occurs:

> Very low, the Endtendant said to her, "Listen, fem. I couldn't stay in the camper last night, so I slept outside. I heard your songs. . . . In the Boyhouse, they taught me that fems' songs are nonsense. They also taught that coupling with a fem out-side of the breeding-rooms is a dreadful peril, but here I am, no different than before; so maybe the songs are not non-sense.
>
> "Now you talk straight to me, bitch, or I'll break your neck, for I'm fed to the teeth with tricks and lies!" (P. 188)

For the first time Alldera responds by saying "I"—"The magical pronoun . . . the equalizing name for the self." The reader and Eykar Bek then receive an indirect narration of childhood and the life of fems who are raised in the "kitpits," where communication is limited to grunting and snarling. Her long conversation with Bek is a unique moment in her life so far:

> Exchanges like these provided them both with distraction. Alldera saw the danger in it and would have stopped, but she couldn't. Even among her own lovers and friends she had

never had any one to talk to like this. There had never been
any security, any time, even when she found another fem with
true verbal facility. This was her first experience of speech as
self-expression with any degree of complexity, eliciting responses of similar quality. It gave her an extraordinary feeling
of power, or reality.

   That was the danger. (Pp. 196–97)

But this breaching of the silence between men and fems ends
abruptly when Bek realizes that although he and Alldera have revealed themselves to each other, "it's worth nothing while I have
the power of death over you" (p. 204). Because his search for his
father is his first priority, he denies the insights he has gained in dialogue with Alldera:

   There must be no horror, no rape, nothing outside of the ordinary, superficial relations between men and fems. Therefore I
   can't permit you to be a person. What you haven't told me,
   keep. The rest I'll do my best to forget—unsuccessfully, if it's
   any comfort to you. Do you understand me?

   She understood him perfectly. She had beaten him into a
   retreat. She bent her head: "As the master says." (P. 204)

Earlier, Alldera's intelligence separated her from the fems. In
the passage above, the connection between language and power is
made clear. Though she finally defers to Bek by playing the obe-
dient slave, they both know the victory in this dialogue is hers.
The sense of power and reality accessible through saying "I" is not
available to most fems, whose speech is characterized as soft,
slurred, and incomprehensible to the masters, whose speech is
"hard-edged" and "manly" (p. 68). When he hears the songs of
the fems Bek realizes that they have a language of their own that
does not easily translate. Alldera's and Bek's positions become
fixed when they each realize that the Holdfast suppresses any real
breakthrough between them.

   Like Odysseus stopping his ears so as not to be distracted by
siren cries, Bek ends the dialogue because he cannot continue to
hear her without giving up his paternal quest; the war between
generations must precede that between men and fems. Recogniz-
ing the need to continue her own journey, Alldera surrenders in

rote fashion to Bek, knowing he will be changed because of their conversation. She has said "I" for the first time. Before she can do so again she must first cross the borders into the Wild, where she hopes to find echoes of her own voice.

The epic proportions of Bek's journey are apparent when the travelers arrive at last at 'Troi, an industrial city for the Holdfast, "built with its back to the Wild, as if in disdain of a conquered enemy" (p. 208). In 'Troi there are the technological advances of electricity and firearms, which confuse, mystify, and frighten the newcomers. Raff Maggomas has spent his life awaiting the arrival of his son. He is the political economist and theorist for the transitional era of famine. With foresight he proclaims a need for new heroes, his son to be first among them. His plan for a "new, better and truly rational society" is elaborated as he, Bek, and d Layo look out over the city at the illuminated streets below. Maggomas considers himself the far-seeing critic of Holdfast power struggles in which the energy of young men is dissipated to prevent change. "The point, young men, is to prevent the Junior population from growing large enough, rich enough, or educated enough to burst the boundaries of the Holdfast, begin a real Reconquest—and perhaps turn around afterward and take the Holdfast for themselves, with their newfound strength and confidence"(p. 220). The drama of the father-son scenario which follows hinges on the future place of fems, who, along with food, have grown scarce. Raff Maggomas's eugenic policies will assure reproduction while they simultaneously maintain a smaller but still enslaved female population. When Eykar Bek emerges as the inevitable victor, one is left to speculate on his own use of power; he fears yet respects fems as a result of his hostile but enlightening dialogue with Alldera after he raped her and then forced her to speak.

"Destination" completes the quest narrative and propels the reader into the suggested future of *Motherlines*.[7] Dialectical movement both within and between each of the two novels offers the promise of a third which might bring together the Holdfast survivors. The end of *Walk to the End of the World* reveals who those survivors might be and how they might deal with the Riding Women and escaped Free Fems of *Motherlines*.

Charnas's long walk takes her readers toward a world of women. Like other utopias composed at approximately the same time, the politics of hope then seemed to have victories everywhere—abortion had been legalized; there was an active movement of women into male-dominated occupations; there was fervor at the grass-roots level; shelters for battered women were being established in cities and towns all over the United States; the need for daycare centers and "equal rights" for women had been taken seriously by enough sectors of the population that feminism (in the form of the Equal Rights Amendment) took root as a question on the national sociopolitical agenda for the first time in some fifty years. This was before the rise of religious fundamentalism and its concomitant political conservatism that would later inform Atwood's *The Handmaid's Tale,* read and rewritten "looking backward" where Charnas had earlier looked forward. What Charnas and Atwood share is a sharp eye for the details in everyday language that disclose the pervasiveness of our gendered subjectivity.

Charnas speaks in a letter of how the writing of *Walk to the End of the World* made its sequel necessary.[8] Alldera is the primary female character through whom the attitudes of the Holdfast men toward fems is explained. Her covert mission is to reach the edges of the Holdfast and then to strike out into the Wild to search for the legendary Free Fems. *Motherlines* presents a dialectical reply to the twist of events which occurs as *Walk to the End of the World* closes. The strict hierarchy of the Holdfast "Brotherhood" has been shaken by the murder of Maggomas, for he had offered Bek the products of patriarchy and its symbols—his accumulation of wealth and power, and, of course, his name. In what may seem a simple breach of codes and manners, Maggomas acquired knowledge of paternity. That taboo was to mark Bek and force his quest, thereby fulfilling a promise of parricide, this particular society's unspoken source of cultural dread, the murder of sons by fathers. Bek's survival and d Layo's escape from 'Troi leave the reader to wonder what the new order of things will become.

Throughout this interchange among the men, Bek has insistently tried to make eye contact with Alldera, so he can be assured by her look that he is not as virulent as his father in his hatred of fems. She finally responds, "smiling a fierce, wild smile." Just as language confers a sense of power and mastery, so does laughter.

Alldera's smile is not obsequious and approving of Bek. It is "fierce" like the laughter of the guérillères was wild, and like Jael Reasoner's smile which revealed her metal teeth. Revitalizing one of many cultural icons of women, Hèlène Cixous's germinal essay on women and language is aptly entitled, "The Laugh of the Medusa." What Cixous does is to reveal the face of the Medusa in her play with language. Classical mythology portrays Perseus planning to behead the Medusa and equipped to defuse her known powers. Athena (who was responsible for Medusa's dreaded visage and who appropriated her power by placing its representation on her own aegis) warns Perseus not to look into Medusa's face but only at her reflection. Overturning the horror of the Medusa, Cixous writes, "You only have to look at the Medusa straight on to see her. And she's not deadly. She's beautiful and she's laughing."[9] She who laughs asserts her mastery over events and language. The most succinct alliance of laughter and power is the social ritual of the joke, which masters language and meaning. Alldera's fierce smile is her first act of defiance against Bek's will to command. Like Charnas's other subtle renderings of Alldera's submission and self-control, her fierce smile simultaneously placates and defies.

In the final chapter of *Walk to the End of the World* Alldera waits, crouched against the outside walls of 'Troi though "she felt no triumph yet at having slipped the leash of the man's authority" (p. 237). Now moving into her own future, she recounts her farewells to the Holdfast and her traveling partners: "Show yourself judiciously among the rocks on the high slopes, and he'll find you . . . if anyone can survive this upheaval it's Servan and whomever he protects!" (p. 242). Like her outlaw companions, she refuses Bek's aid: "Do you think you're the only one with the right to say 'no'?" She then quickly memorizes what Bek shows her of a map with a space marked as the Refuge.

Controlling her fear, she takes her first steps "suddenly buoyant and powerful" into a future of her own making where, as Bek realizes, "there won't be any master along to push you around— or to entertain you," a twist on the usual master-slave lines of use and abuse. As Alldera waits at the walls of 'Troi for her moment to break away, she sees d Layo run by her. The breakdown of law is apparent even in a society as mad and amoral as the Holdfast: "It had been like the passage of some hungry beast . . . so strong was her impression of a hunting predator . . . there was something primeval in the thought of the survivors stalking one another among the ruins—all hunters, all quarry."[10] But Alldera breaks out beyond the ruins making her way into the Wild, braced for her journey "without another glance back . . . warming up for a long, hard run" as the novel closes, and at the same time, opens the utopian space activated by the principle of hope.

With the opening of *Motherlines* Alldera herself has become the "hungry beast" of her vision. Although "[s]he had not seen a living being in the months since her escape from her homeland," she now spies pairs of crescent-shaped tracks which frighten her—the monsters of Holdfast legend. Balancing and answering the ending of *Walk to the End of the World,* "she tried to consider her situation clearly, turning her inner gaze back over the course of her flight" as the future and the past modify each other from the perspective of the present. The Holdfast life has already been burnished by memory and solitude—it is no longer merely the oppressive round of slavery, domination, and survival—it is "her homeland" and "her country." It will be years before contact with the past is renewed. Alldera has only the "rape cub" growing in and feeding off her body to remind her of her past life among humans. Now she will learn the new ways evolved by those who escaped the Wasting and survived the period of Refuge—these are the Riding Women. As Eykar's birthmarking named him the maker of a new order, so too will the child Alldera bears be invested with the hope of the *free* women who raise her—the Riding Women—and those who see her as their successor—the Free Fems—who over the years escaped Holdfast imprisonment—*freed* women.[11] The split between these two groups will be healed in the narrative through Alldera's work as the "messenger" she was trained to be.

Dystopia is defined in *Walk to the End of the World* as that "place" where men still rule and where division by sex and gender is basic to social life. Charnas's utopian vision has its own inner tensions. With its dedication to "J.R." and the call to tell "new stories," the novel asks to be read both contextually and intertextually; that is, in relation to its history as a social and a literary production. Its claim to tell a new story is as much an act of willful rewriting as Wittig's claim in *Lesbian Peoples* for the present as the Glorious Age. Charnas works at healing the mother-amazon split diagnosed earlier in the juxtaposition of Gilman and Wittig. In order to situate Charnas's novel, it will be helpful to return momentarily to Wittig, Russ, and Piercy.

The relationship of storytelling to history making is the main thread in *Motherlines* around which others are gathered. Just as *Walk to the End of the World* inscribes certain structures of fraternal kinship, the title suggests that *Motherlines* posits a collectivity of sisterhood and kinship among women. As in some of the earlier novels examined, most explicitly *Herland* and *Woman on the Edge of Time,* Charnas rewrites the kinship structures of daily life. As in *Les Guérillères* and *The Female Man,* a second major concern is with a new history with women as the makers and recorders of tales, or bearers of fables. Like Piercy, Charnas also presents her readers with a "future family." Not only does Charnas reassemble the mother-amazon duality first studied by Helen Diner in 1932, more recently reworked in Wittig's *Lesbian Peoples,* she also reinvents the conflict examined in *The Female Man* between Jael Reasoner and Janet Evason, two very different women of the future.[12]

The new histories of *Motherlines* arise out of a dialectical interaction with the history of the Holdfast; either within and against it (the Free Fems) or outside it but in reaction to the Wasting. The Riding Women of the Grasslands have also had to adapt to a world "beggared of resources," where scarcity is the basis for their nomadic relation to nature. That these "new histories" are those written by women is an evident concern of all the novels discussed here. In her dystopia Charnas has produced a past against which the new or "future" histories may be read. The symbolic weight of women speaking their own stories in *Walk to the End of the World* was most apparent in the scene where Alldera first said "I." As *Motherlines* opens, Alldera is seen reading others' "writings"—pairs of prints in the dirt, "crescent-shaped, and as big as her fist with a sharp angle sign in the middle of each. Monster's tracks" (p. 3). Alldera assumes that these "tracks," "spoors," and "marks" cannot have been made by men or fems. Yet in her state of near starvation she follows the tracks she knows "would end in food: they would either feed her or eat her" (p. 6).

Charnas's process of defamiliarization is opened up for the reader, but not for Alldera, when the scene changes and we see Sheel riding a horse, carrying a bow and scouting for renegade men. Her knowledge of men comes from years of hunting them as prey: "What a perversity—a creature that would own her if she let it. . . . Men's only good feature was that they were a peerlessly clever and dangerous quarry to hunt. Their terror at the end, when you came up and waited a little way off for the dying to be done with, was wild-eyed and bestial" (p. 9). For the Riding Women men are creatures of a history-become-myth, since they are unknown except through the devastation apparent in the landscape. As the men blamed the unmen for the Wasting, these women presume the world they see was devastated by those they know only through legend—men.

The scene shift from Alldera to Sheel is part of a narrative strategy quite different from the first novel. There, the purposeful quest made for a linear recounting with only the teller shifting in each section of the novel. Here the movement is more contrapuntal than episodic. The rhythm alternates between women and fems through the mediation of Alldera, by her integration with and distance from either group.

Alldera's sense of self after months in the Wild is represented in a mirroring scene which tells a tale quite different from that of the mythical Narcissus. She sees no dreams in the water, her image is roughened in reflection, not idealized: "She glanced down at herself. The only rounded line to be seen was that of her belly. Her hands, feet and joints looked coarse and swollen, surrounding muscle having melted away. . . . She could not pretend to be some proud free fem out of a song; the fems' tales of running off to make a life in the Wild were dreams" (pp. 5–6). This first of the two chapters which make up the prologue ends in a scene reminiscent of the one between Connie and Luciente in *Woman on the Edge of Time*. When Alldera is almost killed and is captured, she assumes her captors are men. Like Connie Ramos, disavowal is her first reaction, since she expects that women do not or would not move this way.

The stranger pulled off his headdress, freeing a thick fall of gray-shot hair. "Don't be afraid," he said again slowly, and Alldera understood. "Don't be scared of me."

He caught up her hand and pressed it against his own body. Under the slick-surfaced tunic Alldera felt the unmistakable soft shape of a female breast.

An identity formed among slavish fems and hierarchically embattled men does not make it possible to imagine action by women; here again is evidence of the internalized self-hatred of a group debased and oppressed, from without and from within. And like Connie Ramos, with the discovery that her pursuer is female, Alldera's fear immediately dissipates.

Alldera travels not through time as do other utopian guests or dreamers, but between histories and identities. For the first part of her life, she was a femmish slave; by the end of this novel, she has spent some twelve years among the women, where her change and growth are paralleled by the growth of the child she was carrying when she was found and who is taken in by the women. Her "cognitive estrangement" among the women provides an entry for us as readers from a world in which we can deny the horrors of the Holdfast and wonder at the community life of the Grasslands. A new family is formed when Alldera is brought back to the camp pregnant with a "rape cub" and so is the hope for a new motherline.

The motherlines are biological groupings which have grown up among the Riding Women since the post-Wasting period of Refuge. Each line is differentiated both by physical and character traits:

> "And I don't like the Ohayars because they're sneaky. The Fowersaths are quick-tempered, the Mellers borrow things and don't return them, the Churrs have ice cold hands, the Hayscalls mumble till you think you're going deaf."
>
> Jesselee joined in zestfully, "The Clarishes are vain, the Perikens exaggerate everything. The Farls are lazy and their fingers turn back in a sickening way." (P. 230)

The tie of the individual to her line is through her "bloodmother," while parenting is taken on by the bloodmother and four sharemothers, among whom the "heartmother" fulfills a tie of special tenderness, affection, or affinity. Ties of blood are not privileged in the choices of affinity. As Alldera's child is told, "liking women has nothing to do with being related to them" (p. 231). This occurs at her naming ceremony where together with Alldera she chooses the name Sorrel for the color of her hair and the horses she likes to ride. If Sorrel can establish a new motherline as a result of being raised among the women, a future resolution of the conflict between those who have not known men and those who have escaped their rule may be possible. Among the Riding Women, tradition gives the bloodmother the privilege of naming her child; for Alldera "the one who gives the name is the master"—causing her to sweat over this responsibility and, even after so many years, to question again her own traditions which still determine many of her difficulties among the women.

Alldera's new family and motherline are established by the group chosen to decide her status and that of her child. In this process begins the narrative unfolding of the long history of conflict between the women and the fems they have rescued over the years, yet who inevitably choose to live among themselves. The Riding Women are pledged to save fems who have survived long enough to be discovered. The reader now hears Holdfast history as retold by the descendants of those who were among those collectively called the unmen. The women insist on the notion that their ancestors were free women, not enslaved fems. "'She's just like the rest of them, the runaways, the "free fems"—they crawl all their lives under the whips of Holdfast men, and those that can't take it any longer run away. We find them, make them a place here on the plains, praise them for their courage—courage to run off and leave the rest of your own kind to rot!' She paused for breath. What a pleasure it was to speak freely against what all the camps agreed was right" (p. 18). Both Sheel and Alldera find the courage and wisdom to overcome much before they accept each other as family. Barvaran, a more generous woman, reminds Sheel of her own contradictory actions and desires: "Some women say you can't tell fems from their masters . . . when you speak of fems, you talk like a woman with no kin" (pp. 19–20).

In part 2, "The Women," Alldera gives birth after a "long dreaming" in her new surroundings. The care, cooperation, and attention given her by the women during the labor and delivery bring about another recognition of her separation from the group: "If she had not been a fem, trained for her life's sake to hide feelings, she would have wept" (p. 26). Alldera's integration into her family is an obstacle course of estrangement. Each woman elicits a response in her which sets the past continually between them. Nenisi Conor, the woman who later becomes Alldera's lover, is black, proving to Alldera how teaching her to despise those with "skin the color of the earth" was yet another lie to serve the purposes of the men. Barvaran, who later becomes Alldera's heartmother, is first seen as ungainly, like the carry-fems; Sheel is an "icy bitch" and easier for Alldera to handle—enmity among fems being familiar to Alldera; and Shayeen is merely polite to Alldera. These impressions are recorded as the women sit facing each other in their tent, passing Alldera's child around as they nurse her in turn.

It takes Alldera some time and courage to ask two questions of the women: "'How do you have children without men?' 'Oh,' Barvaran said, 'we mate with our horses' " (p. 34). Alldera feels the response is meant to mock her ignorance. A fuller explanation will later lead Alldera to leave the women and try to live among other escaped fems with whom she shares a history. How much her years among the women have changed her becomes apparent only then. The second question, long suppressed, is at last spoken to Nenisi:

> "Will you help us?"
>
> "There is no help. . . . It was decided long ago that we women would never risk the free world of our children by invading the Holdfast for the fems' sakes. We all agreed. . . . Besides, it's too late. . . . We think they're all dead. . . ."
>
> She turned away to hide the horror of her feelings: the dark surge of grief for her lost people was shot through with the joy of being truly free of them at last. (Pp. 34–35)

Alldera is released and guilt-ridden at the same time over her "undeserved survival into freedom." The guilt begins to give way to release only when her vast pleasure in running is reawakened by the physical freedom and mobility of the women who travel their lands during the Rainy and Cool seasons. Alldera can then begin the process of seeing herself and her past anew as she learns more about the free fems and their trade relations with the Riding Women.

It is a long time before Alldera speaks publicly among the women. For months she listens, childlike in her curiosity and in her difficulty to adapt to these new voices, as "tangled skeins of events were unrolled." Not a child, however, she wearies at the lack of verbal exchange, since no women ask her to speak of the Holdfast. Still she longs to feel a part "of the ease the women had with each other, the rich connectedness" (p. 49). While Alldera learns with difficulty, her still unnamed child runs free with other prepubescent females in the childpack. In turn, each tent (household) participates in feeding the pack, a noisy, vital, and dirty group who sleep huddled together, are never punished, and need fear only the nightly scavenging of the taboo sharu hordes who feed off the dead. The women subsist on a diet of gathered greens, cultivated vegetables, mare's milk, tea, and the meat of horses regularly culled from the herds. Preparing the meal, the women reminisce about the "free life" of the childpack, which ends abruptly: "You start to bleed, and the younger ones drive you out. . . . There's no place to go but to the tents, where you remember women once carried you and nursed you and mopped your bottom. And sure enough, there they are, all waiting to make you into a proper woman with a name and a family" (p. 52). As in Piercy's and Russ's fictions, adolescence seems less amenable to utopian revision, and more an inevitable process of division and reidentification.

In the trade relations between women and fems their differences need not be confronted. Only when they become partners in more than trade can they begin to recognize each other, glean their likenesses. When the Free Fems appear on a trade visit, Alldera's two histories become rather starkly contrasted in the look, clothing, and bearing of the fems among the women. The fems wear brightly colored clothing, their speech is "grating after the women's liquid speech," their attitude is "truculent," and their avoidance of physical contact with the women all contribute to recreate the old conflict in Alldera—"she felt off balance, flooded with guilt for her abandoned task" (p. 56). What first shocked Alldera about the women—how they reproduce—creates confusion again as she struggles to stay with them, though the insults of the fems frighten her: "Come on, what is it, you like these horse-fuckers, these dirty, rag-tag savages that bathe in their own sweat, dirty beasts, cock-worshippers" (p. 57). From this conflict and Alldera's confusion comes an expanded tale of origins to fill the gaps left by Holdfast men, and to explain the necessary divisiveness between fems and women. The women are descendants of those who survived the Wasting; the "first daughters" managed to learn the genetic technology before the cataclysm. This involved a process of trait-doubling, which started reproduction with the addition of a "certain fluid." These women also learned to breed horses for toughness and speed rather than for looks, which permitted their survival after the Wasting. As for the scavenging sharu, they "were bred up from some tiny animals the men had been using to find out about ferocity, and once let out they flourished—an unhappy surprise, but not bad in the long run. Sharu have their place too" (p. 61). True kinship between Alldera and the women depends finally on whether or not her child will bring "new seed, new traits, the beginning of the first new motherline since our ancestors came out of the lab" (p. 62). This will not be determined until Sorrel leaves the childpack at menarche and attends her first Gather, where mating occurs. The women have already attempted to aid in this process by nursing the child themselves, which relieves Alldera of what she sees as an immobilizing activity, remembering enforced time in the Holdfast Milkery. Unlike her bloodmother, Alldera, who hears with horror of the mating process, Sorrel, the child, will grow up prepared for this Grassland ritual.

The changes which finally bring Alldera into the group in a more intimate way are her learning to ride and her coupling with Nenisi. After this she prepares to speak at the chief tent about the ongoing conflict between herself and Sheel, and she begins again to train for running after some three years among the women. When Nenisi and Alldera go off alone they are able at last to speak of how they each have come to understand their relationship and their ideas of love. Alldera has been hurt by what she views as "Nenisi's apparent unfaithfulness with women of the camp." To Nenisi's explanation/question: "What makes it right for two to be alone, when it's not right for one to be?" Alldera can only reply that "it's different where I come from." Holdfast notions of possession have no place in this shared love. Like Piercy's family of three comothers, Charnas's model of five sharemothers proposes dispersion of intimacy in adulthood and childhood.

Both Charnas and Piercy present models of a utopian family where a child raised collectively learns to love nonpossessively. Without an exclusive parental tie, there is no expectation that one person can or need satisfy all the longings of the heart, thus rewriting parenting along with the myth of romance. In *The Mermaid and the Minotaur* Dorothy Dinnerstein proposes a similar solution through a theoretical and psychoanalytic reading of "human sexual arrangements." Dinnerstein is utopian in her impulse to restructure the workings of the human family. But since her imaginary family is still composed of the heterosexual couple, Dinnerstein and the feminist utopian novelists part company. What they share, however, is an apocalyptic vision in which men, the "desert-makers," ravage the world of resources.

Like Wittig, Charnas remembers and reinvents the Amazon myths in which battle and play merge. Rivalry is not unfamiliar to the women. The prizes of the struggle are horses. In a reworking of the earlier *Totem and Taboo* scenario, the horses function here as the fems did in the Holdfast, with the utopian distinction that the attitude of the women toward their horses is one of connectedness, embodying "the dependence of all beings on each other and the kinship of creatures" (p. 155). The horses are a form of wealth; they are given as gifts and as restitution, they serve as a basis for exchange, along with their role in reproduction. When their time comes to die no part goes unused; they are neither sentimentalized nor mistreated.

When finally the mating with stallions is explained, Alldera feels more strongly her status as an outsider: "[s]he saw it as she knew a Holdfast man would see it: as something titillating." Nenisi explains: "Sheel doesn't want to keep you away to spare your feelings, though we all know how upset fems get about this—you're different anyway, you've lived with us a long time, you'll understand eventually. . . . We do have a bond, of our bodies and theirs. The balance of all things includes us and acts on us. . . . We celebrate it every year at the Gather of all the camps, where young women mate" (p. 87). She cannot believe that "It's nothing at all like a man overpowering a fem just to show her who's master" (pp. 87–88).

Part 2 closes when Alldera tires of her struggle to become a woman among these women and says to Nenisi, "It's no good. I think it would be better if you would just tell me how to find the free fems" (p. 88). And part 3 opens on a scene at the fems's wagon crew where Daya, a former pet-fem, serves as storyteller. Fems call the women "Mares" after their despised habits which the fems know include horses in the process of reproduction. Rumor has spread among them that an escaped fem has been rescued by the women. That she has stayed among them so long arouses a great deal of suspicion, speculation, and, for Daya, fascination and intrigue:

> Maybe she brings a message the Mares don't want us to have. Maybe the men are preparing an invasion, and the Mares are keeping her with them to get information out of her. No, it's the Mares that are preparing an invasion, so they're pumping her all about the Holdfast first. (P. 41)

Daya entertains the fems with elaborate tales of the cruelty of her Holdfast master and her disfigurement at the hands of his treacherous male lover. The insistence with which memory coupled with deprivation rewrite history is highlighted in the late evening reminiscences of the fems around the spare campfire as they longingly remember the variety of foods available in the Holdfast in contrast to the Grasslands.

The fems' camp is dominated by Elnoa's lavishly decorated wagon which, like most mobile homes, never moves. Elnoa has always exercised power from "decades ago when she had first bossed her master's femhold" and had her tongue cut out as punishment for insubordination and denial of the master's accusations. Now communicating in "handspeech" the mute Elnoa still rules the fems with her plans to regain the Holdfast. "Like addicts turning to their drug, the free fems fell to discussing the plan. The great plan. It was Elnoa's idea. According to her, the free fems would one day slip past the Mares' patrols and return to the Holdfast, where they would infiltrate the population and take over, capturing the men and freeing the fems enslaved there" (p. 96). Daya knows the plan serves only as a "useful illusion" for the fems, just as her own stories do. Daya's tales are varied in style, though they all underwrite the necessary notion of strength among the fems, whether they are free or, as in the past, clever enough to outwit their masters. Daya returns from a trading journey to find that Alldera has joined the fems. Though she has been among them for several months, Alldera's "standoffishness" makes her unwelcome: taken in, but excluded. She is needed, for the great plan suffers from the fact that no new fems have escaped the Holdfast in years, and their numbers merely decline. Alldera had scorned tales of "Moonwoman" years ago in the Holdfast; here Moonwoman is the primary subject of Daya's fables and legends.

Like the vying for positions of power among Junior and Senior men, the "freed" fems mock and yet continue the masters' games and contests for favor. Daya knows the games well because of her history as a pet-fem, and she tries her best to maintain her favored status with Elnoa. Having intrigued to stay alone with Elnoa, Daya now begins a furtive plan to keep Alldera at a distance from Elnoa: "Daya had heard Alldera say that the tea camp sometimes seemed just like a big femhold with Elnoa as master. Did Elnoa know that? If not, there might be a profit, sometime, to be made out of the runner's imprudent statement" (p. 106). Daya entertains and distracts Elnoa with lyrical descriptions of the plains she has come to love and which Elnoa refuses to travel.

A surprise visit to Alldera by Nenisi forecasts Daya's future role. She alone among the fems has a love of the new landscape and the mobility it offers, and she alone dares to think enviously of the Mares. Watching Nenisi, with her horse, and Alldera speaking together in the distance, she wonders, "[w]hat did it feel like to be touched by a woman as black as char and to stroke a creature that was not even human at all?" (p. 110). Nenisi's brown skin and the demeanor of the tamed beast fascinate Daya, who hears Nenisi's voice as that of a storyteller and sees her as a "dramatic shadow-person." This inversion of racism—exoticism—represents the limits to which Daya's break from her history can take her.

After Alldera is injured in an aborted escape attempt, Daya sends her to be healed by Fedeka, who lives alone on the plains gathering plants and herbs. The yearly Generation Feast among the fems is a celebration which parallels the women's Gather.

Each year with a potion mixed by Fedeka, the fems hope "to find a starter that will make a new life in us" (p. 123). Each year their hopes go unrealized. At this year's feast, Daya becomes incurably ill from her "fertility douche." She rightly suspects that another jealous fem has poisoned her. She is sent to Fedeka, whom the fems hope will save her. Most of the fems are glad to see her and her intrigues gone. In a farewell handspeech to Daya, Elnoa explains the purpose of the ledgers in which she continuously writes. They are history as remembered and recorded by the one who has lost her speaking voice, yet writes, allying her with Daya, who has lost her looks, yet pleases. "You and I are alike in that; we two have subdued adversity. . . . I will write down what I have done for you, and perhaps a few of your stories, if I can remember them" (p. 130).

The exiled antagonists, Alldera and Daya, are now brought together in Fedeka's care. Arguing over the repetition of Holdfast hierarchy among the fems and their glorification of a false heroic past, Alldera criticizes Daya's romances of "clever fems outwitting their masters! Your romances of the past are as false as your romances of the future. We were slaves. . . . Even when those tales are true they don't mean anything. We were slaves. That's our real history. Better to fight and die" (p. 140). But Daya has the last words: "Of us two, I'm not the one who's ashamed of who she is." Alldera leaves Fedeka and reappears months later with three horses she has tamed while traveling the plains. At first Fedeka fears the horses until she comes to appreciate their use as beasts of burden. Alldera and Daya's enmity fades when, in a replication of Alldera's coming together with Nenisi, she and Daya become lovers. Soon afterward Daya asks Alldera to teach her to ride. For the first time Alldera is in a position to try to merge her histories.

When a group of Riding Women come upon Alldera and Daya, Alldera unhorses one and takes her captive. She demands horses as ransom to increase her child's wealth at the time of leaving the childpack. Alldera now plans to return to the women, and to bring Daya along as her "cousin." Their welcome is eased when two Bawns of Shayeen's motherline accept Alldera as kin and Daya with her. Following the practice among women, "it was the prisoner's right to tell the first version of her own downfall" (p. 168). Storytelling is followed by food, and a special "sweat tent" is set up for Alldera and Daya to "bathe in privacy." Their earlier hostility is long cancelled out. Alldera explains why she first left the Riding Women and how she now hopes to rejoin them: "I demanded too much of them. . . . I liked them even then, and I like them better now. I need to remember who my own people are when I'm here. That's why I asked you to come with me" (p. 170).

As its title "Kindred" indicates, part 5 of *Motherlines* begins to resolve the tensions between the two histories as lived and represented by the free fems and by the women. It is time for the Holdfaster family to reunite for the ceremony of Alldera's child's "coming out" of the childpack. Once again attention shifts to Sheel, who still harbors anger toward Alldera, especially since her return with another fem. Only Sheel's heartmother is able to help her remember her responsibility to the child she has mothered with Barvaran, Shayeen, Nenisi, and Alldera: "You are the only Sheel Torrinor there is. The child has a claim on your mothering right to the end of her childhood, whatever her background may be, whoever her other mothers are" (p. 178). In her dreams Sheel returns to the opening of the story, wishing she'd killed Alldera then. Only later does Alldera find the courage and wisdom to speak up to her at last: "What you and I started in the desert between women and fems is out of your hands and mine now" (p. 187).

When other fems arrive to claim kinship with Alldera, the differences between the two groups erupt into greater hostility. Fems will not eat the women's food, they will not freely share their space, dividing it with a curtain of hides. The women are bothered by the fems's incessant arguing, and their rapid, clipped speech; the storyteller Daya captivates her warring audiences with a tale of taking over the Holdfast together in the ever-present future.

With all the groups finally united in Holdfaster tent, the rituals that mark childhood's end begin. The child must be washed and combed for the first time, leading to physical struggle between mothers and child. Even though Nenisi has explained the ceremony to Alldera, she still feels distant from the others and needs to remind herself that this child is of her own body and to remember her early days with the women. "She was no longer trying to catch up to them. Their distance from her—when she felt it—was now simply part of their nature and their beauty. She found that she did not need Daya to remind her of who she was" (p. 202). Each woman in turn performs a history-telling ritual with her child, pointing out in the sand map of the Grasslands the sites of victory, discovery, and that place where one's own bloodmother was left for the sharu to find. This ritual is called "walking over the world." Alldera's child has chosen Barvaran as her heartmother. Barvaran now leads her to Alldera, whose face she studies for resemblances. Then the bloodmother and child are separated for a time. "The bloodmother looked at her child and saw her own image made young. . . . The child saw in her bloodmother the pattern for her own being. Women said it was best not to let this powerful connection unbalance all the other relationships that guided their two lives" (p. 204).

The naming which follows causes Alldera anxiety since a name has not come to her, and Daya speaks for the fems who think the child should have a femmish name (one always ending in "a"). The ceremony is interrupted by the sudden appearance of Fedeka who intercedes for the fems and their claims on the child's history. Later that night in the fems' wagon, Alldera listens to their reminiscing and feels distant once more from her past and separate from her present and from those women who resent that the fems have come to stay because of Alldera. "Many said they had wished to come to Stone Dancing Camp sooner, but a fading allegiance to Elnoa had held them back, till now; till Sorrel's coming out. The Plan was just the Plan, always in the future, but Alldera's child was real now, and they kept hearing of real things happening now at Holdfaster Tent—free fems on horseback, free fems with bows" (p. 212). Alldera's original mission still haunts her and though she fears endangering the freedom of the women, she allows herself to imagine a takeover of the ruins of the Holdfast.

The fems bring the women knowledge gained during their slavery. When they pave the floor of a granary to keep it safe from sharu, conflicting attitudes surface about work. Daya argues with Shayeen and Jesselee:

> ". . . we aren't afraid of a job that lasts more than a few days or needs careful planning."
>
> "You fems make no sense about what you call work. Women need time to talk and play and ride out hunting, not just

to work. You work all the time, learning something, building something. We do what satisfies us."

"A person is in the world to live in it, not to make it over. Only a creature who belongs to nothing has to keep making things to belong to. A woman isn't like that." (Pp. 218–19)

The skills at riding and the use of the bow which the fems gain from the women feed their plans to retake the Holdfast and to rescue the fems left alive there. Practice for such a struggle comes when the fems join with the women to fight off a swarm of sharu that comes by the camp.

Though Sheel and Alldera have never overcome their distrust and dislike of each other, Sorrel and Sheel form a strong bond. Sheel agrees to plan Sorrel's "maiden raid," which will then prepare her for mating and "familying" with others of her age. Sorrel and Alldera also begin to overcome their temporarily enforced separation: "on one side that cautious attention to the child, a touch perhaps of wary pride, and, on the other, curiosity and eagerness to please. A strange thing, the start of such closeness between a femmish bloodmother and a woman-child" (p. 239). Sheel observes this new intimacy, and through her own closeness to Sorrel she finally begins to let go of her hatred of the fems and their plans:

> [P]lainly the thing Sheel had always feared—that the free fems would truly determine to return to the Holdfast, with unforeseeable consequences for all women—was clearly happening. As a nightmare, the idea had maddened her. Now, with the phantoms of angry imagination vanished in the face of reality, it became simply a fact of the future to be dealt with in its time.
>
> She felt saddened by the loss of her hatred. (P. 240)

In the final chapter of the epilogue, Barvaran dies of a wound received in a duel she fought for Nenisi's sake. Both Sorrel and Alldera grieve and are comforted. Her death will not go unpunished—"Later we will think of who should die for this, which well-loved woman of the guilty line." Alldera is lost in thought as the women return from leaving Barvaran's body for the sharu. Later that night they gather to speak about her. Alldera remembers "the way Barvaran's breast had yielded under her hand, that first touch of a Riding Woman, that first amazement" (p. 243). Nenisi approaches Alldera, who prepares to return to the Hold-fast with her "cousins." Though Alldera goes somewhat un-willingly, Nenisi explains that now women and fems are kindred and promises she will speak in favor of their future return. Before Alldera leaves, Nenisi says: "'I have few of your words from days past to keep with me.' Words, Alldera thought blankly. I was a messenger, and a messenger should know the importance of words without being told" (p. 245). Alldera's function as messen-ger was fulfilled beyond words by her bringing together, because and in spite of herself, two groups of women who were unable to share words or stories.

"This is, alas, a fantasy . . ." is the epigraph to *Motherlines,* where the histories of women and fems were interwoven to make a new history for a potential future. The "not-yet" of the utopian voice of hope reminds us that in a similar gesture, art always says "and yet!" to life.[13] As in *Walk to the End of the World,* the ending of *Motherlines* takes the reader beyond the moment of closure. Even if Alldera and the other fems are unsuccessful, a utopian im-pulse is here transformed into a hopeful future for this child, Sor-rel, and for the new lines she may begin to write into the women's histories.

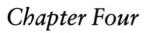

Chapter Four

The Houses of Women

Christiane Rochefort's
Archaos, ou le jardin étincelant
and E. M. Broner's
A Weave of Women

Dreams come in the day as well as at night. And both kinds of dreaming are motivated by wishes they seek to fulfill. But day-dreams differ from night-dreams; for the day-dreaming "I" persists throughout, consciously, privately, envisaging the circumstances and images of a desired, better life. The content of the day-dream is not, like that of the night-dream, a journey back into repressed experiences and their associations. It is concerned with an as far as possible unrestricted journey forward, so that instead of reconstituting that which is no longer conscious, the images of that which is not yet can be phantasied into life and into the world.

Ernst Bloch
The Meaning of Utopia

Hope, defined here as that drive toward change or difference, and as the fundamental impulse of utopian thought, is most commonly mapped onto the territory of the future. But hope may also "look backward" to offer a nostalgic rewriting of the past, as is the case in *Archaos, ou le jardin étincelant* by Christiane Rochefort. Or it can be transformed into the concrete action of an imaginatively lived present, as in E. M. Broner's *A Weave of Women.*[1] This temporal aspect is one contrasting way to read these two novels in tandem. Further contrast is achieved by juxtaposing a fiction located in the unspecified historical past of a Western European Catholic country (Rochefort), and another set in the 1970s in the occupied Old City of Jerusalem (Broner).

Though I have been tracing the phenomenon of the proliferation of feminist utopian fictions in the 1970s, few, if any, lay bare the utopian nexus of religion and politics in so specific a manner as these two novels. Remember the reader of Monique Wittig's *Les Guérillères* who is repeatedly told that "all action is overthrow"; in Broner's novel, the "Daughters of Jerusalem" have overthrown the ritual and language of their "Church Fathers." Through a set of apparent contrasts unexpected comparisons surface, since in Rochefort's novel there are also serious ruptures in the entrenched patriarchal law of Judeo-Christian tradition which introduce a new chaos into the midst of established religious orders and beliefs.

Unlike Marge Piercy in *Woman on the Edge of Time,* neither Broner not Rochefort presents a systematically worked out utopian society. Instead, each represents utopian moments which arise out of a breakdown of social and political orders. These two fictions are also linked by certain narrative concerns which separate them from other recent utopian writings. By bringing together the order of political and religious institutions, both novels question the relations of women to these traditions and the authority imposed on those relations. Broner and Rochefort do not portray the lesbian separatist society of *Les Guérillères,* nor the peaceful world of Charlotte Perkins Gilman's *Herland* into which men suddenly intrude, nor Piercy's genderless world of persons. Instead, we encounter Rochefort's androgynous arcadia of polymorphous perversity, and Broner's mostly Jewish, heterosexual feminist "world-to-come." Since both writers choose to populate their texts with women and men living under established religious doctrines, a case could be made for a shared projection of the tentative path toward utopia rather than the imaginative leap forward into a more fully fictional future. As Joanna Russ reminds her readers of the *The Female Man,* the utopian future of possibility is, after all, never "our future."[2] In this sense Rochefort posits a wished-for past, Broner a potential present, as versions of Bloch's "not-yet."

The contrasts between Broner and Rochefort are already apparent in the pre-textual openings. *Archaos* begins with a prelude, a message from the historians who have recovered the lost past of the kingdom of Archaos. In the prelude Rochefort presents a view of history, historiography, and narrativity.

> One finds no trace in books or elsewhere of the name of Govan-Eremetus, nor of the country of Archaos where he reigned, between the end of the Barbarous Era and the beginning of the Barbarous Era. . . . At this dark corner of History there is something like an abyss. . . . It is irritating for the historian to come against such shadowy zones which make one

think of interference in the course of History; . . . examination . . . reveals deliberate erasures with retroactive falsifications. We have speculated long and hard at the edge of our abyss. In the early morning . . . the idea came to us—scientifically absurd though it may be—to join all the vanishing points of the coordinates. And, wonder of wonders, we thus obtained an image through absence/lack [*image par manque*], a sort of negative. Needless to say this wasn't done in a day. It's not as simple as a dinosaur, and we didn't even have the bones; we only had everything that wasn't the dinosaur when it was there. (Pp. 5–6)

This passage reveals the fantasy space of Archaos as well as the sober tone in which the historians will tell their tale "by negation." The title *Archaos* is multiply suggestive: arche, origins, beginnings, and an "archaeological" view of history; also the Ark, chaos, and finally, and most pertinently, anarchy. The subtitle, *ou le jardin étincelant* ("or the glittering garden"), suggests an edenic representation, a new view of the old garden. In contrast to Rochefort's message from the historians, Broner's *A Weave of Women* opens with a dedication to "Women of the Sword and Sharpened Tongue," suggesting immediate links between language, both spoken and written, and power.

Though superficial as a criterion of resemblance, both novels offer a cast of characters. This marks them, however, as dramatically structured, a structure enacted in the interpolated narratives, dramas, and mystery plays which create a *mise en abîme* [3] of the narratives we are reading. In *Archaos* such effects also come about through description of paintings, "positive proofs" of the existence of Archaos found by the historians. They also discover fragments of poems by Ezéchias, tutor of the child-king and his twin sister-queen, whose verse is in a degenerate linguistic form because Ezéchias had learned the language of Archaos in taverns and from his two royal charges (Onagre and Govan), one of whom still speaks a patois, or "bastard speech." Such statements of verification, like many others in the novel, are often footnoted by the historians: "this did not make our research any easier" (p.5).

Broner and Rochefort draw upon a variety of liturgical, biblical, fantastical, demotic, and earthy languages in order to present their utopian visions. The mystery plays of *Archaos* find their contemporary analogs in the street theater of *Weave*. In *Weave*, Tova and Joan write and stage a play called "The City Between Us" about the conflicts between Jews and Arabs, which no theater will allow them to perform: "Terry has a plan, as usual. She rises in the Knesset the next day and invites her fellow parliamentarians to an event: of political importance (disinterest); of artistic excellence (boredom) . . . an event in which the most beautiful women of the land will participate. Out of courtesy to a colleague, Parliament decides to attend" (p. 178). After watching the play in growing discomfort the police move in to disperse the crowd and end the play. Terry leads the people to the Western Wall (illuminated at night as a historical site, and therefore suitable for the drama), where the performance continues. The play is a success as measured by discussions on television talk shows and in university classes. Finally a permanent location is found, but "The City Between Us" is less successful confined to a theater than it had been in the streets.

Part 1 of *Archaos* (*Le Roi père*, the father king) is named after the current king of Archaos—Avatar II, "an embodiment of a god," ruling by divine right. In need of a male heir to continue his godly rule, he fosters offspring through a violent sexuality usually confined to his forest philandering. His queen, Avanie (French for "insult" or "snub"), conceives after Avatar has forced his way into her chambers. Bruised by this rape, she is ignored by the royal doctors, who are preoccupied with finding a remedy to confer immortality upon the king. Consequently, she is treated by a bonesetter named Analogue, who will heal and comfort the insulted queen. The birth of a son is anticipated by all the royal subjects, and in the first of a series of doubling effects, a daughter is born, "which was of no use." The king commands that she be abandoned in the forest. The bell ringers, on alert all night, are disappointed until, to everyone's surprise, the queen suddenly delivers a male twin. The royal doctors pronounce him stillborn, but Analogue finds him quite alive when he slaps him on the behind. The cry he gives announcing his long-awaited presence cannot be stilled unless he is "constantly caressed" and reunited with his sister.[4] Avanie secretly makes Analogue the doctor to the child.

When the prince, Govan, learns to crawl he makes his way out of the palace, followed by his retinue, into the forest. There the peasants of Archaos are celebrating a holiday to honor the princess, which they have named "The Feast of the Birth of the Prince" in order to fool the royal guards. According to legend, the princess Onagre had been changed into a silver birch. Govan, however, finds her with her nurse and companion, Litote, who is able to translate the child's patois. Both Onagre and Litote are brought back covertly to the castle. This reunion of the royal twins permits a transition to the new Eden Archaos will become after Avatar has abdicated his throne. But until that time, illusion reigns as the princess is dressed in her brother's clothing to keep her hidden from the king, confusing everyone in the palace; this is the cause for the first of Avatar's repressive laws to be passed. Henceforth, visions are punishable by death; if unspoken they are safe, because visionaries are not subject to the laws; this leads to "the greatest disorder" in grammar and language among those who seem to see the prince in more places than one nearly simultaneously (p. 107).

In contrast to the banishment at birth of the daughter born to King Avatar and Queen Avanie and the ringing of bells throughout the kingdom when a son is finally born, in *A Weave of Women,* the birth of a daughter is the first occasion for rewritten celebration and ritual. The novel opens as the women and midwives help deliver Simha's (whose name means "joy") child, who is named Hava (Eve). Rochefort inverts this edenic narrative—her utopia is a path forward into the past, a return to the garden—pre-exile. With Hava, Broner begins to write anew the story of "sanity and madness in the house of women." Unlike the separated and banished but finally balanced pair of twins in *Archaos,* there is no Adam for this Eve; the arcadian may promise more than the future (im)perfect.

The setting of *Weave* is an "old stone house" where fifteen women frequently gather together with Rina and Shula, the so-called wayward girls who live across the street in the Home for Jewish Wayward Girls, which the government keeps trying to close down. The two buildings, house and home, function as op-

posites pointing at and also subverting the traditional confinement of women. Rochefort also produces a traditionally opposed
pair of women's houses. Under the rule of Govan, the prince, the
convent and brothel become one in this "obscene paradise," and
all who wish to participate in the governing council must first present a certificate proving that they have "given pleasure."[5]

The house of Broner's women is a place of warmth, passion,
asylum, and retreat to which women come when need or ceremony require their presence. Sometimes they gather at each
other's houses as well. Only Terry, the director of the Home, and
Simha live permanently in the stone house. Broner has said that
every collective needs a mystic and a Marxist—here Simha and
Terry synthesize the religious and political crosscurrents and tensions in the Palestinian-Israeli situation surrounding the house.[6]
The tension between the religious and the political, the messianic
and the revolutionary has always been integral to utopian
schemes, as it has to critiques of utopia.[7] Both are promissory discourses, visions of due reward. Broner and Rochefort seek ways
to force these discourses into collision, and through language and
fantasy, into collusion.

Hava's birth calls for a new ceremony the women name the
hymenotomy. In imitation of the age-old covenant of Jewish
males in the rite of circumcision, the women gather on the eighth
day. Chapter 3, "Ceremonies on the Throne of Miriam," opens:
"It is during the second orange harvest that Simha's baby has her
hymenotomy. The air smells of orange blossoms. The clementines
are sweet, the grapefruits not tart. Cucumbers are light green and
long. Radishes are large and mild. Nothing growing in this season
is bitter" (p. 20). Simha names her child and acts "upon the command that is not yet written that the daughter of eight days shall
be pierced" (p. 22). The orthodox and traditional women (Hepzibah and Antoinette) are troubled by the "unfamiliar prayers." The
wayward girls are puzzled by the phrases, recalling that as pros-
titutes they, too, were often called "daughters of Eve." The ritual
is not a covenant with a god, but rather a promise and wish the
women make together for the child: "May she not be delivered intact to her bridegroom or judged by her hymen but by the energies
of her life." The vestigial structure is pierced, thus breaking with a
tradition that makes of women objects of exchange whose value is

determined by the proof of virginity. A curious inversion of this gesture, yet similarly protected from and projective of male sexual violence, occurs in *Archaos*; when Onagre is to be married against her will everyone takes to sewing up the carefully placed gaps in her trousseau items to preclude the possibility of penetration.

Broner's hymenotomy undoes the "gynocidal" practices of female circumcision, which seal the female body, keeping it intact and sometimes impenetrable.[8] Opening orifices, the imagined hymenotomy would work to abolish distinctions between outside and inside. The dualistic thinking inherent in ethnocentric and patriarchal societies tends to polarize inside and outside, family and state, private and public, and then to assign one and the other as realms "properly" those of women or men.[9] The essentialism of such thought also "naturalizes" the activities of world-making into those which are the "property" of men or women. The home, the interior, the private, are the spaces in which women are seen moving and acting. Both Broner and Rochefort play in and with "houses of women" and create new values for these interior spaces. These very houses function as "cells" representing utopias to come, bridging both a new poetics and politics of space.

In *The Poetics of Space* Gaston Bachelard writes, "if I were asked to name the chief benefit of the house, I should say: the house shelters daydreaming, the house protects the dreamer, the house allows one to dream in peace."[10] In the above terms, the ties to the house are connected with utopian thought itself as concrete wish fulfillment or daydream. Not only does the house protect dreamer and dream, it also has "maternal features" Bachelard never fully explicates, but which are implied in its "protective" aspects. While the house and the brothel are portrayed as utopian sites in Broner and Rochefort's novels, respectively, the out-of-doors does not remain unaffected by the activities within. Broner's women take their political causes, their dramas, their songs, and their battles into the streets. In Archaos, the prairies and wheat-fields bloom in abundance when pleasure becomes the dominant principle under the new regime of the royal twins, Govan and Onagre.

In a chapter of *Weave* entitled "Street Workers and Street Walkers," the differences between house and home are made public. The state is embarrassed by the existence of a Home for Jewish

Wayward Girls, where illegitimacy is contained and confined. The women demonstrate to "save the home" as a shelter. Under pressure, its name and fortune are simultaneously changed. As the Home for Jewish Future Homemakers, "contributions pour in, also stoves, washing machines, irons, sewing machines" (p. 43). The Home exists to control and suppress female sexuality, whereas in the stone house it is celebrated, protected, cultivated, and expressed. Holy Body Day is a new ritual written into the calendar where all that is needed to make a "counter-holiday" are "a date, a legend, a blessing, and a meal," which the women create. In a parody of reclamation of the Jewish ritual bath Orthodox women must take after the cessation of their "unclean time," the women count this holiday at the twenty-first day after the onset of menstruation. On this day they "speak of the legends of their bodies," write a Women's Song of Songs, and conclude with a meal which recalls the archetypal earliest utopias, or land of Cockayne, where food is plentiful: "They think it is the World to Come with the meal of the Leviathan, for their plates never empty" (p. 262). The ritualized negation of the female body and sexuality practiced in Judeo-Christian tradition is overturned by Broner in the play between these "girls" and the "women." The girls fear and despise sex because it is prohibited and yet a commodity in which they learn to trade, while the women sustain and heal both themselves and others through control of their own sexuality.

Broner and Rochefort portray female sexuality which, when unfettered by convention, is ecstatic and transformative of the already existing "world to come." Vered, the Polish-born social worker, is photographed leading the demonstration for the Home; a newspaper photograph freezes the moment when her fifty-year-old, married, Parliament-member lover grabs her by the hair from out of the parade line. Her brother (and "only living blood relative") goes into mourning to erase the shame of her public humiliation. In his eyes she is his only love, and this is the greatest misery imaginable, equivalent to her death. His mourning ritual is severe: he fasts, retreats from activity, removes Vered's pictures from his walls, and covers all mirrors. When no one has seen him for days, Vered goes to his room in Jaffa where he tells her, "you are dead to me." When she returns to the women for help, they all agree with Vered that "a brother must at all costs be brought back to life" by loving. Vered's lover cannot reach her for several days; in anger he goes to work and votes against abortion: "He votes against the secularization of marriage and divorce. He is considered a Liberal" (p. 85). In an alternating rhythm of languages—rapturous, earthy, and humorous, Broner recounts the ritual seven days it takes to rejuvenate Vered's brother as each of the women goes to visit him at night to make love to him. Finding them gone each morning he begins again to eat, work, and study. Here is how the parodic biblical narrative closes after the visits from Dahlia, Mickey, Tova, Simha, Gloria, and Deedee: "The night of the seventh day the door opens. It is Vered. 'Come in, my sister,' says her brother. 'I have been expecting you.' They lie next to each other. They are family. They are the past. They both can live" (p. 87).

The image of the reunified brother and sister of Broner's novel recalls the unification in Rochefort's *Archaos* which must be achieved before utopia may be situated in time and space. For thirteen years Onagre lives secretly but happily in the castle of Archaos. The conclusion to part 1 announces the new regime of the Son (as) King (*Le Roi fils*). Avatar abdicates after he has raped a shepherdess in the forest who turns out to be his daughter, Onagre, in disguise. Disgusted by his own actions and in a literalization of the symbolic Oedipus narrative, Avatar castrates himself: "How could so little flesh spoil so much virtue! Miserable object, poisonous appendage, stranger to myself . . . and drawing his sword in one blow he cut off the root of evil" (p. 139). During the coronation ceremony the royal scientists interrupt to announce their discovery of immortality; Avatar's final act as king is to throw their potion into the moat, and to order the savants to get busy squaring the circle to keep them out of trouble.

As a result of the rape, Onagre gives birth to twins who are incestuous in utero, and who (continuing Rochefort's play on and with names) are named Fornicato and Copula.[11] Their legal and religious status in the question of baptism necessitates a trip to Rome. Although Govan is the titular head of Archaos, Onagre's departure for Rome brings famine, winter, and scarcity to the country; when she returns she brings back a perpetual spring, and she and Govan say to each other: "Complete me . . . you are my other face" (p. 229). The psychological union of Govan and Onagre is repeated with a difference in the physical union of Fornicato and Copula. Rochefort turns to the pre-Christian mythology of Osiris and Isis, brother and sister who later become husband and wife, and who, in some versions, are said to have fallen in love in the womb.

Early in Rochefort's novel, Avanie, the queen, bemoans her daughter's fate when she says, "the only choice left to a girl is between marriage and the convent . . . there is also the brothel" (p. 44). During this time Avatar had begun to search for Onagre in order to marry her off to a prince of a neighboring kingdom and negotiate a peace settlement. But Onagre had already decided that she would rather found a convent and began instruction for her future life at the convent in Trémènes, capital city of Archaos.[12]

When Govan becomes king, the first invitation he receives is to this "convent" which *is* a brothel (*bordel*) headed by Mme Désirade. "Nothing teaches like pleasure," is the advice Govan receives, and pleasure in all forms becomes the ruling principle under the new king. The brothel is instituted by Govan as a public necessity, and Désirade is empowered to certify that only those who have given satisfaction and pleasure (to be judged by someone who has given and taken it) may serve in the government. Wanting, somewhat disingenuously, to maintain Onagre's innocence for a time, Govan gets all to agree that the brothel will remain the "convent" in name.

Govan's new laws abolish taxes and make all children the king's so that he may take retrospective care of his father's illegitimate offspring. After Avanie and Litote have given and received pleasure at the convent, Govan establishes a "brother" convent (*bordelle*) for women, run by Malafoutre (whose name "makes love/fucks badly" belies his abilities) and assisted by anyone who is interested because "an abundance of constantly fresh workers was necessary" (p. 175), and one for children (*bordelet*) with a child-sized door as well. Henceforth prairies belong to the cows and not to the soldiers who have been practicing maneuvers, and the economy shifts from trading to a system where "everything is free." Both sexual and political economies are ecstatically oversimplified.

Like other contemporary authors of feminist utopian fictions, Broner and Rochefort treat the question of death as well as birth; they represent death in ways as diverse as their earlier representation of the birth of a daughter. The tactic of abandoning Onagre in the forest evokes the literary tradition of the fairy tale. In Rochefort's imaginary history, death is never final—there is always the possibility of resurrection in this pagan/Catholic country where the miraculous is a reliable force. There is also the work of art (this novel) rediscovered by the historians which resurrects Archaos in its flawed entirety; among the other remnants are paintings of the glittering garden (echoing Bosch's "Garden of Earthly Delights") done by Héliozobe. The only characters who actually die are those who have never accepted the new regime of Govan— Ganidan, Avatar's shield-bearer, and Anastème, the archbishop. In most cases, however, death is presumed only to be negated, always bringing the reader back to the pastoral quality of life in Archaos. Setting utopia in the past permits an idealized and suggested vision of what "might be" based on what "was." Broner's setting in the present exposes the problems of situating utopia more concretely both temporally and spatially. In *A Weave of Women* death is always tragic and premature, calling upon the women's continuing assertion of the possibility of spiritual and political rebirth. Hava, Simha's child, is the first to die. The death occurs during the Purim festival. The events surrounding Hava's death are told in chapters 11–13 though they are precipitated by what takes place when Dahlia goes to the desert (chapter 9). In these chapters the making of Broner's textual fabric is most evident as the Purim narrative, Dahlia's story, and Hava's fate are brought to culmination.

Needing a rest and solitude, Dahlia, the singer, goes alone into the desert. There she meets and heals a wounded stork and sexually initiates a young Bedouin prince whose father befriends her after watching her live in the sun for several days. Hava's death, the first of three in the narrative, occurs as a result of the love which, ignited in the mirage of the desert, explodes with violence when the young Bedouin hunts for Dahlia after she returns to the city. With its codes of revelry, transvestism, and socially sanctioned excess, the Purim season of license in the city forms the background against which the women tell the story of Esther and

Ahasuerus. It is intersected by the counterpoint of the young Bedouin and his friend hunting through the raucous crowds in the streets of Jerusalem. The tension builds dramatically. The chapter is called "Count the Stars and Give Them Names." In a litany we hear how each of the women has counted and named the stars for herself. Then:

> To mourners in The Land, the stars are relatives ascending from wars. . . . To children of the development towns, they are the glinting eyes of the enemy. . . . To the young Bedouin prince, lover of Dahlia in the desert, the stars are the first night of his loving, shining on nipples and swells of hip and belly. He searches for Dahlia, not in the Sinai, but first in Beer Sheva and then in Jerusalem. With him he brings a friend of evil counsel. (Pp. 114–15)

The violence and excess of the outdoors is juxtaposed with the activities indoors: "On this day in their little stone house do the women gather to play the games of chance, to deal with the Priestess of the Tarot, the Empress of Justice, to throw dice or move the cup across the Ouija board" (p. 115). Bad omens are forecast when the Ouija board refuses to speak about Simha's future, and the women "drink until the good cannot be distinguished from the bad" (p. 117). Outdoors the Bedouin's friend is dressed as a Hasidic Jew and carries a noisemaking toy hammer. The tragedy and triumph of the Purim feast lead the women to talk of Esther (formerly Ishtar) and her choices in the Persian court as Ahasuerus (Xerxes) planned the killing of Jews. The continued conflict between Israelis and Arabs comes to inhabit and haunt the women's house. Meanwhile "Joan, the playwright from Manchester, and Tova, the American actress" explain the play they are writing, adding another layer to the narratives and histories being interwoven. Inspired by the story of Esther, they envision "an opera like *Samson and Dalila*." Esther's decisions at the court are championed and bemoaned as "the good Jewish girl" ends up "sandwiched between men," her king and her uncle Mordecai, who takes Haman's place as the king's adviser. The Purim tale and ceremonies in the house close as Simha, of the priestly Cohen caste, sings and chants a prayer to Hava, holding her in the air. When the Bedouin and his friend of "evil counsel" burst into the house, the Bedouin wishes to save Dahlia from the violence, and points to Simha. The "toy" hammer hits Hava and kills her.[13] "The quiet streets of the Old City, the deserted streets, are filled with the wail of the siren and the wailings of the mother. The *Magillah,* the tale, is told. In the legend there is relief from the enemy, sorrow is turned into gladness, mourning into holiday. In life, only some of this is possible" (p. 132). Now the women need to remake the rituals of death and mourning as they had first done those surrounding Hava's birth.

After Hava's death and the ritual of mourning is the central chapter, entitled, "Swear a True Oath"; it is the thirteenth chapter where "all will come right." After listing the varied significance of the number thirteen, the narrator discusses the different calendar times that are not shared by women everywhere. Just as there are no laws written for these women, so their time in history is splintered. The women are at work on a political campaign. Terry is running for a seat in the Knesset and has numerous enemies:

> Men are her enemies for they would not share power.
> Women are her enemies for they have adjusted to discomfort.
> Warriors are her enemies for she is a pacifist.
> Pacifists are her enemies for her ways are martial. (P. 149)

Her bitterest enemy is the former lover of Vered, a member of Parliament. He is one of the organizers of the Male Gynecological Conference; a reporter quotes him on the subject of the approaching conference: "'Women, leave your bodies in our hands.' Terry girds for battle" (p. 152). The women of Terry's independent party gird their loins and interrupt the conference after they are denied the right to speak.[14] "For giving battle" Terry wins her seat in Parliament where these forms of militant pacificism will continue to be summoned when necessary. One such moment is the recurring battle to save the Home. If it is dismantled, the girls, like Rina and Shula, will be forced to return to the streets. Terry gathers information to present in Parliament documenting the absence of a space for the prodigal daughter in Israeli society. With fantasies of a "Girls' Town of Haifa" an old Arab house (for which we must read an "expropriated" house) is rented for the girls. Terry recognizes in Rina an organizational skill and places her in charge. For the first time, Rina's parents visit the house and appear to be proud of their daughter. It is designated a "righteous house of women" and it is noted that "the streets have moved indoors" (pp. 207–8).

Birth, death, divorce, exorcism, resurrection, and transubstantiation all occur in these two novels, inhabited as they each are by religious tradition, superstition, and taboo. In *Archaos* the questions of divorce and legitimacy are simultaneously settled by one of Govan's new laws: "I've read in the Law . . . that all children of the country are children of the king. . . . 'But that's not a law that's literature,' says Errata [the registrar]" (p. 189). Govan's new law takes the old one "literally and not literarily" as the castle becomes home for numerous women: those who might have been "lost" but for this law, those whose husbands abuse them, and those who prefer to raise children of the king than to be concerned with proofs of paternity. In *Weave,* divorce and exorcism converge in the story of Mickey, who has been seeking a divorce from the husband who has abused her and has molested a neighbor's child. Nevertheless, the courts demand proof beyond the word of a woman; there is always another delay. Mickey, suffering and "fattening on her anger," is found by Hepzibah in the market and brought to the stone house. There Simha recognizes by Mickey's "nasty laugh" and biblical ravings about forbidden nakedness and defilement that she is possessed by a dybbuk, a wandering dead soul. An exorcism begins made up by the tribunal Simha chooses. The spirit inhabiting Mickey is called Magda, another woman who had sought a divorce: "I said to my husband, 'If you do not separate from me, I will separate from myself.' He only grunted. I walked into the Mediterranean where the undertow was strongest. I did not have to swim far off" (p. 112). Mickey finally does as she is told and cries out three times, "I divorce you," exorcising the demon and finding peace for her own wandering soul. The end of the novel will bring Mickey and Vered's brother together to heal each other's wounds.

A variation on the ritual exorcism of demons is played in the penultimate chapter, "The Excommunication." Gloria, "the convert from California," has not appeared in the stone house for several weeks after a spree of having sex with the present and former lovers of four of the women. Finally she is summoned to a darkened house. She is found guilty of having broken the ten commandments of women: breaking hearts, bringing dishonor, breaking up the family of women, killing feeling, tempting the weak in spirit, stealing "attention, time, affection, memory," bearing false witness, coveting that which is precious and hard won by another, coveting that which has humiliated a friend, and the last commandment, "Thou shalt not replace a trusted woman friend with a new male face." Gloria is divorced from the women, put out of the community, and erased from memory. In the house of women, where Simha has forgiven Dahlia her part in Hava's death, "all is forgiven except for the breaker of commandments" (p. 280). The reversals operated by Rochefort and Broner in the realm of language and naming are among the ways in which a nonpatriarchal system may break with the existing law. This new naming still functions within the limits always circumscribed by language. Now the limits are derived by and for those for whom they are produced. What the feminist body of work on language has amply demonstrated amounts to a vastly more detailed specification of spaces at the center that have gone unnamed (the phallo-patriarchal-andro-misogynist territories) as well as a clearer charting of the borderlines (the gynesis-gynecological-feminine-feminist-womanly horizons). Govan as king may write new laws; the women in Broner's stone house speak the laws which are not yet written and open a new arena of play in language.

Both novels are situated in states whose politics are largely derived from their religious practices. Govan is aided in his administration by Erostase, a monk, and Anastème, a bishop. Among the laws governing Broner's "Israel" are modifications of Talmudic law. The state and the family, in the broadest utopian sense, are always mutually reflecting institutions; in these utopian fictions that reflection is ephemeral at best, and works only by implication. It is in the dystopian representations that the beginnings of an effective critique of the "state" are mounted. Even in Archaos's rule of pleasure, the final determination is to "do that which pleases God." The traditional split between work and play is healed in Archaos's regime of primitive communism where both activities take place in the convent/brothel. When everything in Archaos becomes "free" for the asking or taking, idleness becomes a problem until the citizens begin to produce things they need and which they want to last—finally making art of their work.[15]

By choosing to set their utopian fictions within patriarchal states Broner and Rochefort must work against the social practices that feminism interrogates, which suggests a reading of these two novels as more concretized utopias. Here the not-yet is formulated in a direct response to some of what "is" and what "has been." Other writers treated here have presented alternative and fantastic societies through reliance on generic and narrative strategies. Piercy does so through the use of time travel; Russ has her state operate off stage except as seen through its manifestations in Jael, Jeannine, and Janet, visitors to the imagined futures and pasts; Charnas presents her vision through the Free Fem/Riding Women conflict and the history they can possibly remake; Gilman sketches her state through the distorted mirror effect of Van's questions to the women of Herland; and for Wittig it is the unnamed enemy of the guerrilla women warriors. With Rochefort, Archaos under the rule of Avatar must be brought to an end and a new realm formed and reformed through an upheaval of the laws as written and practiced. The resulting anarchy is set in relief in a proverb which captures the spirit of Govan's new regime. Ganidan repeatedly complains about Archaos, "quel bordel ce royaume," which can be translated as "what a mess this kingdom is," the word *bordel* retaining its meaning of brothel and, colloquially, mess or chaos. The proverb is, *bordel n'est pas mortel* (chaos doesn't kill) then followed by the admonition, *tandis que l'ordre l'est* (but order does), equating order and repression in a revaluation of chaos and freedom.

This proverb is cited at the end of the chapter in which the chaotic implications of Govan's new economics ("Everything is free," Law XIV) become clear to the citizens, who agree, nevertheless, that the new law is better than the old. The free economy creates certain problems of scarcity and unequally distributed abundance. When the people of Archaos discover they have no salt because it is an item which had been acquired through trade, everyone carries a bowl in which tears are collected to fill the lack. Trémènes, the capital city, secedes, declaring itself closed, and passes a law that "everything must be paid for." The unhappy people of Trémènes, who see their former fellow citizens eating without having to work, begin a revolution to have the law revoked, reuniting Archaos and the seat of government. Brimbalon, the mayor, surrenders to the folk wisdom that to speak of liberty can only mean one does not yet have it. In Archaos the standard greeting is now "Vive la liberté" and "one paid no more attention to the meaning of the words than when one formerly said good day" (p. 277).

Prophets abound during the period of conflict. Most significant among them is Jérémias, who attempts to restore order in Trémènes by reconstituting an army. When Govan and his mother, Avanie, visit Trémènes they find Jérémias in the square addressing a group of former members of Avatar's governing council. (Avanie is immediately struck by Jérémias's beauty.) Govan and Jérémias engage in the following dialogue:

> [J:] "Death doesn't frighten us."
> [G:] "I wasn't speaking of death. I'm speaking about justice."
> [J:] "Life without justice is nothing."
> [G]: "The inverse isn't worth much more. The question is rather how to put the second into the first."
> [J:] "By what right does a king speak of justice?"
> [G:] "Divine, obviously. . . . And you?"
> [J:] "I speak in the name of the people."
> [G:] "Why, are they dumb?"
> Laughter was heard proving that at least they weren't deaf. (P. 287)

As the new mayor, Jérémias (called "the firebrand") is portrayed as the revolutionary who finds no followers among the playful people of Archaos. In order to govern with justice and equality he sets out to count everything in sight. Avanie, who has fallen in love with him and certified that he has given her pleasure, begins her own "census of desires" in order to share in his obsession. Frustrated to find no one who will help him govern, Jérémias finally accedes to Avanie's suggestion that he meet with the council (at the brothel), where he will find people to share his burden.

During the period of chaos Onagre and her sisters of the new convent (the "Daughters of Beatitude") begin to prophesy various catastrophes, among them famine; and hunger, "the great regulator," sends the people back to work in order to survive. To remind themselves of "how it was" a new mystery play is performed of "peasant life under the tyrant," and Avatar plays himself in his former role. Progress is measured by the fact that now the people are able to laugh where once they could only weep.

The news of Archaos generates rivalry, jealousy, controversy, and scandal. In a gesture that may recall the chapter in *The Female Man* in which reviews of the book in hand are included, Rochefort quotes some of the things being said about Archaos:

> There the mad are called sane, and the sane mad. The latter are free to do as they wish. . . . Homes are deserted and husbands are left alone. . . . All the children are made by the king. . . . The king [is] constantly drunk. . . . This cruel king, as punishment for a legitimate rebellion in his capital forced the women of a convent (called the Holy Viola) to submit daily to the insults of all the functionaries of the palace. And that's not all. . . . This country is nothing but the devil's stage. . . . And no one works. (Pp. 324–27)

The historians remind us that since there were no documents, this is the view of Archaos which had been left to history for them to undo and redo. Jérémias, like the later historians, leaves Archaos, taking his oratory to the world that does not believe in Archaos, only to become once again the voice in the wilderness. On his way he meets Héliozobe, the painter, dressed as a monk, who is returning to Archaos because the "real" world has been death for him. Inspired by his love for Govan, Héliozobe begins work on the triptych with the glittering garden as the central panel. An anonymous, undated description of the triptych is included with the notes by the historians, indicating that Adam and Eve in the left panel have the face of the "sodomite adolescent" in the central panel, and God the face of the painter who shares in the young man's embrace.

The period of chaos is followed by the time of the glittering garden, part 3, entitled, "The Time (*Heures*) of Beatitude." During the final section of the novel, news of Archaos goes out to the world and the crime of which the country is deemed most guilty is "the reversal of the meaning or direction [*sens*] of history" (p. 436). We are told this by the historians of those "barbarous" times. Approaching armies prepare to invade Archaos, which is said "not to exist," while on the plains and prairies the people of Archaos lay about in an eternal sunshine from which the "future retreated" (p. 443). It seems that the potion of immortality (earlier ordered by Avatar) affected all who had bathed in the waters of Archaos, including Jérémias, who has returned to Archaos to die but is healed by the water and Avanie's love. The novel closes with a litany of fragments and sentences from the text: "Forever intoxicated . . . come to/in us. . . . Listen. . . . Look. . . . You have arrived" (pp. 444–45).

While the narrative structure of *Archaos* is "trinitarian" and ends positing immortality as rendered visible by the work of history, *A Weave of Women* is divided into twenty-four chapters, the number of letters of the Hebrew alphabet. The final chapter combines a battle and a marriage. Once again the battle is to save that space to which the women have devoted time: "Their stone house in the Old City will be destroyed. A high-rise apartment for male yeshiva students will take its place, the annex being across the street in the former Home for Jewish Wayward Girls" (p. 286). Displaced by the demands of the male religious establishment, the women become squatters in a deserted (read "depopulated") Arab village to plan a new kibbutz. In "the Land" this women's commune is refused and the "family of women" denied a home.

> The government sends emissaries. The women refuse them. Other women's groups are sent . . . all begging them to return to the fold. They must enfold their own, date their calendar. . . .
> It is a women's government in exile. (P. 289)

While the women may be in exile, their displacement has exiled those more "other" than themselves—the never-named Palestinians who function as the unstated cause for symptomatic fears of that chaotic space—the outdoors.

Before the closing marriage ceremony, the women gather for the "Time for Sending Forth" alongside "those men who have befriended them" (who, excepting Shlomo Sassoon, always remain unnamed except in relation to the women: Vered's brother, Tova's lover, etc.). The wedding is between Simha and "her kibbutz-nik," who have been joined before in the birth and tragic Purim death of Hava. Now "Simha will divide her time, like Persephone, between the kibbutz and Havurat Shula" (the planned women's commune). The destiny of each of the women is announced in a final chorus, and like Rochefort's ending, this one is full of cautious hope and the ecstatic rhetoric of religious narrative which has produced the core of the struggles in each novel and also the material of transformation:

> What will happen to them, this caravan of women that encircles the outskirts of the city, that peoples the desert?
>   How goodly are thy tents, thy reclaimed ruins, O Sara, O our mothers of the desert. (P. 294)

The utopian strategy aims to insert a future—a what-might-be into a known or imagined past or present. In order to remain strategic it cannot presume to posit a what-will-be, for that would undermine its rhetorical and potentially political force. That would render it static, merely polemical, and would rob it of its dynamic, dialectical dispersion of possibilities. I have examined the kinds of "futures" constructed in each of these fictions for what they may be able to say to us about the shadowy outlines of historical determinants at work in the political imagination.

Chapter Five

No Shadows without Light

Louky Bersianik's *The Eugélionne* and
Margaret Atwood's *The Handmaid's Tale*

She passes by her ancestor
And meets her ancestress.

Hope needs the future tense, which only makes you feel greedy
and a hoarder: the future is what you save up for but like
thunder it's only an echo, a reverse dream.

"Hopeless"
Margaret Atwood

As if to punctuate the proliferation of utopian texts during the
decade marked by the novels grouped here so far, in 1986 Margaret Atwood published *The Handmaid's Tale,* as dystopian a text
as Charnas's *Walk to the End of the World,* and one that is addi-
tionally informed by the antifeminist backlash of Christian fundamentalism and neoconservatism.[1] If Broner's *Weave of Women*
and Charnas's *Motherlines* (both published in 1978) are taken as
the end points followed by ellipsis, then by the time Atwood sets
out to tell her tale, the world is already changed so that a promissory rhetoric of hope is rendered naive. What Charnas imagined, Atwood has seen. What it marks diacritically is the snug sociopolitical fit between the staging of change in everyday life and
in fiction. Atwood's text assures us that what the imagination can
concoct in these times is shaped by "reduced circumstances." The
"what if" has shifted from a terrain bright with daydreams to a
mute field of nightmarish whispers. To set up the echoes and dis-
cords between the mid-1970s and the mid-1980s that signal the
end of a phase of utopian representations, I want to place Atwood's tale in a context with one of her francophone compatriots,
Louky Bersianik, whose 1976 novel, *The Eugélionne,* still called

out to readers with the rhetoric of hope.[2] The two Canadian writers, Atwood and Bersianik, whose ears are tuned to the strains of feminist choruses in the United States and France, make a rereading of the questions at hand possible from another geopolitical perspective within the dominant sphere of the United States and also in the "colonized" sphere from the margins.[3]

The pairing of Atwood's and Bersianik's texts is meant to bring forward questions about the specific conditions of possibility for the production of utopian and dystopian fictions. Geopolitically they are both writers whose identities are framed in terms of the dislocations of Canadian and Quebecois nationalisms which have been shaped by their status as former colonies, but even more pertinently, in recent relation to a grosser form of colonization by market proximity to the United States. Both these novels speak from an elsewhere that knows its enemies to be nearby and, moreover, internalized. A fictive "US SAY" is the planet the Eugélionne visits, where she tries in vain to spread her good news; a fictive Canada is the place to which those in the Mayday movement send fugitives by way of the "Underground Femaleroad" in *The Handmaid's Tale*. By inverting the good and bad place, the good and bad news, Atwood offers a formless but promising "Canada," whose real history as a site for American political fugitives during the Vietnam War is part of the memory of the fictional generation to which the handmaid's mother belonged; the now of Gilead is the mid-1990s.

It is in the attitudes toward language and writing, and their inscription into history, that I think these two novels complement the previous chapters, because they are each working that ground in some detail from different perspectives. The paths they take toward their investigations into the power of language, and language as power, have as much to say about the construction of female subjectivity as about the impact of the discourse of female desire. For it is this discourse that we have been tracking all along, whether from the vantage point of an unrestrained wish that could represent worlds reconceived and restructured by figures of women, from hope concretized in fiction and manifesto, or from a window so shuttered that only flickers of light could fasten upon words barely understood. The handmaid despairs; still she finds reason to engage in the shadow-play of fantasy; it is hope in the register of an enslaved female voice in fiction. That is where we must look to engage as fully as possible the coming-into-writing of a feminist eros—an "I" wanting (simultaneously desire and lack).

If we take language to be one of the strongest measures of oppression-repression, then Atwood's novel shows us with what swiftness and efficiency the rulers of Gilead have enslaved their citizens. We can read this by her narrator's trepidation and apologies about telling this particular story—one she knows is fragmented and shapeless but also one that tells of the renaming of women and the rituals of daily life. Men as well as women in Gilead are divided by function and live out strictly hierarchical relations: Commanders, Eyes, Angels, and Guardians, all words we know though they are shuffled quite thoroughly here. The naming of women by class takes on greater amplitude for horror and comic effect: wives dress in blue, handmaids in red, Marthas in green, the Aunts in brown, daughters (of Commanders) in white, and Econowives in stripes. This renaming is imposed, not chosen, and the reader never knows the "real" name of the handmaid; we, too come to think of her as Offred. As a fiction of a fragmented self *The Handmaid's Tale* offers many strategies that puts its status as a narrative into jeopardy. This is particularly and deliberately the case in the "Historical Notes," an epilogue which represents a historian in 2195 reconstructing through Offred's tale (discovered on cassette tapes) the ways of life in Gilead at a conference, the structure of which is highly suggestive in its redrawing of the map of disciplinary life in universities in yet another future.

Bersianik, writing in French, goes for the grammatic jugular of a language riven by gender distinctions. Following a chapter called "The Unrules of the Language" ("Imprécis de la langue"), there is another called "The Silent Woman" ("La Muette").

> The French language, said the Eugélionne, just like Man, has capitalized the species also for the benefit of Men. . . .
> . . . it's their imperious injunction to women across the centuries to be quiet. . . . That's when I understood the *mute one*. You know, that little vowel in the form of a silent "e" that is found at the end of feminine words? It's always put in invisible parentheses. It represents the silence [*la mutisme*] of women. (P. 220)

Working on grounds other than those which demonstrate how "man" has been meant to exclude woman, and certainly women, the Eugélionne continues: "I present to you a little monologue in which the word '*fille*' represents successively sex, filiation, virginity, celibacy, and prostitution." This monologue, followed by a chart in which "the male is articulated over several registers" (from *homme*, to *garcon*, to *viril*, to *masculinité*), while the female has variations on one form (from *femme* through *féminité*), serves to make Bersianik's point that "the language is so miserly with respect to women."

Both writers are taking up in fiction what has been a most fertile ground of conceptual reworking in feminist theory, and they do so in ways colored by their own mother tongues which flavor how these fictional representations resonate with their counterparts in theoretical feminist discourse. The Eugélionne could be thought of as one of those flying/stealing witches called forth by the voices of Cixous and Clément, among others, in France in the early 1970s; and the handmaid could be the speaker of Adrienne Rich's women in their "lies, secrets, and silence."[4] What I am suggesting is that we can see a variation on the syntheses and synaesthetics of feminist fiction and theory, and on the rich interchange made possible through an analysis of the debates on women, language, and sexual difference as they have developed in the French and English tongues. If we think of the decade between the publication of these two novels, and the different languages of their original production as mirrors facing each other, we might imagine our reading as a way of moving in between and perhaps through these looking-glasses. In so doing we can expect to find multiple and differential refractions and reflections on the spec-(tac)ularity of feminist vision and revisions.

The Eugélionne (the Bearer of good news) is the "record" of a fictive and futile search for a utopian space: a positive planet. In the course of the narrative the Eugélionne herself moves from the position of naive extraterrestrial innocently hoping to find the "male of her species," to the voice announcing doom if the lessons she has learned during her journey go unheeded. What she has found is not the male of *her* species; rather she has confronted evidence everywhere that the species of this planet *is* male—that while "one man out of two is a woman" that womanly half of the species has been massacred, in consciousness if not in fact, and predominantly in language.

In the place the Eugélionne comes from, the legend of sexual difference is inscribed in Latin on the foreheads of the "infawnts": for females the words "I am black but I am beautiful"; for males, "The law is tough but it is the law." The dissymmetry of these mottoes is all too clear; the "but" functions as compensation for females and as rule for males. These words become the "window of identity" (seeing through to), but they also serve as mirrors for (reflecting back at) those who encounter these sexed subjects, and at such a moment the imbalance is even clearer, as the Eugélionne notes:

> "So, the inscription of the Pedalist [females], necessarily read backwards, drives her further into her darkness. It reads: FORMOSA SUM SED NIGRA [I am beautiful but I am black.] Whereas the Legislator [males] benefits in the eyes of his reader, with mitigating circumstance: LEX SED DURA LEX [It is the law but it is tough]." (P. 26)

The law of and as language casts greater darkness over the minds of the female of the Eugélionne's species, those born to be adjectives, that is to say, interchangeable. For the males, born to be nouns (substantive) and verbs, they will not be caught, always in motion, action. The interlude in which these practices are explained is narrated to the Eugélionne by Alysse Bach-Frumm Wonderland, as told to her by Humpty Dumpty, whose meditation on words and their meanings and the ways they will or won't be reshaped comes as the result of her breaking through the mirror. She is a solitary fighter who, reminiscent of Wittig's guérillères, has gone from one imprisoned by mirrors to one who has learned their strategic use for counterattack.[5]

The retelling of the facts, values, and myths of sexual difference plays a central part in *The Eugélionne*. This is done primarily through an allegorical tale of the *psy* laws, given by the prophet, St. Siegfried. While Bersianik takes a strong antipsychoanalytic position, her work demonstrates an attention to the details of oppression and to the consciousness of those oppressed that bears witness to an integration of psychoanalysis in her diagnosis of the difficulty in making change. The phallus, that "tree of rock" whose victories have been "won at the expense of life," is the transcendental signifier of the supremacy of the male of the species of the planet. Its laws are those that silence the females and render them invisible. Bersianik represents a comic opera of the dominion of psychoanalysis in its rewriting of the world. What the Eugélionne gleans from her study of "monolithic phallomorphism" is a reality St. Siegfried might have named, but didn't, and which she calls the *Herrschaft,* or Domination Psychosis. This produces the blind spot of psychoanalysis: the ability, not to analyze, but only to reproduce the history of misogyny. The subsequent smashing of the *psy* law tablets are key scenes in the news the Eugélionne brings to those who listen to her. The construction of proper (clean) female subjects in a phallocratic regime is what she learns in the commandments mothers pass on to daughters regarding how to be a "true woman," as are the beatitudes to the phallus that women learn to embody even as they themselves are disembodied. The laws of the *psy* sciences and the laws of (French) grammar are two of the terrains where Bersianik charts her dystopian site in which the Eugélionne's hope rings hollow. It is finally in praise of the hollow, the hole, that the Eugélionne will find her only hope for both the male and female of her species. The monolithic (made of stone) phallus must be recast as flesh, therefore, porous, and open, as is the female body and flesh that has been disparaged, denigrated, and destroyed. This occurred in the time of St. Siegfried and St. Jacques Linquant, two of the fictive men blamed for blocking women's access to their bodies and pleasures. This critique of phallocentricism is taken up with hilarity in the sobriety of philosophical language:

> Could the Divine Phallus have some hidden fault? Could its famous Preeminence be only a screen to disguise its "primacy," not to mention its piracy? . . . So I asked what this famous "Phallic Primacy" was, for it wasn't the first time I had heard of it.
>
> Exil [one of the Eugélionne's several guides] answered that it was a religion as old as the hills which had made a comeback during the last few decades. One of its most inveterate and well known priests was called St. Siegfried. (P. 153)

Among the episodes in the Eugélionne's visit to the planet is a play she sees, called "In Praise of Filth and Dust," which concerns the daily round of women's domestic tasks. It makes poetry out of everyday language and debased forms of existence which women are asked to take up as their exclusive path to some ephemeral forms of transcendence. Bersianik re-presents in theatrical form those ideas that constitute the diagnostic chapter "The Married Woman" in Simone de Beauvoir's *The Second Sex*; that is, Bersianik dramatizes what de Beauvoir theorized. (Like so many feminist texts this novel is dedicated to Simone de Beauvoir first, among others.) Consider the following from de Beauvoir as a reading of the underside of Bachelard's romantic and maternal sense of the house/home which we noted in the last chapter:

> Such [domestic] work has a negative basis: cleaning is getting rid of dirt, tidying up is eliminating disorder. And under impoverished conditions no satisfaction is possible. . . . Legions of women have only this endless struggle without victory over the dirt. . . . in her war against dust, stains, mud, and dirt she is fighting, wrestling with Satan. . . . She shuts out the sunlight, for along with that come insects, germs, and dust and besides, the sun ruins silk hangings and fades upholstery; . . . she becomes bitter and disagreeable and hostile to all that lives: the end is sometimes murder. (Pp. 425–26)

Here are these insights, translated and rewritten for the Eugélionne's enlightenment:

> Order of the day: The mess of Others is my mess. . . . *Order everywhere!* In papers. In pockets. In laundry. In nooks. In crannies. In the deeper recesses. On the stairs. Under the stairs. . . . In the bottom of cups where the future is written. Order in the ashes of Others. The great Vacuum-Cleaner-Woman. . . . Dust pans. Lamp stands. Eternal Dust. Lucifer the great Vacuum Cleaner. (P. 128)

The vocabulary of women's work is given in alphabetical order in "Behind Every Exploit," a chapter designed to render heroic the mundanity of repetition. Women are the "guardians of entropy"—their involvement is with what is passing, transient—nonproductive labor, as de Beauvoir noted. Cleaning, cooking, even caring, are translated by the drama from the realm of analysis and description into that of theatrical chorus, which produces a poetics rather than a theory of oppression. This drama culminates in an "Ode to the young bride" in which mothers deliver to their daughters, in a ceremony meant to perpetuate the Order of Others, the Ten Commandments of the Married Woman that begin with the consecration of life to "service" of husband and children, and end with the exhortation to let nothing rot, turn foul, become tainted and soiled, worn out, torn: "as long as you keep your place in the home, YOU WILL BE A TRUE WOMAN, MY DAUGHTER" (p. 137).

This play on women's concerns with what is proper and its French proximity to the clean is also cast in terms of woman only being the property of her husband. She is the slave who most clearly knows the master and least cares to aspire to the position of master(y) for that would mean giving up the "inducements to complicity" which the "mystery of the slave" offers as a lure to her own enduring oppression-repression. That, of course, is de Beauvoir's powerful analysis of how women come to participate in their own enslavement. Here, Bersianik has the Eugélionne learn this through its enactment as tragic comedy. Bersianik works some of these notions over in yet another turn to language and the toolkit of words women are given as opposed to those they need to appropriate: the verb "to serve" as opposed to the verb "to claim."

> "SERVE!" There's the keyword for the education of girls of my generation. We had to write it at the head of our exercises. "SERVE!" It was printed on our stationery . . . "SERVE!" It was the password to open our future as "real women.". . .
>
> There is anger in Exil's voice, and the sharp taste of bitterness. (P. 185)

It is this volatile mix of wit and rage that permeates these mid-1970s fictions, and which Atwood cannot afford in the mid-1980s.

In "The Verb: 'To Claim,'" chapter 21 of the third section, which also bears the name "Transgression Is Progression," we need to shift between the English and French; *prétendre* is also linked to "pretense," "pretension." The translation moves between these two areas of the verb and its substantive forms:

. . . Men lay claim to, and get, everything. That is the trait you must imitate. (P. 229)

Make great claims [*soyez de grand prétendantes*], like them, said the Eugélionne.

You seem to be intelligent. You laugh at their jokes at the right time. . . . you seem to admire them greatly. . . .

You only eat at their tables because they have invited you. (P. 230)

Little lady in red at the table of the kings, when are you going to have the great pretension to live by yourself? And will you never [*aurez-vous jamais*] have the pretension to live for yourself? said the Eugélionne. (P. 231)

Women must become the "great pretenders" (transgress) if they are to smash the tablets of the laws (progress). They must take over, lay claim to the verbs.

We need to follow this lexical lead in order to arrive at what constitutes the basis of part 3 of the novel, the sustained assault on the *psy* laws—the rule of the phallus that Bersianik aims to replace with her metaphysics of holes. In the chapter of part 3 which bears the same name as the last of the three parts, Bersianik begins to write new laws that also include a critique of the old. The Eugélionne has by now seen and heard enough about "women of Earth" to speak to them, in the hortatory second person: "You must transgress all commandments, orders, intimidations, whatever they might be. You must transgress the taboos, whatever they might be. You must transgress the dogmas, whatever they might be. For these laws were imposed upon you when you were not free. To resist is good, said the Eugélionne, to transgress is better" (p. 274).

These new orders are given so that women may found a new code of ethics. We can read here another of de Beauvoir's gestures, the one toward an "ethics of ambiguity," if we look backward, and if we read forward we can point toward the work of Carol Gilligan in the United States and Luce Irigaray in France, where the question of ethics in a feminist framework is central.[6]

Bersianik reverses de Beauvoir's order of things which says

that man will "free himself in freeing her," which indicates clearly the extent to which *The Second Sex* is a treatise that emerges from an afeminist discourse though not an antifeminist one. De Beauvoir cannot imagine, as Bersianik can only imagine, women themselves taking up their claims. The Eugélionne often addresses her audience directly:

> "As long as you do not reject, horrified, this coat of dust and garbage which Humanity decks you out in, you will not be free beings, women of the Earth. Women of the Earth, throw off the millennial dust of your species. You will put it on again when the entire species does so with you." . . . This is the only way you will get together: when both of you experience the outside and the inside, when both of you enjoy the advantages and bear the inconveniences of both outside and inside." (Pp. 250–52)

The Eugélionne would redistribute lack among the male and female of the species, in order to make good the "failures of the law." She would have men and women of Earth mutually recognize this contingency and castration (to move between the terms of existential philosophy and psychoanalysis). It is the abuse of psychoanalysis that has made it a "diktat for the inequality of the sexes for the status quo." But there are nevertheless the uses of psychoanalysis. In a passage that works within and against Bersianik's own critique of psychoanalysis there is a character named Ancyl, who has her own version of the Dupe's Complex (*Complexes des Dupes*), and who announces:

> "The orthodox *psys* [always ψ in the novel] wrong women greatly, she said. And yet, it is thanks to one of their number that I am alive today. I arrived at his office and I dissolved into a little moist heap on the floor. In spite of his revulsion, he gathered me up and laid me out on his couch, he dried me off and waited for me to take shape. . . . At last, at long last. . . . I had taken on a certain shape.
>
> They call that living! It is true, they did revive me, but they had confiscated the joy that I saw just oozing from life. No joy for you who are the non-entity, who are the negation of the Penis, who are the lack, who are castration.

And that was when my anger took over and I overturned their offices and their couches and their armchairs. . . .

I have often wondered, said Ancyl, if this confiscation wasn't a clever *psy* tactic to force us to take control of our own star. (P. 291)

Clearly Bersianik wants to retrieve, as did de Beauvoir, some of the insights and, as de Beauvoir did not, some aspects of the methods of psychoanalysis. In the second chapter of *The Second Sex*, de Beauvoir remarks on the power of psychoanalysis to retrieve for language "the body as lived in by the subject," and yet she objects to it as a system which takes Man as the standard and which rejects "the idea of choice." She insists that "psychoanalysis can establish its truths only in the historical context."

We can bring this encounter between feminism and psychoanalysis further by looking at a recent piece of feminist psychoanalytic writing. It is Jessica Benjamin's hope and contention that psychoanalysis can be used by and for women to facilitate the "inward journey."[7] To do so, she recognizes the need for a cluster of metaphors and images that might at least compete with the phallic logos. To search these out she turns, as do many feminists, to theories from the field of object relations and suggests how the realm of otherness might be otherwise inscribed on us as humans, either by us or for us. She seeks out that ever-elusive notion of women's desires and gives up the urge to locate images; instead she reformulates other experiences of desire. She calls the mode of mutual recognition the intersubjective; the intrapsychic (phallic) is the mode of subject/object, the form of domination. She hypothesizes that intersubjectivity may have its counterpart in spatial rather than symbolic representation. This is the key to Benjamin's position, and it may allow us to salvage a way of knowing, of being, of having, from the discourse of the "feminine" in order to explore more widely the range of "gender flexibility." The idea that women associate "desire with a space," a space that is in the in-between, can, I think, be inferred from many of the texts gathered here, especially in the frequent recognition scenes.[8] Benjamin's work points in a newer direction for feminist thought that takes up the dialectic of gender, and by doing so, makes it possible to learn more about the establishment of difference(s) before a new approach to intersubjectivity can emerge. For Benjamin as for Bersianik to talk of sexuality and desire is to talk of power and politics; along the way ethics and metaphysics may take part in the inward journey as we see in all these novels. I want to juxtapose Bersianik's promissory moves toward closure with Benjamin's work on the spatial aspects of gendered (feminine) existence. Her theories, like Freud's and D. W. Winnicott's, both of whom she "recognizes," emerge out of her encounter as an analyst with women's experiences. I had mentioned earlier that Bersianik seeks to replace the rule of the phallus with a metaphysics of holes. This is the task of Ancyl after the Eugélionne has departed our negative planet. It is her departure which signals the assault on the psy laws. Ancyl reclaims holes for the males and females of her kind: *"We are all bodies riddled with holes* thrown into space at the speed of light. Your body is glorious because it is perforated through and through. It is bombarded with holes, like mine. . . . Each function of the body aims to either fill or empty a cavity: breathe, eat, drink, kiss" (p. 339).

The monolithic Obelisk-Phallus is to "become a penis of flesh" and the Hole to be thought as the "opposite of nothingness." Both the unnameable and the physical are returned to consciousness. Bersianik's Hole Trees are to replace the Walking Phalluses that rule by men (patriarchy) has demanded of men and women of Earth.

While Benjamin speaks from a discourse of psychoanalytic practice and Bersianik from a fictive space, I want to point out that they both point toward the intersections made possible through consideration of desire shaped by female subjectivity as lived under conditions of domination—Benjamin's intersubjective space, Bersianik's porous receptivity to others as opposed to the intrapsychic agon, the monolithic phallus. The "uses" made of psychoanalysis and psychoanalytic theory in Bersianik's treatment of the psy laws is unique in this group of texts.

Atwood asks us to return to the intrapsychic with an even more critical position formulated on the workings of power and its desires. The questions of freedom are always shaped by those of necessity at any conjuncture. And Atwood knows from her mid-1980s perspective, as Bersianik writing at the peak of contemporary Western feminism could only know in ways more chiseled by forms of radical hope, that as far as feminism is concerned, too many women are still veiled, quarantined, stunted in body and mind for the struggle to become lost in questions of "high" theory. The desiring "I" of dystopian hope and resistance is an "I" in "reduced circumstances," as Atwood's narrator reminds us repeatedly. We know her by name only as Offred, the patronymic designation that indicates the Commander whose handmaid she has become in the regime of Gilead. Her former name functions like a talisman, something she contemplates only in the safety of the night: that is the covert space of desire where and when she is not seen by the Eyes, spies, that are omnipresent, omniscient. The questions about naming that have been crucial to feminist thought, work, theory, and everyday life are turned on their head by Atwood in this work which tracks down some of the dangerous detours of reaction, not revolution. This is most clear in the rituals which are all part of the state's religious practices: Testifying, Prayvaganzas, Salvagings, and Particicutions—all forms of ensuring order and terror in the hope of smashing resistance. The kinds of alliances formed under such strict surveillance are momentarily firm but finally fragile. On more specifically feminist grounds there are the means by which reproduction is monitored and regulated in the Ceremony (impregnation) and celebrated on the Birth Day (when women are gathered up by Birthmobiles to attend delivery). Attendance at rituals, like changes in name, is mandatory. The handmaid's time unobserved, found in the seven sections called "Night," is time stolen from a daily round of constant observation because handmaids are valuable property. Not many women are fit for the task, both as defined by the white men in charge and their "crack female control agency"—the Aunts. Also, the ecological disasters of the time "in between" have left many women sterile; undoubtedly men have also been affected, but not surprisingly it is women's reproductive capacity which is monitored, blamed, and occasionally celebrated.

In almost a single stroke, the appropriation of women's labor secured the place of the new government of Gilead after the old was overthrown. All the bank accounts and credit cards marked "F" were deactivated, immobilizing women in the midst of daily routine. The narrator indulges in nostalgic revery as she recalls all those women who had "jobs" once; now they have tasks, functions to carry out for the needs of the state, meted out according to the fitness of each woman. We see the restructured domestic economy through the handmaid's view of her place among the women of Commander Fred's household. The regime has multiplied the classes of women, and the handmaid is of supreme utilitarian value to a social structure suffering from severe depopulation. The decline in population is one of many ills blamed on the women of the time before who thought only of themselves—women of a society "dying of too much choice."

Handmaids in Gilead have two tasks: to do the grocery shopping and to reproduce if they possibly can. If they fail to become pregnant they are transferred to a different household where they have another chance; after three such chances, failure means removal to the Colonies, which is the life-in-death punishment that all women work to avoid at any cost. Choices are very limited, but this position of childbearer is one of the more enviable to be had. Atwood suggests some of the ways in which a post- and antifeminist political economy can wrench the core from the ideas which it aims to supersede; this is most evident in the rituals surrounding reproduction and birth in Gilead. As the historians conclude: "Gilead was, although undoubtedly patriarchal in form, occasionally matriarchal in content" producing a "cost-effective way to control women. . . . through women themselves" (p. 308).

Although they are usually kept deeply divided by privilege and function, women, that is, wives, handmaids, and Marthas (those women who cook and clean) come together for the scene of a birth narrated by Offred. The scene echoes the Ceremony, that moment of monthly sexual congress at which the household gathers, with the wife holding the handmaid between her knees while the Commander does his duty, zips up, and leaves. At the birth there are no men present, except in case of emergency. Birthing has been turned back over to the hands of women; it is thought shameful that men used to be present; but now there is a return to the biblical injunction to labor in pain and sorrow, with the added knowledge of how the breath may be controlled to minimize the travail. At this birth we learn that women do the naming; this child is called Angela; she will dress in the white of a Commander's daughter, until such time as she accedes to the blue of Commander's wife.

Offred has lost her name and place in a world she knew. She has lost her own daughter; Luke, her lover; Moira, her closest friend; and her mother. In one of the more compelling ironic juxtapositions of the novel, Moira will finally turn up—as a worker at Jezebel's, a brothel in Gilead for the exclusive use of the Commanders. As a former lesbian feminist, this turns out to be "her version of freedom," as Offred realized the refusal of sexual activity might be for Serena Joy, Commander Fred's wife. As for Offred's mother, it is only as memory that she returns. With love and an admixture of regret, Offred recalls how she and Moira, and even Luke, would laugh at her mother's "pure" feminism—hers was the fight against pornography when Offred was a child, which as an adult she recalls with wonder and terror. What she remembers is "burning photos of women's bodies," not the lesson of their oppression as represented by the photos themselves. This she was too young to understand. She is a somewhat belatedly grateful daughter of this mother. So it is with heavy irony that the narrator, after the birth and naming, says, as if her mother could hear her, "You wanted a women's culture. Well, now there is one. It isn't what you meant, but it exists. Be thankful for small mercies" (p. 127). Her mother's hope is inverted in her own despair—only an impoverished imagination is possible. Again the matriarchal "content" is cut to patriarchal forms. What the handmaid searches out in the course of the story are the cracks in the paranoid surface of this women's culture.

Her regular shopping trips are done in the compulsory company of another handmaid who is her assigned partner, Ofglen. For several weeks they speak only those greetings ("Praise be") and farewells ("Under His Eye") which are sanctioned by the no longer new order. They never make eye contact, for in this society to look and to be seen looking may lead to punishment and even death. It is never safe to assume that your interlocutor is not an Eye; spies are everywhere, and women have been taught by the Aunts to spy on each other during what constituted for this transitional generation a kind of thorough indoctrination—reconditioning for the regime. Those who did not learn the necessary lessons of obedience and submission at the Rachel and Leah Reeducation (RED) Center have disappeared; among the disappeared is Moira. Shopping outings usually include stops by the church and the wall where those executed for current crimes such as Gender Treachery (homosexuality), and Abortion, a "retrospective" crime, are hung for display after death and where the handmaid always searches for signs that none of the victims is Luke.

Ofglen and Offred first exchange furtive glances in the mirror/window of a chain of shops where computer prayers are for sale, the Soul Scrolls. Handmaids have to go to great lengths to see into each other's eyes, not only because they must not, but also because their mode of dress makes it difficult: they wear long red dresses and veils and white headdresses which, based on description and cover illustration are rather like elaborate winged nun's headgear, and which function as blinders. (When the handmaid is prepared for her ritual bath, she finds her nakedness strange, so distant from her own body have the practices of this regime made her.) When the ritual of verbal exchanges between the handmaids is broken by the words "It's a beautiful May day," Offred dimly remembers that the words "May day" used to be a distress signal; it is only later that Ofglen's opening will become fully clear to her; for now she cannot be too cautious: "She holds my stare in the glass, level unwavering. . . . There's a shock in this seeing; it's like seeing somebody naked, for the first time" (p. 167).

When the looks become words, it is Ofglen who asks, "Do you think God listens?" and risking treason they each answer no to her question. The handmaid had dared to imagine in the night, alone, that somewhere there might be a "government in exile" where Luke had perhaps gone. When Ofglen says, "you can join us," there is a spontaneous and mixed reaction to the fact that there is an "us"— Ofglen may be a spy, "a plant, set to trap me; such is the soil in which we grow . . . hope is rising in me, like sap in a tree. Blood in a wound. We have made an opening" (p. 169). In the third interlude, called "Night," we learn some of what forms the basis for Offred's means of survival and how it is bound up with the insistence on memory in conditions of hopelessness. This becomes clear in her reflections on Luke whose whereabouts, and whose existence, are unknown to her. On this night she tries to imagine what sort of quick death or diminished life Luke might have (had):

I believe Luke is lying face down in a thicket. . . . I pray that at least one hole is neatly, quickly, and finally through the skull. . . .

I also believe that Luke is sitting up . . . he's bent like an old man. . . . The body is so easily damaged. . . .

I also believe that they didn't catch him or catch up with him after all. . . . perhaps they were Quakers, they will smuggle him inland.

He made contact with the others, there must be a resistance, a government in exile. Someone must be out there, taking care of things. I believe in the resistance as I believe there can be no light without shadow; or rather, no shadow unless there is also light. There must be a resistance, or where do all the criminals come from, on the television? (Pp. 104–5)

Or those hung out for display at the Wall.

In the face of massive contradictions to which the handmaid is a witness she acknowledges the necessity of splitting—in order to live with contradiction you pay the psychic cost of any shred of a coherent sense of self, identity, integrity. It is not only the cost of political consciousness in Gilead, it also takes on those aspects of split consciousness with which we are familiar in the psychic structures of fascism and the ways resistance is constituted in such times and places; here is the bet that the handmaid keeps placing in the hope of some "version" of freedom:

The things I believe can't all be true, though one of them must be. But I believe in all of them, all three versions of Luke, at one and the same time. This contradictory way of believing seems to me, right now, the only way I can believe anything. Whatever the truth is, I will be ready for it. This is also a belief of mine. This may also be untrue (p. 106).

The chapter then closes:

One of the gravestones in the cemetery near the earliest church has an anchor on it, and an hourglass, and the words, *In Hope*. (P. 106)

In Hope. Why did they put that above a dead person? Was it the corpse hoping; or those alive? (P. 106)
    Does Luke hope? (P. 106)

Luke, her daughter, her mother, and her closest friend, Moira, are all lost to her. Her alliance and collusion with the Commander's wife (to ensure pregnancy) is sealed when Serena Joy offers her a look at a recent photograph of her daughter, indicating she has survived somewhere. Neither Luke's end nor her mother's is known before the handmaid's story ends.

It is some time before the handmaid or the reader will know the nature of this resistance movement. But an indicator of its fragility can be measured by the attempts Ofglen and Offred will make to feed each other information. When the Commander asks what he can do for the handmaid in exchange for her illicit evenings of playing Scrabble with him, she says, "I want to know," and all she can imagine, when he asks for further clarification, is "what's going on?" Similarly, when Ofglen suggests she act as spy for the resistance, she says to Offred, "find out anything you can." Clearly the imagination has been short-circuited by the reduced circumstances to which these women have become accustomed.

How rapidly change can be produced in consciousness is measured in a scene in which Offred in her daily shopping rounds encounters a group of Japanese tourists who want to take her picture. Not only is she deeply embarrassed by their stares, but she is also disgusted by the display of female bodies, which are not fully covered by clothing. The women of the group are wearing high heels and lipstick, both of which she remembers but which seem so obviously designed to make women into appropriately formed bodies for the demands of a culture now distant in time and space from the one she knows. The dizzying circularity of these observations is apparent: there is the narrator, who found her mother's dogmatic pronouncements about appeals to men and their values and desires corrupting, and that same mother, who struggled for a world in which her daughter (the handmaid by another name in the time before) would not have to fight these battles. There is the handmaid, who took this "liberated" world for granted in her own raising of her daughter who has been lost to her under the new order. There is also the question of the gains made by women of other cultures through the adoption of so-called forms of Westernization—the women tourists, for whom the handmaid in her red outfit, long dress, headgear, and veil is both exoticized and eroticized.

It is this kind of theoretical spin on the claims and potential directions of late-twentieth-century feminism that Atwood performs best in this fiction that is both satire and cautionary fable. Atwood means to turn both narrative and feminist commonplaces on their heads and, if possible, inside out, which she manages to do with certain forms of fairy-tale narrative structures: like those, this tale also begins with a "once" and a future, but both have long been lost. Here's how they are set into the tale. In a familiar scenario of collective catastrophe, the novel opens with women sleeping in what was "once" a high school gymnasium; recalling other times in such a place, the desires of adolescence are located as a moment when "we yearned for the future." Both promise and memory have been cauterized by the reeducation in the hands of the Aunts, women who guard those to be sent out as handmaids, who, as a national resource, are tatooed at the ankle, so they cannot escape without identification. The Aunts are as reminiscent of wicked stepsisters and stepmothers as they are of prison or concentration camp guards. They are those b(r)ought in to do the disciplinary work over others of their own kind; they believe only in "either/or," as Offred says of Aunt Lydia. In Charnas's dystopia they were the Matris, and they, too, helped to perpetuate the patriarchal myths about the women-of-the-time-before being responsible for the present suffering and the need for discipline. When Foucault talks of the constitution of "docile bodies" he describes a system of political technology that is meant to turn time and bodies into the forms demanded by capital. This is done through what he calls "exercise," the "technique by which one imposes on the body, tasks that are both repetitive and different, but always graduated." It is a form common to various methods of apprenticeship and initiation: the military, the church, the university, are Foucault's examples. Gilead as a state devises reeducation based on all three of these discursive formations.[9] These devices are familiar to us as readers in a world accustomed to state-sponsored repression and torture. That is one aspect of what makes reading this text disquieting and not nearly as futuristic nor fantasmatic as we might wish.

Whereas utopian thought is founded on a premise of abundance, the dystopian is tied to the rhetoric and economy of scarcity, lack, hopelessness. Among the aspects of everyday life which are reconceived in the utopian form and which are marked by abundance are not only an affective plenitude but also a sense of the spatial as infinitely expandable—a world in which there is room to move. The handmaid in her tale has a room of her very own, but she can never be sure of being alone; there is the eye of surveillance in the ceiling above her, and there are the others in the house who are watching at most times. That is why it comes as such a shock when the Commander summons her to his room in order to be alone with her. She can hardly imagine what she may be asked to do. Both of their imaginations are withered by this order of things—he wants her to kiss him goodnight as if she meant it, and, more than anything else, he wants her to play word games with him, namely Scrabble. Her first request in response to his whim to give her things is to ask for hand cream; we had witnessed her previously stealing a pat of butter to hoard for the purpose of working into her skin. The very idea of soothing the mind with fantasy or the body with oils has been erased from the realm of possibility. With this curious detail Atwood is also having fun with her readers: "*Is there* no balm in Gilead, *is there* no physician there? Why then is not the health of the daughter of my people recovered?" (Jeremiah 8:22). The world of intersubjective relations is utterly debased and degraded in terms of what may be expected from others in the daily surround. This is yet another reason that Offred and Ofglen are so wary of each other until well into their shopping partnership. The ability to care for oneself was cut off with one blow in the time of the takeover—the handmaid was not Luke's companion but his possession when she no longer had her own money. With this went her capacity to care for others and herself. In the present situation her needs are seen to and overseen but never independently so; meals for the handmaid are regimented: "The arrival of the tray, carried up the stairs as if for an invalid. An invalid, one who has been invalidated. No valid passport. No exit" (p. 224). In the late-twentieth-century takeover that founded Gilead, the cancellation of bank accounts, credit cards, and jobs was an extremely effective first measure for the erasure of identity of women across (some) class lines.

The what-if/not-yet that these two fictions pose for feminist readers and readers of feminist history have to do with how they are each grounded in the fictional framing of the historical. For

Atwood there is the epilogue situated two centuries after the events narrated by the handmaid, and offered as scientific/ academic reconstitution of the workings of monotheocratic Gilead; this functions like the voice of the historians of Archaos. For Bersianik there is the use of the French historical present tense (lost in translation into English) which gives her text both an a- and an omni-temporality reminiscent of *Les Guérillères*. While this lack of textual temporal specificity is a conventional privilege of the utopian genre, it is ironically and self-consciously the case that neither writer presumes to use the form programmatically. We never learn how Gilead vanished, but it did—perhaps too terrible a dream. As for the Eugélionne, she vanished as she came— one sad eye, one gay.

We may find it ludicrous and dangerously whimsical that the handmaid dares to ask the Commander for hand cream to replace her stolen rancid butter, but it brings us back to the fundamental condition of lack in dystopian space in short order. There is a way in which Jessica Benjamin's essay may again help us to span the distance between utopia and dystopia, the good and bad places. In *The Handmaid's Tale* the narrator repeatedly finds herself envious of those around her who also share, though with certain differences, her reduced circumstances: "In this house we all envy each other something" (p. 47). Benjamin reminds us in passing that envy, unlike jealousy, is about being, not having. And in Gilead with its stratification of women (and men), envy is the carrier of the intrapsychic mode of domination and control as internalized by those enslaved. The Aunts do the reeducating, but the women soon take over the policing of themselves and their own subjected others. Having is strictly monitored and regulated in Gilead; being then becomes an arena for testing the limits of a shrunken reality. The language of the handmaids among themselves is so circumscribed that variations in delivery and intonations are heard with a kind of attention that is characteristic of the work language is asked to do for subjects imprisoned in body and mind: "But I feel serene, at peace, pervaded with indifference. Don't let the bastards grind you down, I repeat this to myself but it conveys nothing. You might as well say, Don't let there be air; or, Don't be" (p. 291). Until her encounter with Moira, the only confirmations of her being-in-the-world are furtive—she hoards thought and feelings just as she hoards a pat of butter or a single match. The shifting metaphorics of hunger also echo this scenario of deprivation; one of the epigraphs Atwood uses to set her story in a tradition of irony and satire comes from Swift's "Modest Proposal." What Offred hungers after is not food, which is readily available, though variety seems a problem; she hungers instead "to commit the action of touch." Nick, her fellow servant in the Commander's household, potential Eye, and forbidden lover "makes her hungry." And "death makes her hungry," as she learns after the Particicution ritual where Handmaids are let loose to do violence to a man already tortured and said to be a convicted rapist. She also has repeated urges to "steal something" in order to experience forms of greed and avidity. This seems to signal a complete break with any sense of her own desire—it is rather a call to, a wish for, desire to reappear, and with a kind of violent intensity produced by the perspective of disempowerment for these citizens of Gilead.

Certain aspects of desire are reanimated in Atwood's reworking of Charlotte Perkins Gilman's feminist parable, "*The Yellow Wallpaper.*" Where Gilman's confined and also nameless narrator begins to "see" women moving, feminine figures in the paper who lead her to imagine her own escape, Atwood's female figure in the "carpet" has left words carved into the floorboards of the room where Offred sleeps and eats. Her minute examination of her room (as something to do and a place to search for traces of the past) recalls Gilman's narrator searching out difference while cossetted in monotony, and leads Offred to the "Latin" words she cannot translate. Here again she will ask a favor of the Commander—to interpret the vulgar Latin words: they function as an incantation which she knows has been passed down to her from an earlier victim; perhaps the one she has guessed must have killed herself—"don't let the bastards grind you down." It is a minimal pleasure to use these forbidden (because written) words to pray, and to think of the woman before her who scratched them into the wooden cupboard, and to imagine her as Moira, the bold friend.

The importance of recollection and reconstruction is set up in "Night," the first of seven sections so named in the novel. Here the narrator remembers, "We yearned for the future. How did we learn it, that talent for insatiability?" (pp. 3–4). By placing in the foreground the desire for change and the insistence of desire itself,

the narrator begins, in a *mise en abîme* of memories, some not
even her own, to recall adolescents and adolescences past, framed
by the energy of play and expectation. But the limitations on those
urges are located in what we know to be the present in the story:
"We had army-issue blankets, old ones that still said U.S. . . . The
lights were turned down but not out. Aunt Sara and Aunt Eliz-
abeth patrolled; they had electric cattle prods slung on thongs
from their leather belts. . . . We learned to whisper almost without
sound. . . . In this way we exchanged names" (p. 4). This whisper-
ing in near darkness is how the handmaids learn to speak to each
other and is the point of view of the one who seems to be secreting
this tale. The closing frame, "Historical Notes," set at an academic conference of historians, reveals that the narrative we are
reading existed in the form of thirty tape cassettes. The narrator
herself claimed to be involved in the process of reconstruction,
particularly as she conveyed Moira's story; the specialists in Gileadean studies and Caucasian Anthropology themselves take a disciplinary position on reconstruction and the status of the story we
have just been told. They, too, yearn to know what her future held
and are insatiable in what they ask to know of this aberrant period
in history now established and canonized in this Twelfth Sympo-
sium on Gileadean Studies held in 2195. (This closure device as
epilogue resonates with the acknowledgments Atwood makes to
academic granting agencies and to universities for the time and
place to get this story written.) Not only do these intellectual
workers need to reconstruct "a machine capable of playing such
tapes," they also still need to try to reconstruct the components of
this late-twentieth-century monotheocracy which redrew "the
map of the world, especially in this hemisphere" (p. 299).

Unable to "establish an identity for the narrator," just as we
readers never know the name she whispers to Nick, the historians
turn instead to the identity of the Commander about whom there
is enough information to allow for speculation. We, the readers,
seem to be learning both more and less—more about the Commander but less in that our own time frame makes Gilead less re-
mote than we might like. The keynote speaker, Professor James
Darcy Pieixoto, Director of Twentieth and Twenty-first Century
Archives, Cambridge University, England, is drawn to the language of darkness and light to represent the place out of which

The Handmaid's Tale emerged. This is how the novel ends:

> As all historians know, the past is a great darkness, and filled with echoes. Voices may reach us from it; but what they say to us is imbued with the obscurity of the matrix out of which they come; and, try as we may, we cannot always decipher them precisely in the clearer light of our own day.
> *Applause.*
> Are there any questions? (P. 311)

The privileged place Atwood gives to darkness and light as ways of knowing is apparent throughout this novel, and is also forecast in earlier works of hers, in particular, the collection of prose poems, *Murder in the Dark*.[10] But hers is not the conventional association of light with knowledge and darkness with ignorance; there is irony in the historian's belief that the light of his "own day" is clearer than that in Gilead. Here again Atwood's interest is in performing an inversion, so that in darkness another kind of knowledge is available, in this instance, a knowledge against which the daylight hours conspire quite literally. That is another function of the repeated, intermittent chapters called "Night." This inversion where things can be known through other pathways is akin to Atwood's critique of the privilege of human sight as an instrument of knowing; what she suggests is a form of knowing that comes through touch, and she represents this often in the grounding of the feet as closer to a sense of knowing the way things are. During the Ceremony the Handmaid first perceives some potential for a connection to Nick when their feet touch: "the tip of his boot is touching my foot. . . . we are touching, two shapes of leather. I feel my shoe soften, blood flows into it, it grows warm, it becomes a skin" (p. 81). When she is being smuggled into Jezebel's with the Commander she must hide below the back seat where she is eye level with his shoes, which reveal to her the hardness of his corporeal shell/self: "my forehead is against his shoes. I have never been this close to his shoes before. They feel hard, unwinking, like the shells of beetles: black, polished, inscrutable. They seem to have nothing to do with feet" (p. 233).

The metaphysics of touch is presented as an alternative to the long-standing privilege of the optical in the culture of rationalism; it is a variation on the holes and trees as against the phallus of stone. There is a concurrent strain in the writing of Luce Irigaray, which also poses the question of an ethics of sexual difference by suggesting that what may arise from such an epistemological shift (from sight to touch) would constitute another ethics of thought and subjects-in-relation, recalling Jessica Benjamin. For Irigaray in her series of lectures on the question of ethics in a gendered frame, it is in the mutual recognition that women can offer each other through touch and contact that she sees the possibility for women and men to be "open" to each other.[11] This requires remembering the Eugélionne's warnings sounded repeatedly in her determined travels in search of promises. Atwood's text comes wrapped as a warning though it hides so much more. In a personal and political speech Atwood gave at Radcliffe College in 1980, entitled "Witches," we can discern some seeds of the poetic and conceptual field that is *The Handmaid's Tale*.[12] The speech begins with a revery of Cambridge twenty years earlier (also the most likely site of Offred's home in Gilead) when Atwood (as "studentess") had come to study Victorian literature at Radcliffe. She wanted to read "real" poetry, then kept under lock and key, but that did not include Canadian poetry. Her revery and her title take her farther back in time in order to explain her title: Mary Webster, an ancestress hanged as a witch in Connecticut, "more dear to [Atwood's] heart than the privateers and the massacred French Protestants," because when she was cut down, "she was to everyone's surprise, not dead." The anecdote closes thus: "and if there's one thing I hope I've inherited from her, it's her neck." This is a cautionary, not a promissory, version of hope. With a slow turn of her unbent and unbroken neck, Atwood comes to the situation of writers and moves back into the present: "After 10 years of the Women's Movement, we'd like to think that some of the old stereotypes are fading, but 10 years is not a very long time in the history of the world. . . . the old icons, have merely gone underground, and not far at that" (p. 331). She tells her audience that although "in this century, on this continent" women writers "have it rather soft," books, and particularly books by prominent, though unnamed, women writers are being banned in Canada. As a member of Amnesty International, Atwood reminds us of her awareness of daily torture in our world—to be "hunted" it is enough "to be who you are." As for herself and the more general responsibility of writers, she closes: "What kind of world shall you describe for your readers? The one you can see around you, or the better one you can imagine? If only the latter, you'll be unrealistic; if only the former, despairing. But it is by the better world we can imagine that we judge the world we have. If we cease to judge this world, we may find ourselves, very quickly, in one which is infinitely worse" (p. 333). Mostly we have been reading here for the morphology of the utopian where the dystopian becomes the negative space, the unsaid which drives the wish. Atwood's formulation here frames our look, just as her novel demands that we reverse our glance. We've recognized the diminished imagination of the Handmaid and others in Gilead, even the powerful, those in Command. Though Gilead is no more, the fact of the text itself allows us to imagine, with the historians of Gileadean studies, those acts of individual and collective resistance to which the text is meant to bear witness. While the judgments may be partial, naive, even sentimental, the handmaid never stops judging her world, reading its rewritten language for fractured signs of hope.

Afterword

A Klee painting named "Angelus Novus" shows an angel . . .
staring, his mouth open, his wings are spread. His face is turned
toward the past. Where we perceive a chain of events, he sees
one single catastrophe which keeps piling wreckage upon
wreckage and hurls it in front of his feet. . . . But a storm is
blowing from Paradise; it has got caught in his wings with such
violence that the angel can no longer close them. This storm ir-
resistibly propels him into the future to which his back is
turned, while the pile of debris before him grows skyward. This
storm is what we call progress.

> Walter Benjamin,
> IX, "Theses on the
> Philosophy of History"

. . . if we unite our forces as anatomical women it is to destroy
ourselves as sociological women and at the same time to destroy
men as sociological men.

> Editors of
> *Questions Féministes*

In the feminist thinking of the not-yet no one clear future
emerges; what is clear by now, however, is that in the decade under review a "community" of texts was produced whose authors
rewrote significant aspects of the utopian genre as codified in the
nineteenth century and wrote into fiction some of the commonplaces of feminist theory of the time. Borrowing from conventions
of science fiction, travel, picaresque, epic, and other related
genres, they set their novels in the speculative mode and organized
conscious wishes and fantasies. The inherently didactic utopian
form has often served critics wishing to trivialize its literary value;
these works do teach, leading DuPlessis to call some of them
"apologues." Each of the utopian novels studied here offers a
model of how history and the future might be shaped if women
were the subjects, that is, speakers of these histories; the two dystopian fictions represent the deformation of possible histories and
futures when women are silenced.

These novels all tell of the power of speech and naming. They
give evidence of the enabling mastery of writing, suggesting a feminist logos that could be set against the masculine logos quieted by
these narratives. The obvious absence of "sociological" men in

feminist utopian fictions is not only a corrective rewriting of history but also testifies to the need to make a future different from the past. Here, women as speakers also refuse to speak *for* men as men have long assumed they could speak for women. The emphasis on voice and speaking in the French and American debates, and to writing and rewriting, has disclosed much of what had and has been "hidden from history" and what may not-yet have come to be.

These novels construct social systems of community where the will to power is what arouses the greatest suspicion. The "governments" represented are commonly based on consensual decision making. That is to say, the law does not generally exist as inscribed and codified. Earlier writers did not examine how the utopian dweller came into being; for the persons who live in utopian space there is no need to legislate what is practiced by inclination. Questions of the public "spheres" which figured prominently in the earlier utopias—industry, economics, the state—are not evaded; rather they are translated and transposed to another level. Feminist writers begin with the social modes of reproduction and ask instead about work, systems of exchange, and the family.

In these novels change is both necessary and desired. The utopian aspects of feminist theory have always been apparent, from Mary Wollstonescraft to Hélène Cixous. Fictional imagings of what theory has worked and reworked proliferate during the period that followed the "novum" of contemporary feminism, which can be said to have announced itself with the maxim of the "personal is political," a still vital and fruitful insight that keeps feminism in a perpetual dialectic of confrontation between theory and practice. Feminist fictions are the "places" where women speak the desires that frame the anticipatory consciousness of utopia made concrete, bringing the not-yet into the here and now.

Catharine MacKinnon has argued that feminism has no theory of the state and that such a theory must be on the feminist agenda, since both liberal idealist and left materialist analysis of the state fail on the question of sexual politics.[1] I am suggesting that the utopian communities we have seen framed here must be read as implicit critiques and remappings of the state. As in their turn away from power *over* (domination) toward power *to* (enablement), feminists have mostly avoided theorizing the state even while entangled in its workings at the level of the politics of daily reform; this is what leads MacKinnon to say that the "feminist posture toward the state has therefore been schizoid" (p. 643). Power can remain suspect because it is so clearly, like the law, within the realm of domination. But like naming and the law and engagement in or with the symbolic, the feminists we have been reading here *have* given thought to the operations of the state—for example, in their necessarily unfinished reflections on women at war (Wittig, Piercy), women and the social welfare of individuals and groups in the community (Russ, Gilman), required levels of productivity (Rochefort, Russ), and forms of self-government and government of others (Bersianik, Gilman). The level of representation may be microscopic rather than macro-, but I think that is because feminists, women, have been looking and continue to look more closely at how those who inhabit the future are made, or how they are reinscribed in a culture, however real or imaginary, where social, intellectual, and economic possibilities are not arranged by gender but by capacity. What they are looking into are the details of the workings of power. And this is possible in these works because in the imaginative realm women may become "a sex for [them]selves" thereby "mov[ing] community to the level of vision," where MacKinnon realizes they can engage the question of the state (p. 640n).

When feminists fractured the definitions of sexuality, family, kinship, and parenting, as they did in these novels, they did not also imagine that developments in the high-technology of reproduction would so soon bring up debates on banking sperm, fetal monitoring, and surrogate mothering. In these debates we can see how the interests of the ruling class are spotlighted, as, for example, in the increasing numbers of clinics involved in artificial insemination that refuse their services to "single" women, and in the allocation of the most funds for research and development to in-vitro fertilization, the least successful and most expensive of the technologies of reproduction but the one that most closely mimics married heterosexual coupling. It seemed for a time that feminist theory had reached an impasse in the political critique of essentialism, and in the poststructuralist critique that had turned our attention to sexual difference. Some of these critiques have been synthesized in more recent work on "gender," even though that term can all too easily render the political academic. What seems at this moment (1988) to be reanimating the theoretical and political feminist agendas is the work going on in a variety of disciplines to examine what falls under the rubric of "new reproductive technologies."[2] These agendas bring feminism back to its most productive and problematic issues focused on the social and biological reproduction of bodies and their relations of affinity and kinship.

Although the political imagination operates at full tilt in these novels, the life of the white, capitalist, patriarchal polis goes on unimpeded. As Donna Haraway suggests, it has even changed its spots for a better set of camouflage she names the "informatics of domination."[3] Under this rubric, some of the feminist dreams, even those most willfully rocketed into an imagined future, can already be read as yet more arcadias. For example, the full-scale critique of the medical profession as one of the ideological state apparatuses most in control of women's lives—their bodies and their minds—has been outstripped in its rhetoric and concerns by technological developments that have reconsigned women into doctoring hands—the hands are perhaps female, but the controls are still beyond us. Haraway's voice is one that bridges the dialectic at work throughout this text between jeremiad and hope with a necessary twist of irony. We need this particular mix because:

> [f]eminisms and Marxisms have run aground on Western epistemological imperatives to construct a revolutionary subject from the perspective of a hierarchy of oppressions and/or a latent position of moral superiority, innocence, and greater closeness to nature. With no available original dream of a common language or original symbiosis promising protection from hostile "maculine" separation, but written into the play of a text that has no finally privileged reading or salvation history, to recognize "oneself" as fully implicated in the world, frees us of the need to root politics in identification, vanguard parties, purity and mothering. (P. 95)

It is in her "Manifesto for Cyborgs" that she calls for a much-needed "ironic political myth." Published in 1985, this anti-nostalgic utopian call postdates the U.S. antifeminism of the

Reagan years that leaves some of the resolutions proffered here looking hopelessly naive; but Haraway insists that we still must turn to the imaginative impulse if we are to come to terms with the struggle over boundaries—of the self and its partial identities. That is to say, the cyborg—part human, animal, and machine—is a reality that Haraway claims we all already inhabit—some of us closer to centers of "command-control" than others. Citing one of the failures of contemporary political theory, feminist or other, Haraway insists "we lack sufficiently subtle connections for collectively building effective theories of experience"; among the results of this failure is the repeatedly inadequate effort of white-dominated Western feminism to deal with race and class though claims are legion that we must theorize these together with gender. Haraway warns us against the lure of totalizing resolution of contradiction. She proclaims the partial and the monstrous as both necessary to the new machinery of identities which are to be found in writing; two kinds of writing in particular—the writings of women of color and the "monstrous selves" of feminist science fiction: "Cyborg writing must not be about the Fall, the imagination of a once-upon-a-time wholeness before language, before writing, before Man. Cyborg writing is about the power to survive, not on the basis of innocence, but on the basis of seizing the tools to mark the world that marked them as other" (pp. 93–94). This gesture of seizing the tools is a myth for another millennial moment—the late twentieth century. And utopian rhetoric flourishes in such times (think here, for example, about the late nineteenth century, or about Bloch, haunted by hope as he produces his major work on hope in exile in New York while the death machinery of the Third Reich maximizes efficiency).

We are surrounded by millennial discourses, both apocalyptic and utopian; medical science and technology promise us ever-greater control over birth, health, disease, and death, and promote an ethics of perfection reminiscent of late-nineteenth-century eugenic discourse. At the same time we are in the throes of confusion and conflict over what is often described in terms of plague as we watch the spread of AIDS both within and outside of what at first seemed to be contained communities. While projective statistics (for 1991, for the year 2000) force us into *fin-de-siècle* imaginings, the churches, communities, and states struggle over how to support and maintain those already suffering. And this is to limit examples of millennial thinking to the sphere of the lived body—healthy or ill.

While we cannot always read ourselves retrospectively, in the radical shift from the promise of a site like Mattapoisett to the betrayal of Gilead, with a margin of hindsight we can see the need to proliferate partial struggles, to be vigilant in the naming of forms of victimage, and to read novels like those gathered here as partial and partisan skirmishes meant to expand the territories in which we still live as bodies marked by gender.

Notes

Introduction

1. Raymond Williams, *Problems in Materialism and Culture* (London: Verso, 1980), p. 207.

2. Utopian science fictions not included in this study are Ursula LeGuin's *The Dispossessed* and Doris Lessing's *Canopus in Argos: Archives,* both of which privilege what can only be called the "masculine" even as the authors try to interrogate such divisions; and Sally Gearheart's *The Wanderground,* which presents the reverse of this problem in its essentialist "feminist" vision. In a necessary process of elimination, I have also chosen not to work with the following, which are nevertheless part of the phenomenon of literary production I discuss: Dorothy Bryant, *The Kin of Ata Are Waiting for You* (New York: Random House; Berkeley: Moon Books, 1976); Rochelle Singer, *The Demeter Flower* (New York: St. Martin's Press, 1980); Donna J. Young, *Retreat: As It Was, A Fantasy* (Weatherby Lake, Mo.: Naiad Press, 1979).

3. This moment is perhaps best represented in its diversity and controversy in three anthologies: *Coming to Power: Writings and Graphics on Lesbian S/M,* rev. ed., eds., members of SAMOIS, (Boston: Alyson Publications, 1982); Ann Snitow, Christine Stansell, and Sharon Thompson, eds., *Powers of Desire: The Politics of Sexuality* (New York: Monthly Review Press, 1983); and Carole S. Vance, ed., *Pleasure and Danger: Exploring Female Sexuality* (Boston: Routledge & Kegan Paul, 1984).

4. In *The Utopian Novel in America, 1886–1896: The Politics of Form* (Pittsburgh: University of Pittsburgh Press, 1984), Jean Pfaelzer begins her study of a decade with the statement that more than one hundred utopian fictions were published in that short time.

5. I am thinking here of George Kateb in *Utopia* (New York: Atherton, 1971) and Lewis Mumford in *The Story of Utopia* (New York: Viking Press, 1962) but also of articles published in special issues of *Daedalus* 2 (Spring 1965) and *Comparative Literature Studies* 10, no. 4 (Dec. 1973), most of which treat the topic as merely artifactual rather than reshaped by historical conjunctures. The utopian impulse is generally read here as missing in the contemporary situation.

6. See in this context chapter 7, "A State of Her Own; or, What Did Women Want?" of Pfaelzer's *Utopian Novel*, which includes an extensive reading of Mary H. Lane's *Mizora: A Prophecy* (1889), the most often cited of the utopias written by women in this decade.

7. Ernst Bloch, *The Principle of Hope*, 3 vols, trans. Neville Plaice, Stephen Plaice, and Paul Knight (Cambridge, Mass.: MIT Press, 1986).

8. Darko Suvin and Marc Angenot, "Not Only but Also," *Science Fiction Studies* 6, pt. 2, no. 18 (July 1979): 168–79; Joanna Russ, "The Subjunctivity of Science Fiction," *Extrapolation* 15, no. 1 (Dec. 1973): 51–59; Rachel Blau DuPlessis, "The Feminist Apologues of Lessing, Piercy, and Russ," *Frontiers* 4, no. 1 (Spring 1979): 1–8; Paul Tillich, "The Political Meaning of Utopia," in *Political Expectation* (New York: Harper & Row, 1971); Louis Marin, *Utopiques* (Paris: Minuit, 1973).

9. Fredric Jameson, *Marxism and Form* (Princeton: Princeton University Press, 1971), p. 137; until the publication in 1986 of *The Principle of Hope* in its entirety, Jameson and the editors of *New German Critique* were those primarily responsible for translating parts of Bloch's work and thought for English-language readers.

10. Sigmund Freud, "Creative Writers and Day-dreaming," in *The Standard Edition*, vol. 9 (London: Hogarth Press, 1959), pp. 148–49.

11. E.g., in Rita Mae Brown's *The Rubyfruit Jungle* (Plainfield, Vt.: Daughters, 1973), the picaresque; Virginia Woolf's *To the Lighthouse* (New York: Harcourt, Brace, 1927), the Kunstlerroman or psychological novel; Suzy McKee Charnas's *Walk to the End of the World* (New York: Berkley Books, 1974), and *Motherlines* (New York: Berkley Books, 1978), the epic novel.

12. Darko Suvin, "Defining the Literary Genre of Utopia," *Studies in the Literary Imagination* 6, no. 2 (Fall 1973): 138.

13. Joanna Russ, "SF and Technology as Mysification," *Science Fiction Studies* 5, pt. 3, no. 16 (Nov. 1978): 250–60.

14. Elaine Marks and Isabel de Courtivron, eds., *New French Feminisms* (Amherst: University of Massachusetts Press, 1980).

15. Frank E. Manuel and Fritzie P. Manuel, *Utopian Thought in the Western World* (Cambridge, Mass.: Harvard University Press, Belknap Press, 1979); the Manuels move from the "utopian propensity," which they trace from its classical and biblical sources in the West, through to the Christian utopias that follow the Renaissance and on to the rational, philosophical Enlightenment forms of the impulse as they are rewritten in more explicit political discourses of the nineteenth century. They also read the late nineteenth century as the "twilight of utopia" and end their vast work with the question of the "utopian prospect." The feminist utopia makes no appearance in this work.

16. Karl Marx and Frederick Engels, *The German Ideology,* part 1 (New York: International Publishers, 1977), p. 52.

17. Frederick Engels, *The Origin of the Family, Private Property, and the State* (New York: Pathfinder Press, 1972); August Bebel, *Women under Socialism* (New York: Schocken Books, 1971).

18. Frederick Engels, *Socialism Utopian and Scientific* (New York: International Publishers, 1935).

19. Russ, *Subjunctivity,* pp. 56, 58.

20. Suvin, "Defining the Literary Genre," pp. 121–45.

21. Rachel Blau DuPlessis, *Writing beyond the Ending* (Bloomington: Indiana University Press, 1985), p. 5.

22. Anthologies of speculative women's writing, both utopian and science fiction, include Susan Janice Anderson and Vonda N. McIntyre, eds., *Aurora* (Greenwich Conn.: Fawcett, 1976); Virginia Kidd, ed., *Millennial Women* (New York: Dell, 1978); Jessica Salmonson, ed., *Amazons!* (New York: Daw Books, 1979); and three volumes edited by Pamela Sargent, *Women of Wonder* (New York: Random House, Vintage Books, 1975–1978). Critical anthologies that deal with such writing include Marleen S. Barr, ed., *Future Females* (Bowling Green, Ohio: Bowling Green State University Popular Press, 1981); Marleen Barr and Nicholas D. Smith, eds., *Women and Utopia* (Landham, Md.: University Press of America, 1983); Ruby Rohrlich and Elaine Baruch, eds., *Women in Search of Utopia* (New York: Schocken Books, 1984); and Natalie M. Rosinsky, *Feminist Futures* (Ann Arbor, Mich.: UMI Research Press, 1984). Special issues of journals devoted to the utopian include *Extrapolation* 19; *Frontiers* 2; *Littérature* 21; *Minnesota Review,* n.s. 6; *Science Fiction Studies* 7, pt. 1, and a forthcoming issue of *Women's Studies,* "Feminism Faces the Fantastic," ed. Marleen Barr and Patrick Murphy. Conferences that have been devoted to the topic of the utopian include the Colloque de Cérisy, "Le Discours utopique," July–August 1975 (selections from the proceedings were published in Paris by 10/18, 1978); "Women in the Future," held at Indiana University of Pennsylvania in October 1987; and "Women in the Year 2000," sponsored by Indiana University-Purdue University at Indianapolis in April 1988. Special sessions on feminist utopian fiction took place during the meetings of the Midwest Modern Language Association, Indianapolis, 1979; the Modern Language Association, San Francisco, 1979; and the Modern Language Association, Houston, 1980. The Society for Utopian Studies meets annually.

Chapter 1

1. Charlotte Perkins Gilman, *Herland* (New York: Pantheon Books,

1979); Monique Wittig, *Les Guérillères*, trans. David Le Vay (New York: Avon Books, 1973). The French version of the Wittig novel was published in Paris by Editions de Minuit, 1969; all page references will be to the English edition.

2. Helen Diner, in *Mothers and Amazons* (1932; repr., Garden City, N.Y.: Doubleday, Anchor Press, 1973), is the first to work with this distinction in protofeminist ways.

3. Correa Moylan Walsh, *Feminism* (New York: Sturgis & Walton, 1917), p. 74.

4. Ibid., p. 149.

5. Charlotte Perkins Gilman, *The Living of Charlotte Perkins Gilman* (New York: Harper & Row, Colophon Books, 1975).

6. Charlotte Perkins Gilman, "The Yellow Wallpaper," in *The Charlotte Perkins Gilman Reader* (New York: Pantheon Books, 1980).

7. Barbara Ehrenreich and Deirdre English, *For Her Own Good* (Garden City, N.Y.: Doubleday, Anchor Press, 1979). Ehrenreich and English clarify the connections between those physicians specializing in female disorders, nervous or otherwise, and their diagnoses of female invalidism. As for Mitchell, his fame seemed to rest on a combination of a painless if completely submissive "cure" and an extremely dominating personality.

8. George Miller Beard, *American Nervousness* (New York: G. P. Putnam, 1881); Josef Breuer and Sigmund Freud, "Studies on Hysteria," in *The Standard Edition*, vol. 2 (London: Hogarth Press, 1955); Jean Martin Charcot, *Lectures on the Diseases of the Nervous System*, trans. George Sigerson (New York: Hafner, 1962). Two widespread maladies of the late nineteenth century were neurasthenia and hysteria; both, it was claimed, were more apt to occur in women than in men. These three works were all quite influential in their own time and place. For Freud the "Studies" led to the "talking cure," which later became the psychoanalytic method.

9. Charlotte Perkins Gilman, *Women and Economics* (New York: Harper & Row, Torchbooks, 1966).

10. Marge Piercy, "The Grand Coolie Damn," in *Sisterhood Is Powerful*, ed. Robin Morgan (New York: Random House, Vintage Books, 1970).

11. Nancy Hartsock, "Fundamental Feminism," *Quest: A Feminist Quarterly* 2, no. 2 (Fall 1975): 67–80.

12. Walsh (*Feminism*, p. 20) refers here to August Bebel's work *Die Frau und der Socialismus*; this privileging of socialism over feminism is evident in the curious English translation of Bebel's work as *Woman under Socialism* when *Woman and Socialism* would be more precise.

13. Gilman, *Living*, pp. 319–20.

14. Simone de Beauvoir, *The Second Sex*, trans. H. M. Parshley (New York: Bantam Books, 1953). The French version was published in two volumes in Paris by Gallimard, 1949.

15. Gilman, *Women and Economics*, p. 191.

16. *Forerunner* 7 (1916; repr., New York: Greenwood Reprint, 1968).

17. Linda Gordon, "The Struggle for Reproductive Freedom," in *Capitalist Patriarchy and the Case for Socialist Feminism*, ed. Zillah R. Eisenstein (New York: Monthly Review Press, 1979) p. 110.

18. Gilman, *Women and Economics*, p. 174.

19. Gordon, "Struggle," p. 110.

20. Monique Wittig and Sande Zeig, *Lesbian Peoples* (New York: Avon Books, 1979). The book was translated by the authors and the French version was published in Paris in 1976 by Grasset and Fasquelle under the title *Brouillon pour un dictionnaire des amantes*. All page references will be to the English version, hereafter cited as *LP*.

21. For a detailed discussion of contemporary French feminist politics, see Carolyn Greenstein Burke, "Report from Paris," *Signs* 3, no. 4 (Summer 1978): 843–55; Nancy Huston, "French Feminism," *Camera Obscura*, no. 3–4 (Summer 1979): 237–44; and Marks and de Courtivron, *New French Feminisms*, in particular the third introductory essay, "Contexts of the New French Feminisms"; and Claire Duchen, *Feminism in France* (London: Routledge & Kegan Paul, 1986).

22. While we could read this as reproduction through hearsay, it is also worth noting the allusion to Rabelais's Gargantua, who is born out of his mother's left ear.

23. *Écriture féminine* is a term developed and debated early within the French feminist context. Among its ardent representatives are Hélène Cixous, Annie Leclerc, and Luce Irigaray. It suggests an inscription of the female body into the written text and is characterized by a fluid, non-linear, fragmentary discourse. Some of the essays in Marks and de Courtivron, *New French Feminisms* are exemplary of *écriture féminine*.

24. The theoretical position of French materialist feminism is best represented in the journal which first began publication as *Questions féministes* (*Feminist Issues* in an English-language edition) in the summer of 1980. This essay appeared in vol. 1, no. 2 (Winter 1981). It has since become *Nouvelles Questions Féministes* (*New Feminist Issues*) and is now published sporadically, to the best of my knowledge.

25. Maïté Albistur and Daniel Armogathe, *Histoire du féminisme français*, 2 vols. (Paris: Des femmes, 1977). Des femmes, a publishing

house for the politics and psychoanalysis women's group, published this history and simultaneously repudiated it as a reformist work.

26. Alice Jardine, in *Gynesis* (Ithaca: Cornell University Press, 1985), has taken another perspective and given a name, gynesis, to a process whereby the masters have transformed "woman and the feminine into verbs," a valorization "intrinsic to the condition of modernity."

27. Joanna Russ, "When We Were Everybody," review of *Herland*, by Charlotte Perkins Gilman, *New Women's Times Feminist Review* 6–19 July 1979, 10–11.

28. Erika Ostrovsky, "A Cosmogony of O," in *Twentieth Century French Fiction*, ed. George Stambolian (New Brunswick, N.J.: Rutgers University Press, 1975).

29. Fredric Jameson, "Introduction/Prospectus," *Minnesota Review* n.s. 6 (Spring 1976): 53–58.

Chapter 2

1. Joanna Russ, *The Female Man* (New York: Bantam Books, 1975), and Marge Piercy, *Woman on the Edge of Time* (New York: Fawcett Crest Books, 1976). In an earlier novel, *Dance the Eagle to Sleep* (New York: Doubleday, 1970), Piercy sketched a short-lived adolescent utopia of warrior tribes in the middle of Manhattan who organize a city-wide high school strike, and whose practices combine the rhetoric of student revolution and native American ritual.

2. In *S/Z* (New York: Hill & Wang, 1974) Roland Barthes makes the distinction between the readerly text (like Piercy's) in which "everything holds together" and operates by "attaching narrated events together with a kind of logical 'paste'" and the writerly text (like Russ's), where plurality and contradiction in the narrative fabric make it impossible to answer the question of who is speaking? (pp. 140, 156).

3. Erich Auerbach, *Mimesis* (New York: Doubleday, Anchor Press, 1957).

4. Rachel Blau DuPlessis, "The Feminist Apologues of Lessing, Piercy, and Russ," *Frontiers* 4, no. 1 (Spring 1979): 1–8. DuPlessis also does an extremely detailed reading of the names given to characters by Piercy and Russ.

5. Sigmund Freud, "Femininity," in *The Standard Edition*, vol. 23 (London: Hogarth Press, 1964), p. 132.

6. Joanna Russ, "When It Changed," in *The New Women of Wonder*, ed. Pamela Sargent (New York: Random House, Vintage Books, 1978), pp. 227–39.

7. In Samuel R. Delany's introduction to Russ's collection of early stories, *Alyx* (Boston: Gregg Press, 1976), he relates the reason given for

the editorial decision to change the title of Russ's first novel from *Picnic in Paradise* to *Picnic on Paradise*: "so people would know it was science fiction. Otherwise they might think it was a romance" (p. xxii).

8. Darko Suvin, "On the Poetics of the Science Fiction Genre," *College English* 34, no. 3 (Dec. 1972): p. 377.

9. Bertolt Brecht, *Brecht on Theatre*, trans. and ed. John Willett (New York: Hill & Wang, 1964), p. 204.

10. Ibid., p. 194.

11. Joanna Russ, "Towards an Aesthetic of Science Fiction," *Science Fiction Studies* 2, pt. 2, no. 6 (July 1975): 112–19.

12. Ken Kesey, *One Flew Over the Cuckoo's Nest* (New York: Signet Books, 1962).

13. Quoted in Joan B. Landes, "Marcuse's Feminist Dimension," *Telos*, no. 41 (Fall 1979): 158–65.

14. For a more recent apocalyptic reading of this split written in a feminist framework, see Dorothy Dinnerstein, *The Mermaid and the Minotaur* (New York: Harper & Row, Colophon Books, 1977).

15. This easily learned "pan-speech" is reminiscent of the efforts of the seventeenth-century Christian utopians (especially Leibniz) in their search for a universal character to provide a means of communication that would eliminate argument and discord; see Manuel and Manuel, *Utopian Thought*, pp. 392–410.

16. Pp. 104–5. Piercy's decision to treat childbirth via technology takes up the proposal of Shulamith Firestone in *The Dialectic of Sex* (New York: Morrow, 1970), who also equated technological advancement in reproductive techniques with an end to sexual hierarchy and oppression. Firestone, however, saw childbearing as one of the primary sources of women's oppression, not a source of power as Piercy suggests. Here Piercy also replies to the reductive technology of Aldous Huxley's *Brave New World*.

17. Veronica Beechey, "On Patriarchy," *Feminist Review*, no. 3 (1979): 66–82.

18. Ibid., p. 78.

19. Felicity Edholm, Olivia Harris, and Kate Young, "Conceptualizing Women," *Critique of Anthropology* 9 and 10, vol. 3, cited in Beechey, "On Patriarchy."

20. P. 99. This Whileawayan saying finds its way into Monique Wittig's most recent work, coauthored with Sande Zeig, *Lesbian Peoples*, under the entry for "house." The authors speak of the desire to feel at home while not necessarily wanting to settle down. The phrase makes an appearance in the last line of "Bloomingdale's III" in Marilyn Hacker's most recent book of poems, *Love, Death, and the Changing of the Seasons*

(New York: Arbor, 1986). This kind of travel between texts is part of what Elaine Marks has named "Lesbian Intertextuality" in her ground-breaking essay in *Homosexualities in French Literature,* ed. George Stambolian and Elaine Marks (Ithaca: Cornell University Press, 1979), pp. 353–77.

21. Richard Gerber, *Utopian Fantasy* (London: Routledge & Kegan Paul, 1955), p. 47.

22. Juliet Mitchell, *Psychoanalysis and Feminism* (New York: Random House, Vintage Books, 1975), and Gayle Rubin, "The Traffic in Women: Notes on the 'Political Economy' of Sex," in *Toward an Anthropology of Women,* ed. Rayna Reiter (New York: Monthly Review Press, 1975), pp. 157–210. It is to these feminist critics that we must look for such rereadings. Both Mitchell and Rubin work with and against the "fit" between Freud and Lévi-Strauss.

Chapter 3

1. At a conference at Indiana University of Pennsylvania in October 1987, Charnas was a keynote speaker as was Marge Piercy. Charnas spoke of the exhilarating environment at science fiction conferences in the 1970s as each year the women present began to demand rooms and panels of their own. Such settings aided the genesis of what was at first to be one novel called *The Boyhouse Book* and which became instead the first of these two volumes.

2. In a short novel called *The Eye of the Heron* in *Millennial Women,* ed. Virginia Kidd (New York: Dell, 1978), Ursula LeGuin names one of her characters Holdfast. Whether or not the intertextual reference is intended it is noteworthy that LeGuin's emphasis in the name differs from Charnas's. Whereas Charnas's usage comes to be seen as a name given by men clinging to control and fearful of change and what lies beyond their territorial borders, LeGuin's character is one who continues against great odds to struggle against tyranny and domination.

3. In *Writing Degree Zero* (Boston: Beacon Press, 1967), p. 26. Roland Barthes speaks of the eternally repressive content of the word "order."

4. Hélène Cixous, "The Laugh of the Medusa," *Signs* 1, no. 4 (Summer 1976): 875–93.

5. Sigmund Freud, *Totem and Taboo,* in *The Standard Edition,* vol. 13 (London: Hogarth Press, 1950), p. 142.

6. Sigmund Freud, "Dostoevsky and Parricide," *The Standard Edition,* vol. 21 (London: Hogarth Press, 1964), p. 183.

7. Rachel Blau DuPlessis, "The Feminist Apologues," pp. 1–8 DuPlessis says, "Raising the issue of the future is a way of trying to write be-

yond the ending, especially as that ending has functioned in the classic novel: as closure of historical movement and therefore as the end of development." This article has since been revised and appears as the final chapter in DuPlessis's book *Writing beyond the Ending* (Bloomington: Indiana University Press, 1985).

8. Charnas is one of several respondents included in a special issue of *Frontiers*, "Fantasy and Futures," in the article entitled, "Dear Frontiers: Letters from Women Fantasy and Science Fiction Writers," *Frontiers* 2, no. 3 (Fall 1977): pp. 64–68; as recently as October 1987 she tells of the difficulty of bringing the men and women together for a "reconquest" in the form of a finished trilogy (in a paper presented at the conference "Women in the Future," Indiana University of Pennsylvania).

9. Cixous, "Laugh of the Medusa," p. 885.

10. Pp. 245–46 This image of survivors stalking one another seems to have led Charnas not to the promised third novel of this trilogy but to a modern gothic, *The Vampire Tapestry* (New York: Simon & Schuster, 1980).

11. Lynn Murphy, "Prophets of the Futurepast," review of *Walk to the End of the World* and *Motherlines,* in *Body Politic,* no. 65 (Aug. 1980): 29–30. Murphy makes this useful and necessary distinction.

12. Helen Diner, *Mothers and Amazons,* trans. John Philip Lundin (New York: Doubleday, Anchor Press, 1965).

13. Georg Lukács, *The Theory of the Novel,* trans. Anna Bostock (Cambridge, Mass.: MIT Press, 1971), p. 72.

Chapter 4

1. Christiane Rochefort, *Archaos, ou le jardin étincelant,* rev. ed. (Paris: Bernard Grasset, 1972); all page references are to the revised paperback edition and all translations are my own; E. M. Broner, *A Weave of Women* (New York: Holt, Rinehart & Winston, 1978).

2. P. 7. In the theoretical interlude on the subject of time travel, Russ cautions her readers that the "past one visits is never one's own Past"; similarly we are warned that the utopian future she projects is not our own.

3. The phrase suggests the same image, one inside the other—like nested boxes—but two-dimensional.

4. The cry that cannot be stilled at Govan's birth is the first indication that Rochefort is borrowing from the Egyptian mythology surrounding the story of Osiris and Isis; see, for example, Veronica Ions, *Egyptian Mythology* (Middlesex: Hamlyn House, 1965).

5. Lucy McCallum Schwartz, "Christiane Rochefort: Garden of Pleasure" (paper presented at the Annual Meeting of the Midwest Mod-

ern Language Association, Indianapolis, Nov. 1979). The term "obscene paradise" is Schwartz's; she also discusses the etymology and punning on names in Rochefort's text.

6. E. M. Broner, fiction reading (Women's Studies Program Lecture Series, University of Iowa, Iowa City, Nov. 1979). The politics of space and housing is a very charged issue in the context of Israeli-Palestinian relations. In Broner's novel there is a recurring mention of interior space—the indoors is safe, while the outdoors is not. This can be taken as a particular aspect of the gendering of space: the feminine, the inner; it also marks, however, a turn away from the political "now" of Israeli occupation of territory to an imagined "not-yet" where it becomes possible to separate gender from the politics of race. The domestic space of women is the territory under fire, while the "outside" conflict over the "homeland" with its expropriation of Palestinian property is repeatedly effaced in Broner's focus on feminist issues.

7. A thorough treatment of this dialectic may be found in Manuel and Manuel, *Utopian Thought*. Now that Bloch's *Principle of Hope* is available in a complete English translation, readers will also find there the intricate work of a utopian thinker who reintegrates the mystical and the messianic into his Marxism, since it is a mobile, dynamic, and concrete formulation of the utopian and thus is forward-looking.

8. Mary Daly, *Gyn/Ecology* (Boston: Beacon Press, 1978).

9. It is in the work of Jacques Derrida and feminist deconstructionists that one may find the most radical questioning and unfolding of such paired oppositions, and the ways in which they always serve the needs of patriarchal or masculinist thinking.

10. Gaston Bachelard, *The Poetics of Space,* trans. Maria Jolas (New York: Orion Press, 1964), p. 6.

11. Rochefort's doubling of incestuous twins may echo the giant twins (Olyphant and Argantè) of Spenser's *Faerie Queene* 3.7. 37ff. (esp. 48–50).

12. The "convent in Trémènes" recalls Rabelais's "abbey of Thélème" in vol. 1 of *Gargantua,* where the only rule to be observed was "Do what thou wilt."

13. Broner's narrative of Hava's death suggests a feminist rewriting of Albert Camus's *The Stranger,* where a white man kills an Arab on the beach under the desert sun. It is problematic in its own way, which is an ahistorical representation of the "prince" and his friend of "evil counsel"-cum-terrorist who kills a female child.

14. In *Daughters of Rachel* (London: Penguin Books, 1979), Natalie Rein discusses what became known as the Hilton Affair in the history of the women's movement in Israel. Eleven women, including Marcia Freed-

man, feminist and Parliament member, interrupted the convention of the Society of Gynecologists and Obstetricians which took place in June 1976 at the Hilton Hotel in Tel Aviv. Rein describes this as "the most important single event of the whole five years of feminist activity," because it brought to public attention and debate abortion reform and spouse abuse in a setting where the racial aspects of Israeli pro-natalism often go unremarked.

15. See Toril Moï, "L'Utopie féminine" (Ph.D. diss., University of Bergen, Norway, 1980). Moï studies Rochefort in the context of Herbert Marcuse's *Eros and Civilization*, which concentrates on the split between work and play in capitalist societies; she also points out quite clearly the connection between Rochefort's utopia and that of William Morris in *News from Nowhere*, in which work is idealized as artisanship.

Chapter 5

1. Margaret Atwood, *The Handmaid's Tale* (Boston: Houghton Mifflin, 1986).

2. Louky Bersianik, *L'Eugélionne* (Ottawa: Editions de la Presse, 1976; and Paris: Hachette, 1978); *The Eugélionne*, trans. Gerry Denis, Alison Hewitt, Donna Murray, and Martha O'Brien (Victoria: Press Porcépic, 1981).

3. Bell Hooks, *Feminist Theory: From Margin to Center* (Boston: South End Press, 1984). In her preface Hooks declares that the "oppositional world view" she holds as an African American woman is "unknown to most of our oppressors." Knowing the gaps and needs of feminist theory, she suggests that "at its most visionary, it will emerge from individuals who have knowledge of both margin and center." I am making the analogy here to Canadian women writers.

4. Adrienne Rich, *On Lies, Secrets, and Silence* (New York: Norton, 1979). Though it would reduce the complexity of their arguments, it is possible to think of early U.S. feminist theory focusing on the silencing of women by and in history, whereas the French feminists developed the strategy of stealing the language of patriarchy. See in this context Hélène Cixous and Catherine Clément, *La Jeune Née* (Paris: 10/18, 1975), published in English as *The Newly Born Woman*, trans. Betsy Wing (Minneapolis: University of Minnesota Press, 1986); and Claudine Herrmann, *Les Voleuses de langue* (Paris: Des femmes, 1976), to be published in English as *The Tongue Snatchers,* trans. Nancy Kline (Lincoln: University of Nebraska Press, 1989). The handmaid feels herself to be subject to and a subject of both these strategies of silence and subversion.

5. There are also what may be allusions here to Luce Irigaray's essay "The Looking Glass, from the Other Side," which opens the collection

This Sex Which Is Not One (Ithaca: Cornell University Press, 1985), and which first appeared in French in 1973. Like the Eugélionne, who has doubled sight, one sad eye, one gay, Irigaray's Alice (based on a film text) has eyes both blue and red: "eyes that recognize the right side, the wrong side, and the other side." Lucien, a surveyor, and Alice have a relationship "in the zone of the 'not-yet.'" It is a question of missing identity, a missing subject whom Irigaray names with resignation "Alice underground."

6. Simone de Beauvoir, *The Ethics of Ambiguity*, trans. Bernard Frechtman (New York: Citadel Press, 1948); Carol Gilligan, *In a Different Voice* (Cambridge, Mass.: Harvard University Press, 1982); Luce Irigarary, *Ethique de la différence sexuelle* (Paris: Minuit, 1984). In an effort to engage these emerging ethical issues, see also my article "The Question of Ethics in French Feminism," *Berkshire Review* 21 (1986): 22–29.

7. Jessica Benjamin, "A Desire of One's Own: Psychoanalytic Feminism and Intersubjective Space," in *Feminist Studies/Critical Studies*, ed. Teresa de Lauretis (Bloomington: Indiana University Press, 1986), pp. 78–101; see also Benjamin's *The Bonds of Love: Psychoanalysis, Feminism and the Problem of Domination* (New York: Pantheon Books, 1988).

8. This could also be amply documented in the work of feminist film theorists on the look and the specular. While my work in this book takes up the question of the look, it is not primarily in the context of women as objects of the male gaze, women as spectacle. Rather, I am interested in locating precisely the workings of intersubjectivity in the readings of recognition scenes between women. When women recognize themselves and each other in the eyes of other women, another relation to seeing and being seen can be written, a relation of recognition, not one of domination. This is not the place to take up the theoretical problems put into play by such a proposal. This work is being done as feminist film theorists take up the question of female spectatorship. See, for example, Teresa de Lauretis, *Alice Doesn't* (Bloomington: Indiana University Press, 1984); Jacqueline Rose, *Sexuality in the Field of Vision* (London: Verso, 1986); and two articles by Judith Mayne, "Feminist Film Theory and Criticism," *Signs* 11, no. 1 (1985): 81–100, and "Feminist Film Theory and Women at the Movies," *Profession* 87: 13–19.

9. Michel Foucault, *Discipline and Punishment*, trans. Alan Sheridan(New York: Random House, Vintage Books, 1977), p. 161.

10. Margaret Atwood, *Murder in the Dark* (Toronto: Coach House Press, 1983). See also my article "A Fearful Fancy," on Atwood's and Roland Barthes's sublime, *Boundary* 2 6, no. 2 (1986).

11. Luce Irigaray, *Ethique de la différence sexuelle* (Paris: Minuit, 1984). In April 1987 a discussion of an earlier version of this chapter with the feminist theory reading group at the University of Pittsburgh led me to consider how a number of the French feminists as well as Atwood and Bersianik open the space of the in-between to theory. In terms of knowing the center from the margins it seems worth noting the split in national and ethnic identities of a number of feminist theorists and writers: Bersianik and Atwood are from French-and-English-speaking Canada, respectively; Irigaray is of Basque heritage; Cixous is an Algerian Jew; Kristeva transplanted from Bulgaria to France.

12. Margaret Atwood, *Second Words* (Boston: Beacon Press, 1984).

Afterword

1. Catherine A. MacKinnon, "Feminism, Marxism, Method, and the State" part 1, *Signs* 7, no. 3 (Spring 1982): 515–44; "Feminism, Marxism, Method, and the State," part 2, *Signs* 8, no. 4 (Summer 1983): 635–58. This is not intended to be either a full implementation or critique of MacKinnon's call to place the state on the agenda for feminist theory. However, I think, for obvious reasons, these fictions are very rich sources for how feminist discourse might engage such an agenda under more self-determined conditions, imaginary though they may be.

2. The following list of works on the new reproductive technologies is necessarily incomplete, since much of this work is not yet in print: Barbara Katz Rothman, *The Tentative Pregnancy* (New York: Penguin Books, 1986); Rita Arditti, Renate Duelli-Klein, and Shelley Minden, eds., *Test Tube Women* (Boston: Pandora Press, 1984); Gena Corea, *The Mother Machine* (New York: Harper & Row, 1985); Emily Martin, *The Woman in the Body,* (Boston: Beacon Press, 1987); Judith Lasker and Susan Borg, *In Search of Parenthood* (Boston: Beacon Press, 1987); Rosalind Pollack Petchesky, "Fetal Images," *Feminist Studies* 13, no. 2 (Summer 1987), and other articles in this issue; Michelle Harrison, "Social Construction of Mary Beth Whitehead," and Barbara Katz Rothman, "Comment on Harrison," *Gender and Society* 1, no. 3 (Sept. 1987); the forthcoming first issue of *Differences: A Journal of Feminist Cultural Studies,* on "Life and Death in Sexuality," to be published by Indiana University Press.

3. Donna Haraway, "A Manifesto for Cyborgs," *Socialist Review* 15, no. 2 (Mar.–Apr. 1985): 65–107; if my own work here were to be extended over even more time, the theoretical implications and vast bibliographical supports of Haraway's essay would set out some of the boundaries and directions to explore.

Bibliography

Albistur, Maïté, and Daniel Armogathe. *Histoire du féminisme français: Du moyen âge à nos jours.* 2 vols. Paris: des femmes, 1977.

Anderson, Susan Janice, and Vonda N. McIntyre, eds. *Aurora: Beyond Equality.* Greenwich, Conn.: Fawcett, 1976.

Annas, Pamela J. "New Worlds, New Words: Androgyny in Feminist Science Fiction." *Science Fiction Studies* 5, pt. 2, no. 15 (July 1978): 143–56.

Arditti, Rita, Renate Duelli-Klein, and Shelley Minden, eds. *Test Tube Women: What Future for Motherhood?* Boston: Pandora Press, 1984.

Atwood, Margaret. *Murder in the Dark: Short Fictions and Prose Poems.* Toronto: Coach House Press, 1983.

—. *Second Words.* Boston: Beacon Press, 1984.

—. *The Handmaid's Tale.* Boston: Houghton Mifflin, 1986.

Auerbach, Erich. *Mimesis: The Representation of Reality in Western Literature.* Translated by Willard Trask. New York: Doubleday, Anchor Press, 1957.

Auerbach, Nina. *Communities of Women: An Idea in Fiction.* Cambridge, Mass.: Harvard University Press, 1978.

Bachelard, Gaston. *The Poetics of Space.* Translated by Maria Jolas. New York: Orion Press, 1964.

Barr, Marleen S. *Future Females: A Critical Anthology.* Bowling Green, Ohio: Bowling Green State University Popular Press, 1981.

Barr, Marleen S., and Nicholas D. Smith, eds. *Women and Utopia: Critical Interpretations.* Landham, Md.: University Press of America, 1983.

Barr, Marleen S., and Patrick D. Murphy, eds. "Feminism Faces the Fantastic." Special issue of *Women's Studies,* forthcoming.

Barthes, Roland. "The Lesson." Translated by Richard Howard. *October* no. 8 (Spring 1979): 3–16.

—. *S/Z.* Translated by Richard Miller. New York: Hill & Wang, 1974.

—. *Writing Degree Zero.* Translated by Annette Lavers and Colin Smith. Boston: Beacon Press, 1967.

Bartkowski, Frances. "A Fearful Fancy: Reconsiderations of the Sublime." *Boundary* 2, 6, 2 (1986).

—. "The Question of Ethics in French Feminism." *Berkshire Review* 21 (1986): 22–29.

Baruch, Elaine. " 'A Natural and Necessary Monster': Women in Utopia." *Alternative Futures* 2, no. 1 (Winter 1979): 29–48.

Beard, George Miller. *American Nervousness.* New York: G. P. Putnam, 1881.

Bebel, August. *Women: Past, Present, and Future.* New York: Boni & Liveright, 1918.

—. *Women under Socialism.* Translated by Daniel De Leon. 1904. Reprint. New York: Schocken Books, 1971.

Beecher, Jonathan, and Richard Bienvenu, eds. *The Utopian Vision of Charles Fourier.* Boston: Beacon Press, 1971.

Beechey, Veronica. "On Patriarchy." *Feminist Review,* no. 3 (1979): 66–82.

Bellamy, Edward. *Looking Backward,* 2000–1887. New York: Modern Library, 1917.

Benjamin, Walter. *Illuminations.* Translated by Harry Zohn. New York: Schocken Books, 1969.

Bersianik, Louky. *L'Eugélionne.* Ottawa: Editions de la Presse, 1976; and Paris: Hachette, 1978. Translated by Gerry Davis, Alison Hewitt, Donna Murray, and Martha O'Brien, under the title *The Eugélionne.* Victoria, B.C.: Press Porcépic, 1981.

Bloch, Ernst. "Dialectics and Hope." Translated by Mark Ritter. *New German Critique,* no. 9 (Fall 1976): 3–10.

—. *Man on His Own: Essays in the Philosophy of Religion.* Translated by E. B. Ashton. New York: Herder & Herder, 1970.

—. *On Karl Marx.* Translated by John Maxwell. New York: Herder & Herder, 1971.

—. *A Philosophy of the Future.* Translated by John Cumming. New York: Herder & Herder, 1970.

—. *Le Principe espérance.* Vol. I, pts. 1–3. Translated by François Wuilmart. Paris: Gallimard, 1976.

—. *Das Princip Hoffnung.* 3 vols. Frankfurt: Suhrkamp, 1959.

—. *The Principle of Hope.* 3 vols. Translated by Neville Plaice, Stephen Plaice, and Paul Knight. Cambridge, Mass.: MIT Press, 1986.

—. *Spuren.* Frankfurt: Suhrkamp, 1959.

—. *Traces.* Translated by Pierre Quillet and Hans Hildenbrand. Paris: Gallimard, 1968.

Brecht, Bertolt. *Brecht on Theatre.* Translated and edited by John Willett. New York: Hill & Wang, 1964.

Broner, E. M. *A Weave of Women.* New York: Holt, Rinehart & Winston, 1978.

Brown, Norman O. *Love's Body*. New York: Random House, Vintage Books, 1966.

Bryant, Dorothy. *The Kin of Ata Are Waiting for You*. New York: Random House, 1976; Berkeley: Moon Books, 1976.

Burke, Carolyn Greenstein. "Report from Paris: Women's Writing and the Women's Movement." *Signs* 3, no. 4 (Summer 1978): 843–55.

Burton, Gabrielle. *Heartbreak Hotel*. New York: Scribner's, 1986.

Charcot, Jean Martin. *Lectures on the Diseases of the Nervous System*. Translated by George Sigerson. New York: Hafner, 1962.

Charnas, Suzy McKee. *Motherlines*. New York: Berkeley Books, 1978.

—. *The Vampire Tapestry*. New York: Simon & Schuster, 1980.

—. *Walk to the End of the World*. New York: Berkeley Books, 1974.

Chernyshevsky, Nikolai G. *What Is to Be Done?: Tales about New People*. Translated by Benjamin R. Tucker. New York: Random House, Vintage Books, 1961.

Chodorow, Nancy. *The Reproduction of Mothering: Psychoanalysis and the Sociology of Gender*. Berkeley: University of California Press, 1978.

Cixous, Hélène. "The Laugh of the Medusa." Translated by Keith Cohen and Paula Cohen. *Signs* 1, no. 4 (Summer 1976): 875–93.

Cixous, Hélène and Catherine Clément. *La Jeune Née*. Paris: 10/18, 1975. Translated by Betsy Wing under the title *The Newly Born Woman*. Minneapolis: University of Minnesota Press, 1986.

Coming to Power: Writings and Graphics on Lesbian S/M. Rev. ed. Edited by Members of SAMOIS. Boston: Alyson Publications, 1982.

Comparative Literature Studies 10, no. 4 (Dec. 1973). Special issue, entitled "Utopian Thought in Literature and the Social Sciences." Edited by Herbert Knust.

Corea, Gena. *The Mother Machine: Reproductive Technologies from Artificial Insemination to Artificial Wombs*. New York: Harper & Row, 1985.

Daedalus 94, no. 2 (Spring 1965). Special issue entitled "Utopia."

Daly, Mary. *Gyn/Ecology: The Metaethics of Radical Feminism*. Boston: Beacon Press, 1978.

D'Eaubonne, Françoise. *Histoire et actualité du féminisme*. Paris: Alain Moreau, 1972.

De Beauvoir, Simone. *The Ethics of Ambiguity*. Translated by Bernard Frechtman. New York: Citadel Press, 1948.

—. *The Second Sex*. Translated by H. M. Parshley. New York: Bantam Books, 1961.

Delany, Samuel R. *The Jewel-Hinged Jaw: Notes on the Language of Science Fiction*. New York: Berkeley Books, 1977.

—. "The Order of Chaos." *Science Fiction Studies* 6, pt. 3, no. 19 (Nov. 1979): 333–36.

—. *Triton*. New York: Bantam Books, 1976.

De Lauretis, Teresa. *Alice Doesn't: Feminism, Semiotics, Cinema*. Bloomington: Indiana University Press, 1984.

—, ed. *Feminist Studies/Critical Studies*. Bloomington: Indiana University Press, 1986.

Derrida, Jacques. *Of Grammatology*. Translated by Gayatri Chakravorty Spivak. Baltimore: Johns Hopkins University Press, 1976.

Desroche, Henri. *Les Dieux rêvés: Théisme et athéisme en utopie*. Paris: Desclée, 1972.

Diner, Helen. *Mothers and Amazons: The First Feminine History of Culture*. Translated by John Philip Lundin. New York: Doubleday, Anchor Press, 1965.

Dinnerstein, Dorothy. *The Mermaid and the Minotaur: Sexual Arrangements and Human Malaise*. New York: Harper & Row, Colophon Books, 1976.

Le Discours utopique. Proceedings of Colloquium at Cerisy-la-Salle, France, 23 July – 1 Aug. 1975. Paris: 10/18, 1978.

Dowst, Kenneth I., "The Rhetoric of Utopian Fiction." Ph.D. dissertation, University of Pittsburgh, 1979.

Duchen, Claire. *Feminism in France: From May '68 to Mitterrand*. London: Routledge & Kegan Paul, 1986.

DuPlessis, Rachel Blau. "The Feminist Apologues of Lessing, Piercy, and Russ." *Frontiers* 4, no. 1 (Spring 1979): 1–8.

—. *Writing beyond the Ending: Narrative Strategies of Twentieth-Century Women Writers*. Bloomington: Indiana University Press, 1985.

Ehrenreich, Barbara, and Deirdre English. *For Her Own Good: 150 Years of the Experts' Advice to Women*. New York: Doubleday, Anchor Press, 1979.

Eisenstein, Zillah R., ed. *Capitalist Patriarchy and the Case for Socialist Feminism*. New York: Monthly Review Press, 1979.

—. *The Radical Future of Liberal Feminism*. New York: Longman, 1981.

Elliott, Robert C. *The Shape of Utopia: Studies in a Literary Genre*. Chicago: University of Chicago Press, 1970.

Ellman, Mary. *Thinking about Women*. New York: Harcourt, Brace & World, 1968.

Engels, Frederick. *The Origins of the Family, Private Property, and the State*. New York: Pathfinder Press, 1972.

—. *Socialism Utopian and Scientific*. New York: International Publishers, 1935.

Evans, Sara. *Personal Politics: The Roots of Women's Liberation in the Civil Rights Movement and the New Left.* New York: Knopf, 1979.

Extrapolation 19, no. 1 (Dec. 1977). Special issue, entitled "Special Utopias Issue."

Feminist Issues 1. no. 1 (Summer 1980); and following issues.

Firestone, Shulamith. *The Dialectic of Sex: The Case for Feminist Revolution.* New York: Morrow, 1970.

Forerunner 1–7 (1909–1916). New York: Greenwood Reprint, 1968.

Foucault, Michel. *Surveiller et punir: Naissance de la prison.* Paris: Gallimard, 1979. Translated by Alan Sheridan under the title *Discipline and Punishment: The Birth of the Prison.* New York: Random House, Vintage Books, 1977.

Fourier, Charles. *Théorie des quatre mouvements et des destinées générales.* Paris: Jean Jacques Pauvert, 1967.

Freud, Sigmund. *The Standard Edition.* 24 vols. Translated by James Strachey. London: Hogarth Press, 1953–1974.

Frontiers 2, no. 3 (Fall 1977). Special issue, entitled "Fantasy and Futures."

Gearhart, Sally Miller. *The Wanderground: Stories of the Hill Women.* Watertown, Mass.: Persephone Press, 1978.

Gerber, Richard. *Utopian Fantasy: A Study of English Utopian Fiction since the End of the Nineteenth Century.* London: Routledge & Kegan Paul, 1955.

Gilligan, Carol. *In a Different Voice: Psychological Theory and Women's Development.* Cambridge, Mass.: Harvard University Press, 1982.

Gilman, Charlotte Perkins. *Herland.* New York: Pantheon Books, 1979.

—. *The Living of Charlotte Perkins Gilman.* New York: Harper & Row, Colophon Books, 1975.

—. *Women and Economics.* New York: Harper & Row, Torchbooks, 1966.

—. "The Yellow Wallpaper." In *The Charlotte Perkins Gilman Reader.* New York: Pantheon Books, 1980.

Gordon, Linda. "The Struggle for Reproductive Freedom: Three Stages of Feminism." In *Capitalist Patriarchy and the Case for Socialist Feminism.* Edited by Zillah R. Eisenstein. New York: Monthly Review Press, 1979.

Gross, David. "Marxism and Utopia: Ernst Bloch." In *Towards a New Marxism.* Edited by Bart Grahl and Paul Piccone. St. Louis: Telos Press, 1973.

Gubar, Susan. "C. L. Moore and the Conventions of Women's Science Fiction." Paper presented at the Annual Meeting of the Midwest Modern Language Association, Indianapolis, 7 Nov. 1979.

Hacker, Marilyn. "Science Fiction and Feminism: The Work of Joanna Russ." *Chrysalis,* no. 4 (1977): 67–79.

Haraway, Donna. "A Manifesto for Cyborgs: Science, Technology and Socialist Feminism in the 1980's." *Socialist Review* 80, vol. 15, no. 2 (Mar.–Apr. 1985): 65–105.

Harrison, Michelle. "Social Construction of Mary Beth Whitehead." *Gender and Society* 1, no. 3 (Sept. 1987).

Hartsock, Nancy. "Fundamental Feminism: Process and Perspective." *Quest: A Feminist Quarterly* 2, no. 2 (Fall 1975): 67–80.

Hays, H. R. *The Dangerous Sex: The Myth of Feminine Evil.* New York: Putnam's, 1964.

Herrmann, Claudine. *Voleuses de langue.* Paris: Des femmes, 1975.

Hertzler, Joyce Oramel. *The History of Utopian Thought.* New York: Macmillan, 1923.

Hirsh, Marianne, Mary Jean Green, and Lynn Anthony Higgins. "An Interview with Christiane Rochefort." *L'Esprit Créateur* 19, no. 2 (Summer 1979): 107–20.

Holquist, Michael. "How to Play Utopia." In *Game, Play, Literature.* Edited by Jacques Ehrmann. Boston: Beacon Press, 1971.

Huizinga, Johan. *Homo Ludens: A Study of the Play Element in Culture.* Boston: Beacon Press, 1950.

Huston, Nancy. "French Feminism." *Camera Obscura,* no. 3–4 (Summer 1979), 237–44.

Huxley, Aldous. *Island.* New York: Harper & Brothers, 1962.

Ions, Veronica. *Egyptian Mythology.* Middlesex: Hamlyn House, 1965.

Irigaray, Luce. *Ce Sexe qui n'en est pas un.* Paris: Minuit, 1977. Translated by Catherine Porter under the title *This Sex Which Is Not One.* Ithaca: Cornell University Press, 1985.

—. *Ethique de la différence sexuelle.* Paris: Minuit, 1984.

—. *Speculum de l'autre femme.* Paris: Minuit, 1974. Translated by Catherine Porter under the title *Speculum of the Other Woman.* Ithaca: Cornell University Press, 1985.

Jameson, Fredric. "Introduction/Prospectus: To Consider the Relationship of Marxism to Utopian Thought." *Minnesota Review,* n.s. 6 (Spring 1976): 53–58.

—. *Marxism and Form: Twentieth Century Dialectical Theories of Literature.* Princeton: Princeton University Press, 1971.

—. "Of Islands and Trenches: Naturalizations and the Production of Utopian Discourse." *Diacritics* 7, no. 2 (Summer 1977): 2–21.

—. *The Political Unconscious: Narrative as a Socially Symbolic Act.* London: Methuen, 1981.

Jardine, Alice. *Gynesis: Configurations of Woman and Modernity.* Ithaca: Cornell University Press, 1985.

Jenness, Linda, ed. *Feminism and Socialism.* New York: Pathfinder Press, 1972.

Johnston, Mary. *Sweet Rocket.* New York: Harper & Brothers, 1920.

Kateb, George, ed. *Utopia.* New York: Atherton Press, 1971.

Kellner, Douglas, and Harry O'Hara. "Utopia and Marxism in Ernst Bloch." *New German Critique*, no. 9 (Fall 1976), 11–34.

Kesey, Ken. *One Flew Over the Cuckoo's Nest.* New York: Signet Books, 1962.

Kessler, Carol Farley, ed. *Daring to Dream: Utopian Stories by United States Women, 1836–1919.* Boston: Pandora Press, 1984.

Key, Ellen. *The Woman Movement.* Translated by Mamah Bouton Borthwick. New York: Putnam's, 1912.

Kidd, Virginia, ed. *Millennial Women.* New York: Dell, 1978.

Koedt, Anne, Ellen Levine, and Anita Rapone, eds. *Radical Feminism.* New York: Quadrangle Books, 1973.

Kress, Susan. "Politics of Time and Space: The Utopian Vision in *Woman on the Edge of Time*." Paper presented at the Annual Meeting of the Modern Language Association, San Francisco, 27 Dec. 1979.

Kristeva, Julia. "Women's Time." Translated and introduced by Alice Jardine. *Signs* 7, no. 1 (Autumn 1981). Special issue, entitled "French Feminist Theory."

Lakoff, Robin. *Language and Woman's Place.* New York: Harper & Row, Colophon Books, 1975.

Landes, Joan B. "Marcuse's Feminist Dimension." *Telos*, no. 41 (Fall 1979): 158–65.

Lane, Mary E. Bradley. *Mizora: A Prophesy.* 1890. Reprint. Boston: Gregg Press, 1975.

Lasker, Judith. *In Search of Parenthood: Coping with Infertility and High-Tech Conception.* Boston: Beacon Press, 1987.

Lasky, Melvin J. *Utopia and Revolution.* Chicago: University of Chicago Press, 1976.

Leclerc, Annie. *Parole de femme.* Paris: Grasset, 1974.

LeGuin, Ursula, K. *The Dispossessed.* New York: Avon Books, 1974.

—. "Is Gender Necessary?" In *Aurora: Beyond Equality.* Edited by Susan Janice Anderson and Vonda McIntyre. Greenwich, Conn.: Fawcett, 1976.

—. *The Left Hand of Darkness.* New York: Ace Books, 1969.

Lessing, Doris May. *Canopus in Argos: Archives.* New York: Knopf, 1979.

Lipshitz, Susan, ed. *Tearing the Veil: Essays on Femininity*. London: Routledge & Kegan Paul, 1978.

Littérature, no. 21 (Feb. 1976). Special issue, entitled "Lieux de l'Utopie."

Lukács, Georg. *The Theory of the Novel*. Translated by Anna Bostock. Cambridge, Mass.: MIT Press, 1971.

Lyotard, Jean-François. "One of the Things at Stake in Women's Struggles." *Sub/Stance*, no. 20 (1978): 9–17.

Macherey, Pierre. *A Theory of Literary Production*. Translated by Geoffrey Wall. London: Routledge & Kegan Paul, 1978.

MacKinnon, Catherine. "Feminism, Marxism, Method, and the State: An Agenda for Theory." Part 1. *Signs* 7, no. 3 (Spring 1982): 515–44

—. "Feminism, Marxism, Method, and the State: Toward Feminist Jurisprudence." Part 2, *Signs* 8, no. 4 (Summer 1983): 635–58.

Mannheim, Karl. *Ideology and Utopia: An Introduction to the Sociology of Knowledge*. New York: Harcourt, 1936.

Manuel, Frank E., and Fritzie P. Manuel, eds. *French Utopias: An Anthology of Ideal Societies*. New York: Free Press, 1966.

—. *Utopian Thought in the Western World*. Cambridge Mass.: Harvard University Press, Belknap Press, 1979.

Marcuse, Herbert. *Eros and Civilization: A Philosophical Inquiry into Freud*. Boston: Beacon Press, 1966.

—. *Five Lectures: Psychoanalysis, Politics, and Utopia*. Translated by Jeremy J. Shapiro and Shierry M. Weber. Boston: Beacon Press, 1970.

Marin, Louis. *Utopiques: Jeux d'espaces*. Paris: Minuit, 1973.

Marks, Elaine. "Lesbian Intertextuality." In *Homosexualities and French Literature: Cultural Contexts/Critical Texts*. Edited by George Stambolian and Elaine Marks. Ithaca: Cornell University Press, 1979.

Marks, Elaine, and Isabelle de Courtivron, eds. *New French Feminisms*. Amherst: University of Massachusetts Press, 1980.

—. "Women and Literature in France." *Signs* 3, no. 4 (Summer 1978): 832–42.

Martin, Biddy. "Feminism, Criticism, and Foucault." *New German Critique*, no. 27 (Fall 1982): 3–31.

Martin, Emily. *The Woman in the Body: A Cultural Analysis of Reproduction*. Boston: Beacon Press, 1987.

Marx, Karl, and Frederick Engels. *The German Ideology*. Part 1. New York: Morrow, 1949.

Mayne, Judith. "Feminist Film Theory and Criticism." *Signs* 11, no. 1 (Autumn 1985): 81–100.

—. "Feminist Film Theory and Women at the Movies." *Profession 87*: 13–19.

Mellor, Anne K. "On Feminist Utopias." *Women's Studies* 9, no. 3 (1982): 241–62.

Millett, Kate. *Sexual Politics*. New York: Avon Books, 1969.

Minnesota Review, n.s. 6 (Spring 1976). Special section, entitled "Marxism and Utopia."

Mitchell, Juliet. *Psychoanalysis and Feminism*. New York: Random House, Vintage Books, 1975.

Moï, Toril. *Sexual/Textual Politics: Feminist Literary Theory*. London: Methuen, 1985.

—. "L'Utopie féminine: Une étude des romans utopiques de Christiane Rochefort." Ph.D. dissertation, University of Bergen, Norway, 1980.

More, Sir Thomas. *Utopia*. Translated by Ralph Robinson. London: Routledge & Kegan Paul, 1925.

Morgan, Robin, ed. *Sisterhood Is Powerful: An Anthology of Writings from the Women's Liberation Movement*. New York: Random House, Vintage Books, 1970.

Morris, William. *News from Nowhere; or, An Epoch of Rest*. 1890. Reprint. London: Routledge & Kegan Paul, 1970.

Morson, Gary Saul. *The Boundaries of Genre: Dostoevsky's Diary of a Writer and the Traditions of Literary Utopia*. Austin: University of Texas Press. 1981.

Moylan, Tom. *Demand the Impossible: Science Fiction and the Utopian Imagination*. New York: Methuen, 1986.

Mumford, Lewis. *The Story of Utopias*. New York: Viking Press, 1962.

Murphy, Lynn. "Prophets of the Futurepast." Review of *Walk to the End of the World* and *Motherlines*. *Body Politic*, no. 65 (Aug. 1980): 29–30.

Oakley, Ann. *Sex, Gender, and Society*. New York: Harper & Row, Colophon Books, 1972.

Ostrovsky, Erika. "A Cosmogony of O." In *Twentieth Century French Fiction: Essays for Germaine Brée*. Edited by George Stambolian. New Brunswick, N.J.: Rutgers University Press, 1975.

Pearson, Carol. "Women's Fantasies and Feminist Utopias." *Frontiers* 2, no. 3 (Fall 1977): 50–61.

Petitfils, Jean-Christian. *Les Socialismes utopiques*. Paris: Presses universitaires de France, 1977.

Petchesky, Rosalind Pollack. "Fetal Images: The Power of Visual Culture in the Politics of Reproduction." *Feminist Studies* 13, no. 2 (Summer 1987): 263–92.

Pfaelzer, Jean. "Feminism as Ideology: Women in American Utopias,

1880–1900." Paper presented at the Annual Meeting of the Modern Language Association, San Francisco, 27 Dec. 1979.

—. *The Utopian Novel in America, 1886–1896: The Politics of Form.* Pittsburgh: University of Pittsburgh Press, 1984.

Piercy, Marge. *Dance the Eagle to Sleep.* New York: Doubleday, 1970.

—. "The Grand Coolie Damn." In *Sisterhood Is Powerful.* Edited by Robin Morgan. New York: Random House, Vintage Books, 1970.

—. *Hard Loving.* Middletown, Conn.: Wesleyan University Press, 1970.

—. *Woman on the Edge of Time.* New York: Fawcett Crest Books, 1976.

Plato. *The Republic.* Translated by Desmond Lee. Baltimore: Penguin Books, 1974.

Plattel, Martin G. *Utopian and Critical Thinking.* Translated by Henry J. Koren. Pittsburgh: Duquesne University Press, 1972.

Plekhanov, Georgii V. *Utopian Socialism of the Nineteenth Century.* Translated by Julius Katzer. Moscow: Foreign Languages Publishing House, n.d.

Poster, Mark, ed. *Harmonian Man: Selected Writings of Charles Fourier.* Translated by Susan Hanson. New York: Doubleday, Anchor Press, 1971.

Rabkin, Eric S. "Atavism and Utopia." *Alternative Futures* 1, no. 1 (Spring 1978): 71–82.

Raulet, Gérard, ed. *Utopie-Marxisme selon Ernst Bloch: Un système de l'inconstructible.* Paris: Payot, 1976.

Raymond, Janice G. *The Transsexual Empire: The Making of the She-Male.* Boston: Beacon Press, 1979.

Reiche, Reimut. *Sexuality and Class Struggle.* New York: Praeger, 1971.

Rein, Natalie. *Daughters of Rachel: Women in Israel.* London: Penguin Books, 1979.

Rich, Adrienne. *On Lies, Secrets, and Silence: Selected Prose, 1966–1978.* New York: Norton, 1979.

Rochefort, Christiane. *Archaos, ou le jardin étincelant.* Revised ed. Paris: Bernard Grasset, 1972.

—. "J'ai perdu mes utopies." *Magazine Littéraire,* no. 139 (July–Aug. 1978): 42–43.

Roemer, Kenneth M. *The Obsolete Necessity: America in Utopian Writings, 1880–1900.* Kent, Ohio: Kent State University Press, 1976.

Rohrlich, Ruby, and Elaine Baruch, eds. *Women in Search of Utopias: Mavericks and Mythmakers.* New York: Schocken Books, 1984.

Rosaldo, Michelle Zimbalist, and Louise Lamphere, eds. *Women, Culture, and Society.* Stanford: Stanford University Press, 1974.

Rose, Hilary. "Dreaming the Future." *Hypatia* 5, no. 1 (Spring 1988): 119–37.

Rose, Jacqueline. *Sexuality in the Field of Vision.* London: Verso, 1986.

Rosinsky, Natalie M. *Feminist Futures: Contemporary Women's Speculative Fiction.* Ann Arbor: UMI Research Press, 1984.

Rothman, Barbara Katz. "Comment on Harrison: The Commodification of Motherhood." *Gender and Society* 1, no. 3 (Sept. 1987).

—.*The Tentative Pregnancy: Prenatal Diagnosis and the Future of Motherhood.* New York: Penguin Books, 1986.

Rowbotham, Sheila. *Women, Resistance, and Revolution: A History of Women and Revolution in the Modern World.* New York: Random House, Vintage Books, 1974.

—.*Women's Consciousness, Man's World.* London: Penguin Books, 1973.

Rubin, Gayle. "The Traffic in Women: Notes on the 'Political Economy' of Sex." In *Towards an Anthropology of Women.* Edited by Rayna Reiter. New York: Monthly Review Press, 1975.

Russ, Joanna. *Alyx.* Reprint. Boston: Gregg Press, 1976.

—. *Extra(ordinary) People.* New York: St. Martin's Press, 1984.

—. *The Female Man.* New York: Bantam Books, 1975.

—. *How to Suppress Women's Writing.* Austin: University of Texas Press, 1983.

—. "The Image of Women in Science Fiction." In *Images of Women in Fiction: Feminist Perspectives.* Edited by Susan Koppelman Cornillon. Bowling Green, Ohio: Bowling Green University Popular Press, 1972.

—. *Magic Mommas, Trembling Sisters, Puritans, and Parents: Feminist Essays.* Trumansberg, N.Y.: Crossing Press, 1985.

—. "Reflection on Science Fiction: An Interview." *Quest: A Feminist Quarterly* 2, no. 1 (Summer 1975): 40–49.

—. "SF and Technology as Mystification." *Science Fiction Studies* 5, pt. 3, no. 16 (Nov. 1978): 250–60.

—. "The Subjunctivity of Science Fiction." *Extrapolation* 15, no. 1 (Dec. 1973): 51–59.

—. "Towards an Aesthetic of Science Fiction." *Science Fiction Studies* 2, pt. 2, no. 6 (July 1975): 112–19.

—. "What Can a Heroine Do? Or Why Women Can't Write." In *Images of Women in Fiction: Feminist Perspectives.* Edited by Susan Koppelman Cornillon. Bowling Green, Ohio: Bowling Green University Popular Press, 1972.

—. "When We Were Everybody: A Lost Feminist Utopia." Review of *Herland,* by Charlotte Perkins Gilman. *New Women's Times Feminist Review,* 6–19 July 1979, 10–11.

Ruyer, Raymond. *L'Utopie et les utopies*. Paris: Presses universitaires de France, 1950.

Salmonson, Jessica Amanda, ed. *Amazons!* New York: Daw Books, 1979.

Sargent, Lyman Tower. "Utopia—The Problem of Definition." *Extrapolation* 16, no. 2 (May 1975): 137–48.

—. "Women in Utopia." *Comparative Literature Studies* 10, no. 4 (Dec. 1973): 302–16.

Sargent, Pamela, ed. *Women of Wonder*. 3 vols. New York: Random House, Vintage Books, 1975–1978.

Scholes, Robert, and Eric S. Rabkin. *Science Fiction: History, Science, Vision*. New York: Oxford University Press, 1977.

Schwartz, Lucy McCallum. "Christiane Rochefort: Garden of Pleasure." Paper presented at the Annual Meeting of the Modern Language Association, San Francisco, 27 Dec. 1979.

Science Fiction Studies 7, pt. 1, no. 20 (March 1980). Special issue, entitled "Science Fiction on Women—Science Fiction by Women."

Sherzer, Dina. "Christiane Rochefort: *Archaos, ou le jardin étincelant*." *French Review* 47, no. 4 (Mar. 1974): 837–38.

Singer, Rochelle. *The Demeter Flower*. New York: St. Martin's Press, 1980.

Snitow, Ann Barr. "The Front Line: Notes on Sex in Novels by Women." *Signs* 5, no. 4 (Summer 1980): 702–18.

Snitow, Ann Barr, Christine Stansell, and Sharon Thompson, eds. *Powers of Desire: The Politics of Sexuality*. New York: Monthly Review Press, 1983.

Staicar, Tom. *The Feminine Eye: Science Fiction and the Women Who Write It*. New York: Ungar, 1982.

Stambolian, George, and Elaine Marks, eds. *Homosexualities and French Literature: Cultural Contexts / Critical Texts*. Ithaca: Cornell University Press, 1979.

Studies in the Literary Imagination 6, no. 2 (Fall 1973). Special issue, entitled "Aspects of Utopian Fiction."

Sturgeon, Theodore. *Venus Plus X*. New York: Dell, 1960.

Suvin, Darko. "Defining the Literary Genre of Utopia: Some Historical Semantics, Some Genology, a Proposal, and a Plea." *Studies in the Literary Imagination* 6, no. 2 (Fall 1973): 121–45.

—. *Metamorphoses of Science Fiction: On the Poetics and History of a Literary Genre*. New Haven: Yale University Press, 1979.

—. "The Mirror and the Dynamo: On Brecht's Aesthetic Point of View." *Drama Review* 12, no. 1 (Fall 1967): 56–67.

—. "On the Poetics of the Science Fiction Genre." *College English* 34, no. 3 (Dec. 1972): 372–82.

—. "On the Poetics of the Science Fiction Theory: Determining and Delimiting the Genre." *Science Fiction Studies* 6, pt. 1, no. 17 (Mar. 1979): 32–45.

Suvin, Darko, and Marc Angenot. "Not Only but Also: Reflections on Cognition and Ideology in Science Fiction and Science Fiction Criticism." *Science Fiction Studies* 6, pt. 2, no. 18 (July 1979): 168–79.

Thompson, Edward. "Romanticism, Moralism, and Utopianism: The Case of William Morris." *New Left Review,* no. 99 (Sept.–Oct. 1976): 83–111.

Thorne, Barrie, and Nancy Henley, eds. *Language and Sex: Difference and Dominance.* Rowley, Mass.: Newbury House, 1975.

Tillich, Paul. *Political Expectation.* New York: Harper & Row, 1971.

Tristan, Anne, and Annie de Pisan. *Histoires du M.L.F.* Paris: Calmann-Lévy, 1977.

Vance, Carole S., ed. *Pleasure and Danger: Exploring Female Sexuality.* Boston: Routledge & Kegan Paul, 1984.

Venalut, Philippe. *"Archaos, ou le jardin étincelant* par Christiane Rochefort." *Magazine Littéraire,* no. 69 (Oct. 1972): 30–31.

Volosinov, V. N. *Marxism and the Philosophy of Language.* Translated by Ladislav Matejka and I. R. Titunik. New York: Seminar Press, 1973.

Walsh, Chad. *From Utopia to Nightmare.* New York: Harper & Row, 1962.

Walsh, Correa Moylan. *Feminism.* New York: Sturgis & Walton, 1917.

Weinbaum, Batya. *The Curious Courtship of Women's Liberation and Socialism.* Boston: South End Press, 1978.

Weininger, Otto. *Sex and Character.* New York: A. L. Burt, n.d.

Williams, Raymond. *Problems in Materialism and Culture.* London: Verso, 1980.

—. "Utopia and Science Fiction." *Science Fiction Studies* 5, pt. 3, no. 16 (Nov. 1978): 203–14.

Wittig, Monique. *Les Guérillères.* Paris: Minuit, 1969. Translated by David Le Vay under the title *The Guérillères.* New York: Avon Books, 1973.

Wittig, Monique, and Sande Zeig. *Brouillon pour un dictionnaire des amantes.* Paris: Grasset & Fasquelle, 1976. Translated by the authors under the title *Lesbian Peoples: Material for a Dictionary.* New York: Avon Books, 1979.

Wollstonecraft. Mary. *A Vindication of the Rights of Woman*. New York: Norton, 1975.

Young, Donna J. *Retreat: As It Was, a Fantasy*. Weatherby Lake, Mo.: Naiad Press, 1979.

Zaretsky, Eli. *Capitalism, the Family, and Personal Life*. New York: Harper & Row, Colophon Books, 1976.

Index

Abundance. *See* Food; Economy

Adolescence, 58, 68, 72, 99, 105, 151, 155. *See also* Children

Amazon, 23, 34, 36, 38–39, 94, 101. *See also* Lesbian

Atwood, Margaret, 4, 15–16, 18, 82, 91, 133–58

Auerbach, Erich, 50, 52

Bachelard, Gaston, 117, 139

Barthes, Roland, 37, 59

Beauvoir, Simone de, 8, 27, 33, 36, 139, 141–43

Beechey, Veronica, 70–72

Bellamy, Edward, 7, 9, 14, 52, 54

Benjamin, Jessica, 143–44, 153, 157

Bersianik, Louky, 4, 18, 133–58, 163

Birth, 68, 145–47, 165; of daughter, 97, 121, 129; of son, 114–15; of twins, 119. *See also* Reproduction

Bloch, Ernst, 10–11, 13, 64, 74–75, 111–12, 165

Brecht, Bertolt, 14, 59–61

Broner, E. M., 4, 18, 111–30

Charnas, Suzy McKee, 4, 16–17, 81–108, 126, 133

Children, 5, 40–41, 98–100, 106, 113, 115, 147; freedom for/of, 55, 99, 105; responsibility for, 100, 120, 124, 128. *See also* Family; Reproduction

Cixous, Helene, 85, 92, 136, 162

Closure, 38–39, 107, 155

Clothing, 40–41, 99, 135; and sexual difference, 29–30, 115; and sexuality, 148, 150, 156

Community, 5, 15, 18, 44, 60, 66, 161–63, 165; becoming a member of, 68, 70, 83, 125. *See also* Family; Kinship

Consciousness, 13, 50, 54, 87, 137, 149; coming to, 59, 61–62, 150; utopian, 10–11

Daydreams, 10–11, 16, 52, 117, 133

Death, 54, 70, 88–89, 118, 121, 148, 165; of a child, 123, 125, 129; and femininity, 85; and hunger, 154; and power, 89

Desire, 4, 85, 127, 151, 154; and representation, 3, 49; sexual, 58; and utopia, 7, 10; of women, 5, 9, 134–35, 143. *See also* Hope; Language; Power; Sexuality

Diner, Helen, 34, 94

Dinnerstein, Dorothy, 64, 69, 101

DuPlessis, Rachel Blau, 10, 14, 50, 52, 161

Dystopia, 4, 7, 18, 49, 61, 69, 125, 134, 158; and hopelessness, 145, 151, 153; as world ruled by men, 17, 81, 93, 133. *See also* Utopian discourse; Utopian genre, history of

Economy, 61, 83, 120, 146; and kin-
  ship, 72, 77; and utopia, 8, 87,
  125–26, 151. *See also* Food;
  Hunger
Engels, Friedrich, 13–14, 71
Exile, 35, 39, 104, 115, 129, 148

Family, 53, 60, 71–73, 83, 97–99, 107,
  129; ideology of, 16, 34, 71;
  redefinition of, 5, 49–50, 65–69,
  76, 96, 101, 104; and state, 15, 18,
  125, 162–63. *See also* Children;
  Community; Kinship; Mothers;
  Reproduction; State
Feminism. *See* Women's liberation
  movement
Firestone, Shulamith, 17, 64, 71
Food, 33, 90, 95, 99, 102, 118–19,
  144. *See also* Hunger
Foucault, Michel, 37, 151
Freud, Sigmund, 10–11, 25, 37, 85–86
Future, 10, 38, 51, 61, 74, 78, 90, 93,
  97, 105–7, 122, 126, 151, 155; and
  the family, 72, 94; men in the, 69;
  and time travel, 54, 65, 161; and
  utopian discourse, 129–30, 133;
  women in the, 9, 83, 90, 94; in
  writing, 7, 11, 12, 24, 52, 94, 111–
  12, 135, 164. *See also* Hope; Not-
  yet; Time; Space; Speculation

Gaze, 28, 63, 91, 93, 147–48, 158
Gilman, Charlotte Perkins, 4, 15–16,
  18, 23–45, 49, 64, 66, 72, 94, 112,
  154, 163
Goodman, Paul, 8, 63
Gordon, Linda, 30, 33–34
Governing, 78, 116, 148, 163

Haraway, Donna, 164–65
History: and memory, 28, 84, 104,
  128; and narration, 38–39, 50,

106, 112–13, 121, 153; and women,
  161–62. *See also* Time
Home, 50, 60, 115, 123–24, 129; and
  femininity, 29, 32, 117; and travel,
  74
Hope, 7, 58, 91, 130, 134, 138, 147,
  164–65; capacity for, 3–4, 53, 93,
  158; for change, 10, 19, 108, 111,
  133; and resistance, 145, 157. *See
  also* Desire; Future; Time
Hunger, 87, 94, 119, 126–27, 154. *See
  also* Food

Identity, 18, 137, 149, 152, 165; gender
  and, 66, 68, 96, 143. *See also*
  Lesbian; Sexual difference;
  Subjectivity; female
Ideology, 17, 42–44, 164; and the
  family, 16, 66; and motherhood,
  31, 33; and narrative, 14, 39
Irigaray, Luce, 141, 157

Jameson, Fredric, 10, 44

Kinship, 17, 49, 83, 94, 101;
  redefinition of, 5, 14, 34, 77, 85,
  163; among women, 97, 100, 104–
  5, 107. *See also* Community;
  Family; Mothers; Reproduction
Kollontai, Alexandra, 25, 38, 44

Language, 41, 86, 91–92, 99, 105, 111,
  114–16, 119, 125, 139, 155, 165;
  language change, 8–9, 14, 44, 64,
  83, 127; language learning, 30, 40;
  oppression and, 153; power and,
  89, 91–92, 113, 134–35;
  transgression and, 148, 154;
  women and, 5, 36–37, 99, 102,
  124, 136–37. *See also* Desire;
  Names; Power; Subjectivity,
  female

Laughter, 40, 43–44, 91–92, 127–28, 141

Law, 137–38, 142–44, 162–63; breakdown of, 92, 125; and repression, 114–15, 148; rewriting of, 124, 126–27, 141; rule of, 32

Lesbian, 33–36, 39, 112, 147. *See also* Amazon; Identity; Sexual difference; Subjectivity; female

Levi-Strauss, Claude, 49, 77

Look. *See* Gaze

Love, 32, 60, 100–101, 118, 120; romantic, 75, 127–29

MacKinnon, Catharine, 162–63

Marcuse, Herbert, 8, 13, 63

Marriage, 31, 34, 75, 77–78, 120, 129, 139–40

Men, 3, 69, 95, 112, 122, 136, 157, 161–62; arrival in utopia, 28–32, 54–55, 125; rule by, 82, 93

More, Sir Thomas, 9, 14, 52

Morris, William, 4, 8, 52, 70

Motherhood, 30, 35, 40, 66, 72. *See also* Sexuality

Mothering, 16, 68, 72–73, 163–64

Mothers: and amazons, 23, 39, 45; redefinition of, 105–6; and women, 15, 34–35, 45, 72, 94, 123, 147, 150. *See also* Family; Kinship; Reproduction

Names/Naming, 125, 129, 135, 147, 154–55, 161, 163, 166; giving of, 31, 91, 97, 106, 145–46 *See also* Language; Power

Not-yet, 4, 10–11, 15, 107, 112, 126, 152, 161–62. *See also* Future; Speculation; Utopian discourse

Patriarchy, 64, 77, 117, 126, 146–47; and capitalism, 71; history of, 38, 84; and paternity, 91, 114

Piercy, Marge, 4, 16–17, 25, 49–78, 94, 101, 112, 126, 163

Pleasure, 33, 50, 58, 116–17, 120, 138, 154

Power, 14, 72, 82, 87, 91, 103, 144, 158, 163; and feminism, 5, 88, 163; instruments of, 29, 57; and language, 5, 88, 92, 113, 134, 161, 165; uses of, 6, 85, 88, 90, 102, 106, 154, 162. *See also* Desire; Language; Names/Naming

Psychoanalysis, 85, 101; and change, 137–38; and the family, 68, 76; and female subjectivity, 142–44; and French feminist politics, 35, 37. *See also* Subjectivity, female

Racism, 17, 26, 98, 103, 165

Rape, 32, 88, 119. *See also* Violence; War

Religion, 18, 30, 32, 35, 111, 130

Reproduction, 86, 90, 107, 146, 163–4; feminism and, 15, 33–34, 71–72, 162; modes of, 30, 36, 41, 66, 70–72, 76, 83, 98, 100–102, 104; representation of, 15–17, 96, 145; sexuality and, 35. *See also* Birth; Children; Family; Kinship; Mothers; Sexuality

Ritual, 50, 111, 118, 145–46, 148; adolescence and, 105; birth and, 115–16, 146; death and, 123; history and, 106; religion and, 111, 145; reproduction and, 100, 103, 146

Rochefort, Christiane, 4, 17–18, 111–30, 163

Rubin, Gayle, 17, 77

Russ, Joanna, 4, 10, 12, 14, 16, 17, 40,

Russ, Joanna (*cont.*)
49–78, 81–82, 93–94, 112, 126, 163

Scarcity. See Economy; Hunger
Science fiction, 7, 12, 14, 17, 45, 60, 81–82, 161–65
Sexual difference, 6, 27, 57–58, 136–37, 143, 166; demand for, 29–30, 57–58; and recognition, 66–68, 143. See also Clothing; Identity; Lesbian; Subjectivity; female
Sexuality, 15, 17, 40, 60, 121, 163; female, 37, 41, 118; and motherhood, 32; and reproduction, 31, 34. See also Clothing; Motherhood; Reproduction
Slaves, 17, 86–87, 90, 102, 104, 140, 153
Socialism, 7, 13, 24–26, 72
Space, 4, 12–13, 50, 59, 82, 117, 119, 123, 136, 152, 158, 162. See also Future
Speculation, 5, 9, 45, 52, 155. See also Future; Not-Yet
State, 15, 18, 77, 125–26, 145–46, 151, 162–63, 165. See also Family
Subjectivity, female: and feminist theory, 24, 26, 164–65; and language, 5, 12, 91, 134–35, 153; and recognition, 56–57, 59, 67, 87, 143–44, 152, 157. See also Identity; Language; Lesbian; Psychoanalysis; Sexual difference
Suvin, Darko, 9, 14

Taboo, 75, 77, 84–85, 91, 99, 124, 141

Technology, 44–45, 61, 71, 90, 151, 165; reproductive, 17, 72, 163–64
Time, 4, 12–13, 17, 50, 59, 82, 119, 121, 126. See also Future; History; Hope
Travel, 9, 53, 82, 103, 126, 157, 161

Utopian discourse, 14–15, 27; and didacticism, 9, 12, 44, 50, 161; and political imagination, 39, 116, 130, 164–65. See also Dystopia; Not-yet
Utopian genre, history of, 6, 9, 11, 13, 17, 24, 73, 81, 126, 153; and feminism, 23, 44–45; in nineteenth century, 7–8, 24, 45, 161. See also Dystopia

Violence, 121–23, 145; men and their relation to, 86, 114, 117; women and their relation to, 34–35; Women as agents of, 16, 53, 73–74, 107, 126, 137, 139, 163; women as victims of, 16, 32, 62. See also Rape; War

Walsh, Correa Moylan, 24, 26
War, 39, 42–44, 61, 89, 129, 163. See also Violence
Wittig, Monique, 4, 16, 18, 23–45, 49, 58–59, 94, 101, 111, 126, 163
Women's liberation movement, 8, 16, 33–34, 49, 66, 82; history of, 5–6, 25, 37, 62, 64, 91, 133, 144–45, 164
Work, 50, 60, 84, 88, 106, 155; and play, 73–75, 125–26; and survival, 127–28; and women, 139, 145